THE UNIVERSITY OF
WINCHESTER

D1424615

SPRINGTIME

The New Student Rebellions

---◆---

EDITED BY CLARE SOLOMON AND TANIA PALMIERI

VERSO
London • New York

First published in English by Verso 2011
The collection © Verso 2011
Individual contributions © The contributors 2011
Translation, Section 2 © Arianna Bové and Pier Paolo Frassinelli

All royalties will be donated to PalestineConnect
www.palestineconnect.org

Every effort has been made to obtain permission to use copyright material, both illustrative and quoted, in this book. Verso apologizes for any omissions in this regard and will be pleased to make the appropriate acknowledgements in future editions.

1 3 5 7 9 10 8 6 4 2

Verso
UK: 6 Meard Street, London W1F 0EG
US: 20 Jay Street, Suite 1010, Brooklyn, NY 11201
www.versobooks.com

Verso is the imprint of New Left Books

ISBN-13: 978-1-84467-740-5

British Library Cataloguing in Publication Data
A catalogue record for this book is available from the British Library

Library of Congress Cataloging-in-Publication Data
A catalog record for this book is available from the Library of Congress

Typeset by Hewer Text UK Ltd, Edinburgh
Printed in Great Britain by Bell & Bain Ltd, Glasgow

CONTENTS

CONTENTS

CONTENTS

CONTENTS

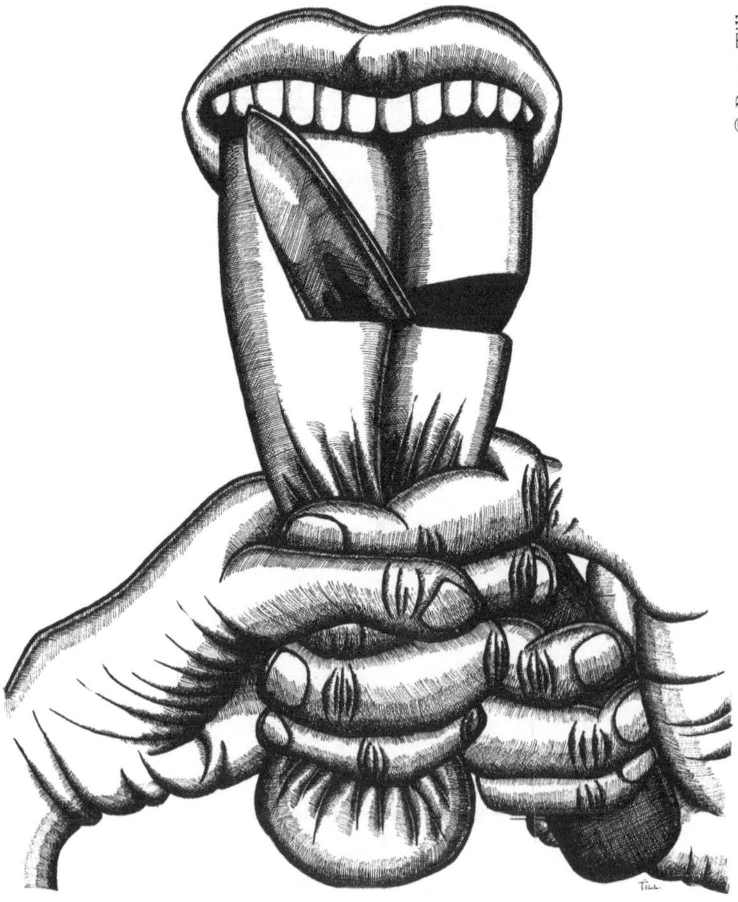

INTRODUCTION

Our rulers thought that now was the perfect moment drastically to restructure higher education (and much else besides) by institutionalizing a form of specialization that simultaneously imparted ignorance and knowledge, and restricted higher education by imposing a financial bar. They hoped that students would drown in specialized research and ignore the fact that their intellectual development was being stunted. Education has never been delinked from the overall structures and needs of a society, whatever its character, but students have often transcended the limitations imposed on them. Western universities changed dramatically over the last sixty years as the post–Second World War period ushered in reforms that included the right to a free education for all, paving the way for a huge expansion of the universities.

Before the twentieth century, the British state (and its peers elsewhere) had existed to protect property and privilege, and educated those who agreed to do the same. Unsurprisingly, education was a preserve of the well-off and the church orders that buttressed and spiritually nourished injustice and inequality. The democratic rights fought for by the Chartists and the suffragettes for over a hundred years included the right to vote. Free education came later – and now, they're taking it away again. The resulting tension has produced an opposition from below, a resistance that is also premonitory. For if a good education is once again to become the preserve of a few, might this not herald a further hollowing out of the democratic process itself, already in a bad way with moderate Republicanism an agreed consensus in the States, and its equivalents in Britain and in Europe? The students who marched on the streets to protect their rights are fighting for something larger.

The governors of Britain were not prepared for the response that greeted its 'austerity measures'. This book that Verso is proud to publish consists largely of accounts by student participants in the wave of struggles that have stretched from the West Coast of the United States to much of Western Europe. It is a chronicle, but not just a chronicle. It is the formulation of an experience. We hope that its cumulative impact will be to develop alternatives that challenge the priorities of capitalist society. What is this society that, having promised and for a time provided its citizens many satisfactions, now threatens to turn around and crush them if they demand rights that were once taken for granted?

It is too early yet to draw any definitive conclusions as to the final outcome of the resistance against capitalism's assault on students and the underprivileged, but the fact that a new generation is learning, through its own experiences, the priorities of the world in which they live, augurs well for the future. We no longer live in a time where capitalism guarantees full employment. Many who graduate will be without work and thus difficult to integrate – as was the case with the student generation of the 1960s and 1970s. Times are much harsher now, not because they need to be, but because Capital determines the conditions under which we live.

Contemporary politicians and their followers are still besotted with the system they created in the closing decades of the twentieth century. The collapse of Communism, and subsequently of Social Democracy, laid the foundations for a return to a no-holds-barred, fang-and-claw capitalism. Greed, legitimized in theory and practice, overpowered all else. Institutionalized in Wall Street and the City of London, it was happily mimicked elsewhere. Bankers, corporations and politicians were content to carry out each other's orders, blind to the human misery they were creating and sensitive only to their corporate and individual needs.

Then came the Wall Street crash of 2008. Its arrival had been predicted by a few courageous economists, while the majority of that breed wallowed in wealth and helped launch Tina (there is no alternative), a fear-based dogma, short-sighted and foolish, but defended in the media with the same vigour that *Pravda* deployed to defend the most irrational excesses of the Soviet politburo. At first, shameless politician blamed shameless banker, but these visionless leaders and their vacuous camp-followers needed to unite with the hard-faced finance-capitalists for whom conscience had always been regarded as a dirty word. Both sides agreed – how could they not? – that the less well-off and the poor must bear the brunt of the crisis. Bush–Obama and Brown–Clegg–Cameron were in denial, refusing to accept the fact that the Reagan–Thatcher era was over.

There are no mysteries attached to the Wall Street collapse of 2008. It's foolish to waste too much time trying to understand the character and motives of the politicians, bankers and speculators whose combined complacency led to the crash. Mostly they were a self-seeking, incompetent and single-minded bunch who contributed fairly equally to the crisis. Till then, with the exception of a few sober voices, the excesses of neo-liberal capitalism were widely celebrated, and nowhere more so than in the land of its birth – the United States – and that of its loyal British satrapy. Market-fundamentalism became the mantra of Republicans and New Democrats, Conservatives and New Labour and their friends in the global media networks. Privatization and deregulation were the new virtues. Helping them forcibly, if legally, to violate hitherto hallowed spheres of social and public provision was hailed as 'courageous', 'far-sighted', 'reformist', and so on. The state was the enemy, the problem. The market was the only solution. Those who opposed the strangulation of the welfare state experienced a double liability: they were dinosaurs wedded to the state and they refused to accept their defeat. They were on the wrong side of history, and the choice offered to them was to capitulate to bourgeois order, possibly prosper, and remain silent. To understand that there has been a defeat does not mean that one celebrates or accepts the outcome.

As the crisis exposed the weaknesses of the system, the much-maligned state, denounced over the last three decades, including by the more fashionable sectors on the left, was needed once again to prevent a complete systemic collapse. Money unavailable for education, health, public housing, transport and other necessities of life suddenly flowed in to rescue the banks. In 21,000 transactions, the Federal Reserve Bank released taxpayers' money to the tune of $9 trillion so that Wall Street's finest, as well as a wide variety of banks and corporations, could carry on as before. A similar process took place in Britain where, it appears, there was no Private Finance Initiative available to step in and save the banks. The state, without consulting the taxpayer, provided billions of pounds. Even the more astute defenders of capitalism cheered. Here is Martin Wolf in the *Financial Times*:

> In the case of this crisis, the failure lies not so much with the market system as a whole, but with defects in the world's financial and monetary systems . . . Happily, governments and central banks have learnt the lessons of the 1930s and decided, rightly, to prevent collapses of either the financial system or the economy. That is precisely the right kind of 'piecemeal social engineering'.

It wasn't long before the blood burst through the sticking plaster. Greece collapsed just as Argentina had done at the end of the 1990s. These were not simply aggravated liquidity problems, but something that went far deeper, that was much more structural. This time the euro was threatened. The German banks were required to bail out Greece. Then Portugal tottered on the brink. Might Spain collapse? Ireland did, like Iceland before it. Its corrupt political and economic elite went on its knees before the EU: we fought against the instinct of our citizens and intimidated them in order to push through everything you wanted. Don't let us down now. The 'piecemeal social engineering' is reducing much of Europe to the status of a debtor's prison, with politicians and bankers as the warders and ordinary citizens – students, public-sector workers, the unemployed and the elderly, serving as inmates.

Verso decided to produce this book to mark a significant revival of dissent, protest and anger against the system, spearheaded by students from schools and universities across Europe and North America. This is no surprise. The problems they face are not a result of economic crises or the supposedly necessary cuts in social expenditure. The needs of twenty-first-century capitalism require universities that subordinate intellectual creativity, discourage individual initiatives and restrict the number of disciplines with which higher education has usually been associated. The United States, as the only global empire, requires a layer that can serve imperial needs (just as Britain once did), and therefore the study of world history, languages, philosophy cannot be dumped as easily as in Britain. Here they want simultaneously to restrict knowledge, hoping that those who are taught in this fashion will soon become so intellectually stunted that they will not realize what they are missing. Some hope. Specialized technicians is all they want, young people who never question the purposes of the technology and who are rewarded for bottling their independence. On the humanities front, the number of departments in 'Terror Studies' and 'Human Rights' reveals the instrumental pattern of corporate education. The university is becoming closely linked to corporations: pharmaceutical industries and the military-industrial complex, to give but two examples, are increasingly connected to education, disturbing the social and educational structure of the university. Once regarded as the embattled outposts of intellectual freedom, the campus managers who run these institutions under various titles have abjectly surrendered to economic and political power, which is why they were appointed in the first place.

Students seeking to combat this subordination have a long struggle ahead of them, and not just while they remain students. The capitalist system, as currently organized, is simply not capable of employing every graduate. Hence the financial barriers that are being erected to limit access to education, with a few sops designed largely for public relations. Capitalism's future lies in its past.

What were the students protesting about? Tuition fees, certainly, but also against the trilateral consensus that dominates British politics. The Thatcherization of the Labour Party, followed by the Blairization of the Tories and the Cameronization of the Liberal Democrats, has created a monstrously homogenized electoral monolith. The tri-partisan consensus is evident in every aspect of government policy. Thus:

- Welfare benefits and pensions: in 2007, investment banker David (now Lord) Freud, appointed by New Labour to reduce the benefits bill, recommended replacing the various crumbs – housing benefit, incapacity benefit, disability allowance – with a single, means-tested payment linked to harsh 'incentives to work'. Tory welfare minister Iain Duncan-Smith is enthusiastically driving the plan forward, implementing at the same time an £18 billion reduction in payments and the downgrading of inflation-linked benefit increases.
- Higher education: in 1998, Blair's government imposed fairly nominal tuition fees on students (a policy earlier resisted by the former Conservative PM John Major) as the thin end of the wedge; in 2004 it hiked the fees substantially, claiming that 'those who benefited' from higher education should fund it themselves, and set up low-interest student loans to pay for them – fresh fields for the financial sector. Responsibility for universities was duly shifted from the Department of Education to the Department of Business. In 2009, New Labour appointed the ex-CEO of BP, Lord Browne, to 'reform' higher education. His proposals – that teaching subsidies be cut by over 70 per cent; students pay commercial rates on their loans; universities be free to hike fees at will, or compete like businesses in price-cutting against each other to attract students, with inevitable college bankruptcies and closures – will now be implemented by the LDP minister for business, Vince Cable. The Liberal Democrats, who promised to abolish tuition fees altogether in their 2010 manifesto, have been bought off, as cheaply as Labour's 'left' under Blair and Brown, with low-level – but well-salaried – parliamentary appointments.
- Health: Since New Labour had already insisted that the Natinoal Health Service (NHS) find £20 billion in savings within its current budget to cope with the expanding number of elderly patients and drug price rises over the next four years, the Coalition could claim to be ring-fencing health expenditure. But health secretary Andrew Lansley has already broken the Coalition pledge to put an end to New Labour's permanent revolution in top-down administrative restructuring, which has brought a vast increase in form-filling, to the detriment of patient care, as medical personnel are forced to spend their time managing the NHS's 'internal market'. Lansley was formerly employed by a private health outfit.

- Defence: famously, New Labour's two brand-new aircraft carriers will be spared from the Chancellor George Osborne's cuts, at a cost of some £5 billion, since it would be 'too expensive' to break the contracts.

As this book reveals, it is experience, the society in which we live, the lives we lead, that determines consciousness. It is always thus: yesterday and today, as the events in Tunisia, Egypt and Yemen demonstrate. The flashbacks that we have included from previous struggles indicate a continuity: an account of the actions of German police in Berlin, utilizing 'wedge tactics' against the young in 1967, reads just like the descriptions of 'kettling' from British students in London in December 2010.

Wisdoms old and young, however, mix admirably well. There is a new mood in the air, an anger that melts the snow. All hail the new, young student Decembrists who challenged a complacent government and simultaneously fired a few shots across the bows of an opposition and its toadies in the media, all still recovering from a paralytic hangover, a consequence of imbibing too much Nouveau Blair.

The young Decembrists occupied, they sang, they blogged, Facebooked, tweeted and marched to show their contempt for the politicians who lied. The fires lit in Parliament Square to keep the kettled Decembrists warm were also symbolic, turning the heat on a rotting Coalition that might not last the full term so joyfully imagined. The hard-faced Cameron can no longer boast to his European counterparts that this country is a politico-economic Guantánamo where everything goes. No longer.

In times of struggle it is possible to transcend the ideological limits imposed by bourgeois society in which democracy itself is becoming increasingly hollow, with the established political parties of the West operating, together with the mediacracy, essentially as a capitalist collective, incapable of even thinking about any serious alternative. Britain is a country without an official opposition. An extra-parliamentary upheaval is necessary not simply to combat the cuts, but also to enhance a democracy that at the moment is designed to do little more than further corporate interests. Bailouts for bankers and the rich, an obscene level of defence expenditure to fight Washington's wars, and cuts for the less well off and the poor. A topsy-turvy world produces its own priorities. They need to be contested. These islands have a radical past, after all, one that is not being taught in the history modules on offer. We will have to educate ourselves. We need a social charter that can be fought for and defended, just as Shelley advised almost two centuries ago:

INTRODUCTION

Ye who suffer woes untold
Or to feel or to behold
Your lost country bought and sold
With a price of blood and gold.

[. . .]

Rise like Lions after slumber
In unvanquishable number,
Shake your chains to earth like dew
Which in sleep had fallen on you.
Ye are many, they are few.

January 2011

1

UK: DECEMBER DAYS

WE FELT LIBERATED

Clare Solomon

The closing months of 2010 saw the sudden reappearance of the British student movement. In early 2009, a burst of around thirty-five occupations expressing solidarity with Gaza had marked a partial revival of student direct action and solidarity with an oppressed people. During 2010 the long-running occupation at Middlesex University, in defence of its philosophy department, and protests and occupations at a small number of other universities facing cuts, like Sussex, were signs that a student movement was in the making.

What emerged in November 2010 was on quite a different scale, with a truly national reach and mass participation, including FE and school students alongside university students. It's impossible to discuss each and every experience. But the stories you're about to read provide a snapshot of a political revival within the entire education system. This section provides testimony, facts and analysis from a wide variety of people, the majority of whom were participating in political direct action for the first time.

'Demolition 2010' was called for by the National Union of Students (NUS) with the support of the lecturers' University and College Union (UCU) for 10 November. For years, activists from the student left had tried to persuade the Labour-dominated NUS leadership to hold a national demonstration in defence of higher education. It was, after all, Blair and Brown who had decided to introduce tuition fees. But as long as New Labour was in power the NUS leadership was not inclined to organize any serious show of strength. This refusal to take on New Labour was disastrous. Had the NUS done so, we would have been in a much stronger position to take on the Tories and Lib Dems in 2010. At National Conference in April, mindful of the impending Browne Review of higher education funding (a review set up by New Labour), the argument was finally won. A motion was passed, and support for a national demonstration promptly backed by UCU and UNISON, the main union for support and administrative staff. The hope lurking in the back of bureaucratic minds was no doubt that a respectable campaign against likely funding cuts and fees hikes could be kept within the safe confines of official NUS politics – very much part of the trilateral consensus that permeates British politics today.

The arrival of a Tory–Liberal coalition government in May meant that there could now be a serious show of strength, safe in the knowledge that New Labour's boat would not be rocked. Significant NUS resources were, for once, poured into the mobilization, matched by the work of activists on the ground. The NUS leadership hoped for a pleasant stroll through central London to hear a parade of safely, implicitly pro-Labour speakers, before dispersing to letter-writing campaigns, or, more likely, passivity. Activists on the ground realized something bigger might be in the offing, and perhaps secretly began to hope that (say) a sit-down protest could be staged or a token breakaway march launched. The police and, it would seem, the government idly assumed that business would be much as usual – Metropolitan Police press officers insisted to journalists, the day before the demo, that 'no more than' 10,000 could be expected. The police, realizing the unpopularity of the Lib Dems among the student population, duly despatched a squad or two to guard their headquarters. Conservative HQ, sitting on the demo route at Millbank, was left virtually undefended.

November 10 blew all expectations away. At 8 a.m., 2,000 students from Scotland and Northern England settled down to a breakfast at the University of London Union (ULU). At midday, a 10,000-strong march of students from London colleges set off from ULU into the main demo – instantly politicizing a student institution notorious for its apolitical irrelevance. By 2 p.m., some 50,000 students were on the move, crammed in from Trafalgar Square to Millbank. Student apathy, fostered by New Labour tradition inside the NUS, had been the supposed rule. Students were simply not supposed to care about their own education. And yet here was the biggest student protest for generations. And here were thousands of sixth-form and FE students, protesting in unprecedented numbers against the scrapping of the Education Maintenance Allowance (EMA) – up to £30 a week paid to poorer students. And here, unbelievably, was an unplanned mass occupation of Millbank Towers. Tory HQ was almost entirely unguarded. A number of us walked into the reception and began chanting. Protestors flooded in behind us and into the courtyard. A crowd of around 5,000 crammed in, ignoring NUS stewards. It was this creative spontaneity that galvanized the public. Despite tabloid fury, a majority of public opinion was on our side.

Around fifty students made it onto the roof of the seven-storey building, including one wheelchair user who dragged himself up the stairs. They hung banners and sent text messages in solidarity with public-sector workers. And on the ground the atmosphere was electric: a combination of anger and complete disbelief at what was actually happening. It didn't feel 'radical', it felt inevitable. Around fifty police arrived, but this only added to the anger. Hostile gestures by both them and Tory staff inside the building provoked demonstrators, and before we knew it windows were being broken and fires lit to keep warm while we celebrated the rebirth of the student movement. Inside the foyer of another building we could see large TV screens showing live news coverage. How the media chose to represent the events shocked us. We saw dancing, they showed flames. We chanted angry slogans and danced; they showed repeatedly a couple of images or incidents which made the demonstration look like all hell had broken loose.

People felt liberated. In a moment of madness, a young, first-time demonstrator threw a fire extinguisher from the roof. He later received a jail sentence of thirty-two months, intended to make an example of him. A solidarity campaign has been launched for him and another seventy or so students arrested either on the demo or in a series of dawn raids after the media witch-hunt that followed.

With night falling, the crowd began to thin. We headed for post-demo celebrations at the London School of Economics. Spirits were high, though the magnitude of what we had done had not yet sunk in. The news was showing repeated footage of the day. And then we heard that the NUS president, Aaron Porter, condemned the actions of 'this violent minority'; 'despicable' he called them. To students at LSE and on campuses across the country, it was unacceptable for him to condemn his own members – that he chose to highlight an isolated incident of stupidity rather than explain the causes of the anger.

That evening I was invited on *Newsnight*, the BBC current affairs programme hosted by the combative Jeremy Paxman, with fellow guests Simon Hughes MP and Aaron Porter. 'Do you or do you not condemn the violence?' was the line of questioning. Of course, we would like to achieve our demands peacefully, but would we have even had the air-space if a few windows hadn't got smashed?

The support from the wider public has been overwhelming. This book includes examples of how wide that support is. Media polls range from 56 to 76 per cent in support of the students. We called on trade unionists to support us. A few brave lecturers' union representatives spoke out in our defence and received the almighty backlash of the media, with erroneous accusations that they endorsed 'violence'.

University students also spoke out in solidarity with each other. As students returned from the protests to campus, they discussed next steps. Occupations were argued for. The School of Oriental and African Studies in London won a union motion to occupy after a tense debate. Elly Badcock, in this section, explains how and why they did it, and how the fifty following university occupations became critical bases for the movement.

This was, as all those involved knew, and as all those cheering the students on now realized, only the beginning. The National Campaign Against Fees and Cuts (NCAFC), one of the existing left-led campaigns, had before 10 November called a National Day of Action for 24 November, anticipating it would be a way of keeping up momentum after the 10 November demo. NUS and education unions refused to back it, especially after the events at Millbank. However, we on the left were even more certain that it should go ahead. This was the first major demo that we had organized ourselves, without endorsement from the official movement in the shape of the NUS. After attacks and arrests of students on the 10 November, activists convened a London Student Assembly (LSA), aiming to provide coordination and support between groups and campuses. A start point of midday at Trafalgar Square – historically associated with political rallies – was announced on Facebook, and a Carnival of Resistance organized from ULU to the main assembly.

We invited Lowkey MC to organize an open mic, rather than a rally of speakers, in order to encourage younger students to engage in the speeches and take the lead. Reports from the Trafalgar Square meeting point explained how thousands upon thousands of mainly FE students began swarming. Every minute or two yet another group of young students arrived over the horizon, like the cavalry coming over the hills, from every corner. Each group, upon arrival, excited to see banners and flags all over the iconic statues and thousands of fellow students, ran into each other's arms, hugging, cheering and dancing.

Unfortunately, the police contained our Carnival at the mouth of Aldwych, en route to Trafalgar Square. The rear of the demo was forced down the Strand. Those who were waiting at the Square, meanwhile, were largely unaware that there was a feeder march on its way and, with a roar, headed down Whitehall before we arrived

Police lines moved swiftly. They kettled us – a method which the police call 'containment' – in the freezing weather, without food, water or toilet facilities, for nine hours. Students as young as ten were in attendance. Many were on their first demo. They were clearly not expecting to be kettled. The hours passed. Thank goodness for Lowkey and the sound systems: they kept the music and carnival atmosphere going right up to the end. A mass hokey cokey was started, and people danced all over the walls and statues to keep warm. Building works at the site had left a dug-out well which was filled with placards, newspapers and any bits of rubbish, and turned into a makeshift fireplace.

'Revolution', spray-painted on the walls by a first-time young protester, encapsulated the feeling among many of the crowd.

Towards the end of the kettle, police charged horses into the crowd, then denied they had done so – a lie exposed by YouTube footage. Some tell similar stories of police brutality. University of Manchester Students Union (UMSU) Welfare Officer Hannah Paterson said that, despite earlier student cooperation, police had knowingly 'charged horses into a crowd of peaceful students, some of whom were as young as twelve and thirteen'.

The NUS and UCU, once again, issued statements condemning student violence, which infuriated students – and indeed many sympathetic or outraged parents.

Yet it was the response from the rest of the country that revealed the true scale of the movement. From across the country, reports flooded in of student walkouts and protests of a size unseen for decades. The BBC estimated that 130,000 protested nationwide.

Cat and mouse

Another protest was called on Facebook for 30 November. At the next LSA, some discussed cancellation, to avoid being kettled again. But the pull of the movement was too strong. Many thousands turned up, with attendance dominated by younger students. Across the country, often braving threats of expulsion, students walked out of classes and lessons to join their own protests. Trafalgar Square was again the focus.

In London, we were not prepared to be kettled again. As soon as police lines formed, the crowd heading down Whitehall turned and ran the opposite way. Then another police line, and we turned again. This went on all day, in snow and freezing cold. We broke up into smaller groups and marched all over London: down to Victoria station, to Hyde Park Corner, up and along Oxford Street. Another group made it to St Pauls and the Barbican; another over to Waterloo and on to Piccadilly Circus. Someone tweeted out to converge at Trafalgar Square, to which we all responded.

A small number were kettled; scores were beaten. The police said it was in order to 'facilitate peaceful dispersal'. They made arrests, bringing the total detained during the protests to over 150.

The vote in parliament: glowsticks and glass-houses

On 3 December it was announced that the tuition fees vote would take place less than one week later, on 9 December. The NUS, having seemingly hidden for weeks, and the national UCU dutifully announced a polite lobby of MPs, and a 'glowstick vigil' on the Embankment at 3 p.m. The movement, some way ahead of its official leaders, aimed to be at parliament in large numbers. The LSA agreed to march – aiming to beat the kettle through strength of numbers. ULU and London Region UCU provided logistical support.

Fraught negotiations with the police produced a route that led us into Parliament Square, and out again to the 'official' demonstration. The mood was determined. Police formed solid lines along the length of the demonstration, riot helmets at the ready. A few speeches, and we were off. Thirty thousand students surged through central London, police running to keep up. The raucous, unrestrained crowd arrived in Parliament Square well ahead of the police schedule – and, much against police wishes, they stayed. Parliament was the target. No need for a vigil: we were celebrating the birth of a movement, not the death of education. The fences were torn down and the whole Square occupied. Again there was music and dancing and chanting. BBC *Newsnight*'s Paul Mason coined the term 'Dubstep Rebellion' after this day.

This is a personal snapshot of those days. There are many thousands of stories from the new student rebellions. I wish I could share them all. This movement has gained even more confidence: as we go to print, we hear of the uprisings in Tunisia, Egypt and Jordan. Our solidarity goes out to all those standing up to our bully governments, and may the struggles continue.

Freedom for Palestine and a warm welcome to the old mole that has emerged again: the revolution.

THE REBELLION IN CONTEXT

James Meadway

The great student revolt appeared as if from nowhere. From out of the campuses and colleges a generation shook off its long-assumed apathy and roared into the streets. Its energy and idealism have become an inspiration for all those confronting austerity. It has thrown up new ways of organizing and offered a vision of a different society. But this emergent rebellion had material roots.

The bare facts are well known. The provision of higher education has dramatically expanded in the last forty years – from a bare 5 per cent of eighteen- to nineteen-year-olds attending HE institutions, to 45 per cent today. With the 1.7 million sixth-formers and FE students, there are 4.2 million students registered in UK institutions today. Aside from a minority of Tory recidivists, it is accepted by all that attendance will now remain high.

This expansion was and is linked to the transformation of capitalism over the same period: the creation of a mass, service-sector working class necessitated a different form of education – in particular, the provision of generalized information-processing and comprehension skills, as provided by the bulk of arts, humanities and social science degrees, and – alongside that – the increased specialization of definite vocational qualifications in sciences and engineering. The workforce, on average, has become more skilled.

Government, not private firms, took the leading role in this. Private capital transferred the costs of educating its own workforce onto the state. Previously, relatively stable employment in firms that could not easily uproot themselves had created the conditions in which job-specific training and apprenticeships could be provided in-house, despite their expense. The workforce would be unlikely to move jobs, and the provisioning firm would itself expect to be tied to long-term investments in specific locations.

The disintegration of traditional manufacturing, gathering pace from the 1970s but devastating through the 1980s, broke open that system. Numbers in apprenticeship training declined from 240,000 in the mid-1960s to 53,000 by 1990. More informal post-school training, provided in the workplace, diminished as increased numbers undertook formal, state-provided education. The proportion of sixteen- to eighteen-year-olds in further education rose from 35 per cent in 1985 to close to 70 per cent by 2009.

This represented a massive socialization of the costs of education beyond school age. These costs were transferred away from the private sector – either individual households or firms – and onto the state. Education as a whole became a growing concern for the state, verging on an obsession: between 1944 and 1979 there were four Education Acts passed; between 1988 and 2007, there were seventeen.

The HE system was continually prodded and poked, with new and more onerous targeting and assessment regimes introduced, like the much-loathed Research Assessment Exercise. These are a reflection of the state's new concern with the content of education itself. Where once it could be left to private institutions, and therefore largely ignored by government, post-sixteen education itself was now a direct concern. Academic autonomy, once prized as virtually the essence of a free university system, came under direct attack.

The state attempted to perform functions that had until then largely been left to either private or highly autonomous institutions: either private firms, or the universities themselves. As the state incorporated their functions, it attempted to ape the market. Mark Fisher has described what he calls the 'business ontology' of education: the drive to make everything fit to a presumed business ethic: so standards and targets are applied, and incentives structured to ape, badly, the way markets behave – while state control and ownership are retained.

Public costs over the initial period were held down, while expansion was attempted, so that spending per student collapsed by 40 per cent from the mid-1970s to the mid-1990s.

New Labour, elected in 1997 promising to prioritize 'education, education, education', offered its own solution – the re-privatization of those costs. These fell not on private firms, but onto the individual student – or, more likely, the students' parents. The removal of grants and the introduction of university tuition fees in 1998, and of top-up fees in 2004, were both motivated by efforts to sustain levels of spending per student within the HE system.

It was, in its own terms, a success. Funding per student stabilized, even as expansion continued. Graduate employment, often to the public sector, remained high. There were even some limited reforms elsewhere in the system – most notably the introduction of the Education

Maintenance Allowance (EMA), up to £30 a week paid to students from lower-income families attending college. This was the material basis for New Labour in student politics: tuition fees were inevitable, but would be kept low; expansion would continue, with funding; and jobs would be forthcoming on graduation. For as long as those conditions held, there would be no serious challenge to its dominance. Flickers of revolt sometimes flared – the anti-war protests of the early 2000s, occupations over the invasion of Gaza at the end of the decade – but the sodden blanket of Blairism smothered all.

It was the financial crisis beginning in 2007/08 that blew the entire, finely balanced structure wide open. The crisis forced governments around the world into bailing out their stricken banking systems. In the UK, the total cost of this operation has been reliably estimated, by the Bank of England, as around £1.2 trillion – an unimaginably large sum, close to the entire output of the economy for a year. And it is this cost that has pushed the recent increase in debt and rising deficits.

These debts have nothing at all to do with supposedly 'excessive' state spending on public services – despite insistent claims to the contrary. Between 1997 and 2007, before the crash, Labour spent on average 38.9 per cent of GDP on public expenditure. Between 1979 and 1997, Tory governments spent on average 43.8 per cent of GDP. Tory governments were more 'profligate' than Labour.

But in any case the point is nonsense: it is the exceptional spending arising from the failure of the banking system that has produced the increased national debt. And it is the failure to reform the banking system in any way that is driving the generalized cuts now. Bailing out the banks meant, to all intents and purposes, that the bankers got away with it. They are behaving exactly the same now as they did before. That is the meaning of this year's £7 billion bonus pot. The status quo has been restored – at our expense.

Like spoiled children, if they're not punished for doing something wrong, bankers carry on doing exactly the same thing. The same gambles and delusions are all still there. The risks now building up inside the banking system are substantial. There are strong reasons to expect a further crisis. But states are weakened after the last bailout. They cannot afford another.

The Bank of International Settlements, in last year's annual report, said very clearly that 'highly indebted governments may not be able to act as a buyer of last resort to save banks in a crisis'. Balance sheets in France, Germany, Spain and the UK may all be too 'fragile' to cope.

The New Economics Foundation provided some figures to back this up. British banks will face a funding shortfall of £156 billion over 2011, as current public assistance dries up. They will be driven to look for another bailout. Even the International Monetary Fund has called the banking system the global economy's 'Achilles heel' – a continual threat to stability. The first bailout will spawn children.

This situation defines the crisis now. It creates a very particular problem: having agreed to socialize the costs of the banking system in the last crisis, we have also implicitly agreed to take on the costs of the next crisis – and the next, and the one after that. But British capitalism simply isn't big or dynamic enough to afford both a financial sector of this bloated size and other public services. The state cannot fund both.

So a question is posed: Do we fund the City of London, or do we fund public services?

This Coalition of millionaires has unabashedly chosen the former. That compels it to squeeze as much spending out of the state as possible. That means, for higher education, a lurch towards outright privatization – throwing universities back into the private sector, with all the consequences for access and inequality this creates. It means trashing one of New Labour's genuine reforms by scrapping EMA.

The students have provided a different answer. The shattering of New Labour's consensus opened the space for radicalism on a scale not seen in the UK for decades. Against the logic of bailouts and bonuses, the students demanded funding for public services. Against Cameron and Clegg's vision of a liberal market society, where value would be defined solely by price, they offered a different vision of a broader, inclusive education, valued for its own sake.

In doing so, they broke the consensus on cuts that had held since the Coalition was formed. They have cleared the path for others to follow. The outcome of 2011 will be decided by how many take their lead.

Flashback:

CAPITALISM'S DISCONTENTS[1]

Eric Hobsbawm

The students rebelling against a society which offers them all its prizes, the workers forgetting about their HP debts to establish, by their spontaneous mass action, that life is more than overtime earnings and holidays in Palma: these are not French but potentially international phenomena.

We knew – though the politicians didn't – that people are not contented. They feel that their lives are meaningless in the consumer society. They know that, even when they are comfortable (which many of them are not) they are also more powerless than before, more pushed around by giant organizations for whom they are items and not men.

They know that the official mechanisms for representing them – elections, parties, etc. – have tended to become a set of ceremonial institutions going through empty rituals. They do not like it – but until recently they did not know what to do about it, and may have wondered whether there was anything that they could do about it. What France proves is that when someone demonstrates that people are *not* powerless, they may begin to act again. Perhaps even more than this: that only the sense of impotence is holding many of us back from acting like men and not zombies.

---

1   From the second issue of *Black Dwarf*, published on 1 June 1968 in London.

Flashback:

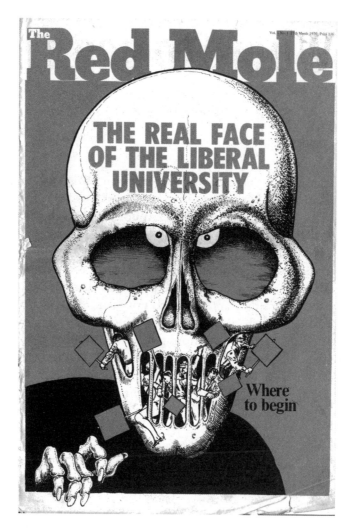

Front Cover of *The Red Mole*, Vol.1 No. 1 17th March 1970

EDUCATION CUTS, CLASS AND RACISM

Kanja Sessay

The day of 10 November 2010 was a sea-change moment for the student movement, with over 50,000 students, lecturers and parents taking to the streets of London to oppose the tripling of tuition fees. This will have a devastating impact on students and the wider society, as our education system has become one of the most expensive in the world, pricing out the most disadvantaged in our society. The NUS Black Students Campaign represents over one million African, Asian, Arab and Caribbean students, and has had a longstanding policy in favour of free education, which it has defended and promoted against successive governments and, unfortunately, successive leaderships of the National Union of Students (NUS), which repeatedly failed to back, let alone call, days of action in the weeks leading up to the vote.

The cuts of the Tory-led government will impact on the life chances of British people in every area, but particularly on the poorest and most vulnerable. The waves of student protests, occupations and opposition, despite police brutality against young people and an NUS leadership that was forced to label itself both 'spineless' and 'dithering', are just the beginning of the opposition to the Tory-led government's agenda. Despite the votes to increase fees and to end the Education Maintenance Allowance (EMA), the student movement is repeating that 'this is just the beginning'. With support from union leaders such as Len McClusky from Unite and Billy Hayes from the Communication Workers Union (CWU), it is clear that this has been the first of many points of resistance to protect vital public services and a quality education that is accessible to all.

The vote for a hike in fees to £9,000 was far closer than many had anticipated, showing the level of pressure that parliamentarians faced on this issue. On the day of the vote, my campaign was proud to join the tens of thousands of students who marched on parliament, facing kettling, horse charges and police batons. Meanwhile, the NUS leadership called a forlorn candle-lit vigil on the same day, mourning the loss of free education, with President Aaron Porter even failing to step up and condemn the brutality, which saw forty-three students injured over the course of the protests. The police actions led to injuries, including a Muslim woman who was knocked unconscious on one demonstration and then faced insulting comments about her headscarf from medical staff when she was being treated for concussion. Aaron's silence was one of many betrayals, which included urging Simon Hughes to decrease the fees hike rather than simply oppose it, and then refusing to back further student-led demonstrations in January. But this has not stopped the emerging new student movement from grabbing the attention of the media or capturing the mood of the moment.

This is a movement that is younger and broader than we have ever seen before – from school-children and sixth-formers right up to university lecturers, teachers and parents. This reflects the brutal impact that the cuts will have on generations to come. Facebook and Twitter have made it more dynamic than ever before – getting the facts out has been more important, given the media bias against students. Demonstrations, occupations, teach-ins, sit-ins and flash-mobs are keeping the issue of fees constantly in the headlines – these are now the common language of the anti-fees movement, which has not gone away despite the votes in parliament and the brutal treatment of peaceful demonstrators at the hands of the police.

These cuts are ideological and regressive. That has had a galvanizing, rather than a demoralizing effect, as there is now a coherent understanding within the movement that opposing these cuts is in the best interest of the economy. That is very dangerous ground for any government to have to concede, as it undermines from the outset the authority of its proposals with entire sections of society.

Investing in education gives the country a return: it stimulates growth and would tackle the deficit. The £23 billion that was spent on higher education produced an economic return of £60 billion, arising from a variety of sources, including jobs, exports and innovation.[1] For every pound invested in higher education, the economy expands by £2.60. Treasury models indicate that half of this – around £1.30 – comes back in tax revenue, giving the government extra income on each pound to pay off the national debt or invest in other public services.[2] The

---

1   Speech by Lord Mandelson, 'The Future of Higher Education – The Peering Lecture', 11 February 2010.
2   Treasury Economic Working Paper No. 5, November 2008.

reduction in investment will reduce the number of graduates. Britain was a world leader for graduate rates in 2000. It is now below the OECD average.

The anti-fees and labour movements understand that these cuts are economic vandalism, hitting the poorest and most disadvantaged hardest, saddling students with debts. With 75 per cent of black people in this country living in the eighty-eight poorest wards, black students are among those set to fare the worst. The majority of black students study in further education, so the loss of the EMA will impact disproportionately upon our life chances. The loss of the EMA will also have a regional impact. Almost 647,000 of England's sixteen-to-eighteen-year-olds receive the allowance. In Birmingham and Leicester, four-fifths of sixteen-year-olds receive the allowance. It is already estimated that the scrapping of the EMA will mean that 70 per cent of those at sixth-form college will drop out.

These cuts will bring nothing but more misery for this generation, a much heavier burden on our shoulders – and we can expect to see a continued rise in youth unemployment, especially for young black people. Discrimination in the workplace means that black people already take longer to pay back their student debt. Black people earn less than their white counterparts. For example, the pay penalty for black African women, even when skills are taken into account, is 27 per cent according to government research.[3]

This is compounded by the fact that black graduates are more likely to be unemployed than white graduates. A government sting operation in 2009 found that there is widespread racial discrimination against workers with African and Asian names. It found that an applicant who appeared to be white would send nine applications before receiving a positive response, while ethnic minority candidates with the same qualifications and experience had to send sixteen applications before receiving a similar response.[4]

All of these factors are set to become more pronounced under the current government and its proposals for cuts. The rising activism and anger that was sparked by the government's moves are set to continue to be part of the political landscape. The impact of unfair economic policies on young people and students is providing a flashpoint not just in Britain, but has been part of the resistance to similar austerity measures in parts of Europe. More recently, the price rises in Tunisia had a galvanizing effect on young people as part of the uprising against the corrupt Ben Ali government. Just as the students involved in the education funding protests here are saying

---

3 'An Anatomy of Economic Inequality in the UK', report of the National Equality Panel, January 2010.
4 *Observer*, 18 October 2009.

'this is just the beginning', it looks like the baton will be passed to other sectors of society as the Tory-led cuts target other parts of the public sector. What is clear is that the breadth of opposition to the education cuts demonstrates the socio-economic and political centrality of education to our society. The struggle to save our education continues.

PAST AND PRESENT: THE LONDON SCHOOL OF ECONOMICS

Ashok Kumar

The Pandora's Box of British student resistance broke open on 27 October 1968.

Vietnam was ablaze. The West, after decades of expansionary policies eastward, found itself mired in internal acrimony. The young and passionate, shipped off to fight wars for the old and powerful, had had enough. Universities of the 1960s emerged as breeding grounds for resistance, reclamation and revolution. Berkeley students emboldened free speech, the Sorbonne's championed a general strike, and Berlin's led massive sit-ins. It was London's turn. On a brisk October day, 3,000 students broke through the Houghton Street gates, barricaded themselves in university premises, and rekindled the spirit of a seemingly lost democracy at the hallowed halls of the London School of Economics.

Déjà vu running on forty-two! On 10 November 2010, in response to government-instituted education cuts and the trebling of tuition fees, 1,400 inspired students marched down LSE's Houghton Street, brandished 'Spirit of '68' placards, and united with the 'Free Education Bloc' in the largest student demonstration in British history. The '60s chants of 'London, Paris, Rome, Berlin – We will Fight! We will Win!' had been replaced with the modern-day '1-2-3, L-S-E, We don't want no fucking fees!' The memory of '68, its dissent and protest, had been indelibly etched into our psyches. In other words, although the ends were different, the means remained the same.

Pioneering civil rights leader and ex-slave Frederick Douglass asserted, 'Power concedes nothing without a demand; it never did and it never will.' As an elected organizer at the LSE Students Union, I couldn't agree more, prompting the following reflection. Do resistance-based student actions of the past have a direct effect on what it means to be a student today?

Prior to the 1960s, Western institutions of higher learning often remained relegated to elites who, in social conflict, sided with structures of power. From the 1960s, as diverse layers of society finally gained university access, things began to change. In many cases, a student culture of inclusivity burgeoned in opposition to the very forces that had previously been exclusive, i.e. institutionalized racism, global violence, and political suppression.

At the London School of Economics in 1968, for example, this transformation was manifested in anti-war marches and student-led protests. Avenues of dissent were no more defined according to professorial diktats, textbook protocols, or historic precedent. Instead, students were able to use their institutions to fight entrenched powers rather than deepening their roots. The legacy of an institution did not remain confined to the stones and mortar of the building; instead, it lay within the very consciousness of the students who decided to shape it and make it their own.

Until recently, the mass activism at the LSE was something we could only read about in history books and talk about in class. The spirit of the Fabians who founded the LSE in 1895, and the radicals of the movements who ignited that torch in 1968, seemed of the distant past. Their iconic images, seared into our collective memories and peppering today's LSE brochures, are an inspiration for our present-day struggles.

Although the LSE's major student movements are separated by more than forty years, parallels between the two are clear: the mass march down Houghton Street, the passionate Union General Meetings in the Old Theatre, occupations by hundreds of students and lecturers, and many others . . . together, we're the LSE: learning from and building our own (hi)story.

LECTURERS, DEFEND YOUR STUDENTS!

Nina Power

In times of occupation, or the fear of it, university management routinely circulates documents to lecturers with titles like 'General Security Measures' and 'Student Disruption: General Guidance for Staff'. These documents instruct us in the following ways: 'Individual staff should not engage/debate with protestors'; 'decline, politely, to enter into argument (whether with those involved in the disruption or those not involved or opposed) over the rights and wrongs of the case'.

Lecturers are further instructed to 'keep College plans confidential – do not divulge information to those NOT involved in the disruption or to staff unconnected with the action', and to 'secure all doors, secure all confidential papers in locked cabinets, possibly removing the most sensitive items, close down all computers – if action is not imminent, keep one open for messages'.

Don't talk to students, don't listen to them, certainly don't try to understand why they might be angry. The common cause of lecturers and students in opposing education cuts and fee increases haunts these desperate internal communications. The message is clear: students are at all times moments away from becoming a feral mob out to destroy university property, mess with internal communications and disrupt the smooth running of the contemporary marketized university.

In early January 2011, an officer from Scotland Yard's counter-terrorism unit sent an email to staff at London universities which reads as follows: 'I would be grateful if in your capacity at your various colleges that should you pick up any relevant information that would be helpful to all of us to anticipate possible demonstrations or occupations, please forward it onto me.'

Lecturers are to become informants; their students the enemy within – 'terrorists'. Lecturers involved in supporting the student protests in November have their photographs splashed across

29

newspaper covers: 'Full Marks for the Riots say Lecturers', attacking staff at Goldsmiths who had defended the occupation of Tory Party HQ at Millbank. Just as staff and students were suspended by their own management as a consequence of supporting the Middlesex philosophy protests in 2010, a clear divide has opened up between those who understand that their cause is the same as that of their students, and those who see students as little more than tiresome (if profitable) units to be shuffled through on their way to jobs that increasingly don't exist. (It should be noted, though, that some institutions have managers who understand and share the concerns of staff and students: in early December Paul O'Prey, Vice Chancellor of Roehampton University – alongside Les Ebdon of the University of Bedfordshire and Caroline Gipps of the University of Wolverhampton – refused to sign a letter originally intended to be signed by all English Vice Chancellors supporting the fee increases.)

The idea that staff and students are opposed on the question of fees and cuts, and should operate in mutual suspicion of one another, is indicative of a broader and more fundamental confusion in the way students and staff are supposed to relate to each other in the contemporary university. The introduction of fees, and the university's description of students as 'clients', has led to a disastrous, mutually destructive compact. Are the students buying a degree? Are lecturers selling them a product? Should students expect lecturers to provide them with whatever they want because they are told to feel that they are paying for a service? When staff and students march together on protests, when staff support occupations and students defend their lecturers, then the true stakes of the current university system are made manifest. They are attacking us, all of us, and, no matter how many police requests and paranoid internal documents we receive, we must defend our students at all costs.

ALBION ROSE

Susan Matthews

Since 9 December, when my son was injured at the student protests in London, I have been haunted by a print by William Blake known as 'Albion Rose'. It is one of those images that are too familiar, too clichéd even, to see properly – forever owned by the 1960s. Although created in the 1790s, it was inscribed by Blake with the date 1780, the year in which rioting mobs ruled London for a week, burned down prisons and threatened the Bank of England. For most contemporary observers, the Gordon Riots of 1780 were an ugly outbreak of fanaticism, a horror best swiftly forgotten. Yet Blake's image is strangely exultant, a collective figure of the nation (or the world) reborn.

Since 9 December, I've been contacted by people I would never otherwise have met. Parents tell me of their pride in their children's commitment to defending education. Activists write to warn of the difficult road to psychological recovery. Political economists have shared their analysis of the government's destructive project. Some, as well, reveal their scepticism. One such was the fellow academic concerned that many of the protesters were not themselves affected by the cuts – to him, a sign of bad faith. Unbuttoned by the anonymity of the web, others pour scorn on the middle-class protester – drawn to the melee, perhaps, by the buzz of chaotic energy; or worse, unwilling to fund bursaries for the poor.

For some, it is hard to see protest as anything other than a collective outbreak of madness. For too long the educated few have imagined themselves as standing against the forces of unreason embodied in the mob. This story is well told in Adam Curtis's BBC series, *The Century of the Self*, or in John Carey's 1992 account of the snobberies underlying modernist aesthetics in *The Intellectuals and the Masses*. Exactly this fear emerged in David Cameron's response to the student protest in which my son was injured. So careful up to that point to appear the voice of consensus and compassion, Cameron now took sides: it was 'us' against 'them'. Protesters had behaved in an 'absolutely feral way' and violence (he claimed) pervaded the protest.

Like Cameron I am a product of Oxford, but unlike him I have a wider experience of education, having taught for twenty years in a post-1992 university. I know that educational excellence is not the preserve of elite institutions. In the marketing of universities, students are encouraged to choose according to facilities or reputation or glossy advertisements. Working in a university, I would instead choose according to evidence. My son chose to study at the leading department for the study of modern European philosophy, which was at Middlesex, a post-1992 university. His department was closed because it offered a high staff-to-student ratio and a large proportion of postgraduate students: the kind of educational experience that is normal for Russell Group students.

Walking to Parliament Square on 9 December I felt out of place, and wondered whether to stop off at Tate Britain instead. But the collective punishment of 'kettling' makes no distinctions among protestors. My loyalty is to those who waited: cold, fearful, angry and baffled at the apparent determination of the police to provoke. It is the voice of the protestors that demonstrates logic, cutting through the smokescreen of 'reform'. I am moved that so many of the protestors will not themselves be hit by the hike in fees or the loss of EMA. To doubt the possibility of altruism is to imagine a bleak future.

Since 9 December I see Blake's hackneyed image in a new way. Blake witnessed the riots; he was caught up inadvertently in the mob. Being there, he must have seen things that contemporary accounts did not record. The images that stay with me from the student protests are not those of the violence splashed over the front pages (which I did not myself witness) or of 'victims' injured and beaten (though I sat by the bedside of my son). Instead, what I remember is the determination of a varied group of people to resist unfair treatment, to question a false narrative of necessity, and to protect the fragile gains of decades of expansion of higher education.

Flashback:

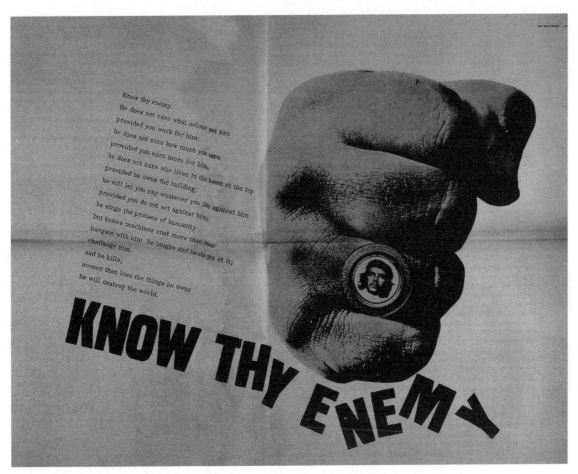

Know thy enemy.
He does not care what colour you are
provided you work for him;
he does not care how much you earn
provided you earn more for him,
he does not care who lives in the room at the top
provided he owns the building;
he will let you say whatever you like against him
provided you do not act against him;
he sings the praises of humanity
but knows machines cost more than men
bargain with him he laughs and beats you at it;
challenge him
and he kills;
sooner than lose the things he owns
he will destroy the world.

KNOW THY ENEMY

A Poster Poem by Christoper Logue (*Black Dwarf*, 1968)

REBIRTH OF STUDENT ACTIVISM

Hesham Yafai

One of the most remarkable features of the present wave of student activism has been its ability to place itself within a wider struggle: both with other areas of UK society under attack from the Coalition government, and with people in other parts of the world fighting for the right to education. We can see the former in events such as Goldsmiths' occupation of Deptford town hall to protest at council cuts, King's College London students joining RMT workers at tube stations to protest ticket office closures, and LSE students joining the fire-fighters on picket lines in solidarity with their efforts to prevent unfair contract changes. But to appreciate the movement's internationalism, we need to return to 27 December 2008.

On that date Israel began its 22-day offensive against the besieged Gaza strip, in what Amnesty International has since called the '22 Days of Death and Destruction'.[1] The official United Nations investigation into the attack found that Israel had committed war crimes and possibly crimes against humanity. While international leaders the world over trotted out their usual, tired chorus of rehearsed 'condemnation', in the UK hundreds of thousands of people joined demonstrations across the country as anger spilled out onto the streets.

Yet the anger did not end there. Students returned to their campuses and began to organize. There was an acknowledgement that the conventional democratic channels had failed them. To effect real change students realized they needed to self-organize and move to unconventional channels to fight the battles that lay ahead. In early 2009 students from the School of Oriental and African Studies occupied one of the university's largest galleries in solidarity with the people

---

1   'Israel/Gaza: Operation "Cast Lead": 22 Days of Death and Destruction', Official Amnesty International Report: at www. amnesty.org

of Palestine. The myth of the so-called 'iPod generation' had been exploded; suddenly, there was talk of the reawakening of the spirit of '68. Dozens of universities soon followed, including Essex, Birmingham, Oxford, Cambridge and Manchester.

Students at the occupations began to organize effectively, ushered along by the visitations of experienced campaigners and activists from Tariq Ali and Alex Callinicos, to Ghada Karmi and Lindsey German. Lecture shut-outs, walkouts, demonstrations, stalls, stunts, planning meetings and large-scale events embraced colleges and universities up and down the country. It was truly a rebirth of student activism, transforming disempowered students to front-line resisters, spurred on by an injustice committed halfway across the world and signalling a new era in student politics.

The fact that British students were protesting in their name was not lost on the Palestinians, who sent thousands of messages of support and gratitude. Today, education in Palestine continues to come under attack from a variety of directions: the cantonization of the West Bank severely delays and periodically prevents students from reaching classes via check-points; the controlled Palestinian economy means tens of thousands of students wishing to study cannot afford to do so; strikes by UNRWA workers mean classes have to be cancelled; students constantly face risk of arrest and trial before a military court; schools and universities face closure and transmutation into military barracks; and so on. Despite these many adversities the Palestinians continue to struggle on and, remarkably, still exhibit the second highest literacy rates in the Arab world.[2]

An international Right To Education campaign, which has its roots in Birzeit University, is gathering momentum: in the summer of 2010 it held an international conference in the West Bank. Right to Education week is slowly becoming a permanent fixture, and is helping to link up the various struggles across the world for a free and fair education. It is a struggle that crosses national borders, as has also been seen through the acts of solidarity with French and Greek students and workers.

So from Gaza to Golders Green, via Greece and beyond, a collective struggle is beginning to take place. International solidarity is back on the agenda and the sentiment of a shared cause is pervasive. Perhaps this sense of unity is best expressed through the statement most manifested in messages of solidarity between different groups across the world: 'Our struggle is your struggle, and your struggle is ours.'

---

2   Human Development Report 2009, *Overcoming Barriers: Human Mobility and Development*, at: http://hdr.undp.org.

A NEW STRATEGY IS NEEDED FOR A BRUTAL NEW ERA

Peter Hallward

On 9 December, the government passed one of the most reactionary and ill-conceived pieces of legislation in this country's history. At a stroke, the increase in tuition fees promises to destroy publicly funded further and higher education in England, and to consolidate one of the most far-reaching shifts of power and opportunity that has ever been engineered in a so-called democracy. Camouflaged by vacuous reference to 'student choice' and a few token concessions to the less affluent, the new law will rig the entire system in favour of the privileged few. It will accelerate the conversion of genuine education into market-driven job training, and it will do irreversible damage to arts, humanities and social science subjects in particular.

Students and staff have mobilized in unprecedented numbers and unprecedented ways to oppose these disastrous education cuts. Unable to sustain, let alone win, the argument in public debate, unwilling to devote even minimal time for general consultation and discussion, the government has instead opted to quash our demonstrations with naked force, intimidation and collective punishment. Up and down the country, secondary school students have been threatened with expulsion for joining local protest marches. Scores of protesters have been injured by riot police, hundreds have been arrested and many thousands have repeatedly been corralled and detained (and then photographed) against their will.

Attempts to portray the protests as 'riots' provoked by a frenzied few are a clichéd evasion of the real issues at stake here. Anyone who has participated in these demonstrations knows that each one has been a massive and powerful expression of revulsion for the government's plans, an uncompromising rejection of the cuts and the neo-liberal priorities they represent. It takes some nerve for a government that is destroying our education system (while waging war in Afghanistan, investing in new nuclear weapons and using 'anti-terror' laws to persecute large swathes of its own population) to treat the tens of thousands of students and lecturers defending it as if they were guilty of collusion in violence.

In reality, the great majority of the violence has been suffered rather than inflicted by the protesters. In reality, given the calamity that confronts us, protesters have acted with remarkable discipline and restraint. In reality, although police justify the use of 'containment' as a means of preventing violence, most of what violence there was during the 9 December rally began well after the vast kettling operation was set up.

I imagine that the experience of my own students (studying philosophy at Kingston University, or at Middlesex University, where I taught until summer 2010) is typical of that of many others. Most of them have already committed huge amounts of time and energy to the anti-cuts campaign, and many have attended all of the major London rallies over the past month.

Shortly after the 9 December vote, a policeman hit one of my current MA students on the head with his truncheon. He said it felt like he was struck by a solid metal bar. After being bandaged by other students and released from the kettle on account of his obvious injuries, police medics took a quick look at him, and checked that his eyes were still responding to light. According to my student, they recommended that he make his own way to his local hospital in North London, where he received stitches.

At least a dozen of the students I work with didn't escape the kettle so quickly, and were among the thousand or so people who were eventually forced back on to Westminster Bridge shortly after 9 p.m., without water or toilets, without information or explanation, in the freezing cold and wind, long after the media had gone home. They were then crowded together for a couple of hours between solid lines of baton-wielding riot police. Many students say they were beaten with truncheons as they held their open hands high in the air, in the hope of calming their attackers.

'I was standing at the front of the group with nowhere to go', Johann Hoiby, a Middlesex philosophy student, told me. 'My hands were open and visible, when a riot police officer, without provocation, hit me in the face with his shield, screaming "get back" when I clearly couldn't move. The most terrifying thing was the fact that everyone was screaming that people were getting crushed, yet the police kept pushing us backwards when we had nowhere to go.'

Around the same time, one of Johann's classmates, Zain Ahsan, was 'hit in the abdominal area with a baton; I shouted back at the officer that my hands were in the air and I was being pushed by the people behind me'.

37

My Kingston students say they saw people having panic attacks, people seized up with asthma, people who fell under the feet of the crowd. 'The fact that there were no deaths on that bridge', one says, 'is a true miracle.'

Some students claim that they were then kicked by police as they were slowly released, single-file, through a narrow police corridor. Everyone was forcibly photographed, and many of the people detained on the bridge were then taken away for questioning.

The story of one Middlesex undergraduate who used to sit in on my MA classes, Alfie Meadows, is already notorious. He received a full-on blow to the side of his skull. My partner and I found him wandering in Parliament Square a little after 6 p.m., pale and distraught, looking for a way to go home. He had a large lump on the right side of his head. He said he'd been hit by the police and didn't feel well. We took one look at him and walked him towards the nearest barricaded exit as quickly as possible. It took a few minutes to reach the taciturn wall of police blocking Great George Street, and then convince them to let him through their shields; but they refused to let me, my partner or anyone else accompany him in search of medical help. We assumed that he would receive immediate and appropriate treatment on the other side of the police wall as a matter of course, but in fact he was left to wander off on his own, towards Victoria.

As it turns out, Alfie's subsequent survival depended on three chance events. If his mother (a lecturer at Roehampton, who was also 'contained' in Parliament Square) hadn't received his phone call and caught up with him shortly afterwards, the odds are that he'd have passed out on the street. If they hadn't then stumbled upon an ambulance waiting nearby, his diagnosis could have been fatally delayed. And if the driver of this ambulance hadn't overruled an initial refusal of the A&E department of the Chelsea and Westminster hospital to look at Alfie, his transfer to the Charing Cross neurological unit for emergency brain surgery might well have come too late.

With each new protest, we learn a little more about what we are up against.

For decades, the corporate interests that promoted and then implemented their neo-liberal 'reforms' sought to present them as a form of modernizing improvement, one carried by the inexorable progress of history towards the untrammelled pursuit of profit 'for the benefit of all'. For decades, this grotesque distortion of reality has helped to mask a relentless assault on the remnants of our not-yet-for-profit services and resources, and to persuade many of those sheltering in the more privileged parts of the world to tolerate such 'development' as a necessary price to be paid for their comfort and security. Not any more. The days of 'there is no alternative' are rapidly becoming a distant memory, and all over Europe the bankers' masks have begun hiding behind police visors.

On Thursday, 9 December, the government converted its assault on further and higher education into law, but only additional reliance on police truncheons will allow them to enforce it. To judge from the government's response so far, it is now only a matter of time before truncheons are reinforced by water cannon and rubber bullets, and before near-fatal injuries become fatalities. As Michel Foucault understood, however, the successful exercise of power is 'proportional to its ability to hide its own mechanisms'. If the neo-liberal programme has never yet pushed so deep into the British public sphere, rarely have the means to impose it looked so exposed. No amount of police brutality can enforce an unpopular measure in the face of massive non-compliance. If threats to expel students may intimidate an isolated few, they soon become risible if ignored en masse.

The government has no mandate to treble fees and eliminate the Education Maintenance Allowance, and parliament offers no credible alternative. The only way to block implementation of the Tory cuts is to mobilize schools and campuses over the coming months in ways that will oblige the government to back down. The Tories have called the question; as Howard Zinn reminds us, you can't be neutral on a moving train.

Flashback:

KETTLING, BERLIN STYLE 1967[1]

Fritz Teufel

Those who wished to avoid giving the impression that they agreed with the imperialist complicity with which Bonn and Washington supported all regimes in the Third World that are inimical to emancipation, who wished to avoid giving the impression that they approved of illiteracy, hunger, disease and exploitation in Persia, had no alternative but to demonstrate when the 'greatest reformer of all times', the operetta gangster of Teheran, the Viceroy of the American oil companies in Persia, was received in Berlin with pomp and circumstance. Unfortunately, the Commune could not think of much that could be done apart from the demonstration paper bags which were, above all, to protect the Persian fellow students from the secret service of their country. Nevertheless, we took part in the demonstration against the Shah in order to see what would happen. After all, there had to be some occasion when somebody else besides the Commune produced ideas.

One thing has become particularly clear in connection with state visits: official politics assumes more and more the character of a circus; the politicians become interchangeable with ham actors. It is no accident that we talk of the political stage. (Some actors, of course, are quite cute; for instance Heinrich Lubke, the West German president. One could hardly believe that, once upon a time, he designed concentration camps; one could, at most, think of him as a former head-waiter at the Führer's headquarters.) The population is being degraded to the status of the theatrical audience. T. thinks that the audience in a theatre has good cause to throw eggs and tomatoes if they don't like the play.

---

1 Extract from Fritz Teufel, 'Prophylactic Notes for the Self-Indictment of the Accused', in Tariq Ali, ed., *New Revolutionaries: Left Opposition* (London: Owen, 1969), pp. 198–201.

The evening in front of the opera house

T. arrived some time after seven-thirty. He felt some misgivings when he saw the barricade through which the police were herding the demonstrators into a narrow gangway between a railing and a building-fence. In addition there was a gigantic police force. T. believed, however, that these preparations had been made to intimidate the demonstrators, but not in order to facilitate beating them systematically, as was in fact done later. Clashes began at seven-forty-five when policemen, who had been placed on the building-site behind the fence, moved against the demonstrators who were sitting on the fence. Rubber rings flew over the fence on to the demonstrators – some fell on the street, since the gangway was so narrow. No stones were thrown. Some demonstrators threw things back. When the VIP appeared, eggs and tomatoes were thrown in front of the entrance to the opera house. Smoke-bombs were thrown on to the street, which were then thrown back into the tightly packed mass of demonstrators. T. can say with absolute certainty that he did not throw a single stone, still less incite others to do so; nor did he see any policemen or demonstrators throwing stones.

Relations with the police

We have nothing against the police. On the contrary: in December 1966 we demonstrated in favour of the introduction of a thirty-five-hour week for the police. However, we do have misgivings when we see the police being misused for political purposes, or when the consciousness industry makes deliberate attempts to incite the police against the students. When one sees pictures of uniformed men using their truncheons to beat a woman who is lying in the street, it is understandable if stones are thrown, even if one does not approve.

However, one thing is certain: people who show themselves to be inhuman to such a degree cannot even themselves have been treated as human beings. These were no free citizens of a democratic society, but rather bloodhounds trained to savagery, like the American elite troops in Vietnam.

Tomatoes, eggs, smoke-bombs

T. declares his solidarity with all those who have thrown objects suitable for demonstration purposes (that means objects incapable of inflicting injury), such as eggs, tomatoes and smoke-bombs. Even though he cannot prove having thrown, for instance, a tomato, he would like to encourage the Court to treat him as it would those who have thrown tomatoes, eggs or smoke-bombs.

Arrest

Shortly after eight o'clock there occurred what has been referred to as 'driving in the main wedge' – a task-force of policemen used their truncheons to beat a gap into the mass of demonstrators. In order to see more clearly what was happening, T. advanced some way towards the scene of action. After the 'driving of the wedge' had been achieved, the police began to drive the demonstrators like a herd of cattle towards Krumme Street. In order to escape a similar fate, those demonstrators who were standing in the vicinity of Sesenheimer Street sat down. T. was sitting near the events, approximately half-way between the building-fence and the railings, facing in the direction of Krumme Street.

When, a little later, a second 'wedge' was driven in the direction of Sesenheimer Street, he turned round to see what was going on, so that he was facing the demonstrators. The police then began to advance against the sitting demonstrators as well. T. tried to ignore the policemen and continued to turn his back on them. Suddenly he was pulled by the hair, and somebody said, 'Move on, get up!' He did not get up, and received blows from the truncheons, as well as kicks. He took no counter-action but confined himself to protecting his face and his arms, while attempting to put away his spectacles away, which, however, were broken nevertheless.

T. was carried away. When he was carried over the middle of the road, he heard a man in civilian clothes (this appears to have been CID officer Böhme) call out as he approached the group – 'Why, that is Teufel' – followed by words to the effect that he was one of those who had prepared a dynamite attack against Humphrey. While T. was still being carried across the road, he was beaten. He shouted loudly. The beating stopped.

T. was transported in a police car to Keith Street police station. He was accompanied by two policemen. One of them, who wore a white uniform jacket (T. later learned that this was Hessner), continued to beat him during the drive with both his fists and his truncheon, all the while demanding hysterically what sort of people they were who prepared dynamite attacks and threw stones – for each policeman, a thousand SDS swine should be done in; we should not imagine that the police did not know us, they had pictures of all of us. All this, and more besides, he shouted several times over. The other policeman (Mertin) sat there and pretended that the whole thing was none of his business. Once T. attempted to explain that he had not thrown stones; whereupon Hessner attacked him again and shouted that all of them had thrown stones.

T. was glad when the drive was over. In the writ of indictment, it says: 'Nothing of note happened during the drive to Keith Street police station.'

WHO CAN PAY FOR THE DEFICIT?

John Rees

The practical effects of the student movement are well known. It significantly raised the level of active resistance to the Coalition government's plans to tens of thousands of people, and resulted in the first open split between the Liberal Democrats and the Coalition government. But in the long run, the ideological impact of the student movement may prove to be as important. Until the student movement began, the Coalition government had been smothering opposition to its deficit-reduction plan with its 'nobody likes it but it's inevitable' rhetoric. Any concession to popular dislike of this policy ran along the lines of 'well, you can choose which cuts you would like'. Those who said that welfare cuts and job losses were not inevitable were, in the words of a *Guardian* editorial, 'deficit deniers'. The student movement suddenly took the 'deficit denier' argument from the margins of political debate to centre-stage.

On the streets, arguments were expressed in slogans and sound bites: 'make the bankers pay', 'make the corporations pay', 'cut warfare not welfare', 'stop tax evasion'. But is there substance behind the slogans? Is there enough money elsewhere in the system that could meet the deficit and make welfare cuts unnecessary? Is it enough? First, let's look at the facts.

Can the banks pay?
The banks and the financial institutions certainly *should* pay. And that's not just because they got us into this mess. The Bank of England estimates the total cost of the bailouts to be £1.3 trillion. That's the same value as all the goods and services produced by the economy in a single year. But financial sector debt alone is over half the value of GDP. Corporate sector debt accounts for another 30 per cent and household debt is only 20 per cent of the value of GDP. So if, as the

43

politicians keep telling us, we are in this state because 'the country has maxed-out on its credit card' we can see that some members of this 'family' have rather more to pay back than others.

The banks can certainly afford to pay. The smallest of the top four British banks, Lloyds, which is now 41 per cent state-owned, has assets worth 74 per cent of the country's GDP. The next biggest, HSBC, has assets worth 105 per cent of GDP. Barclays have assets of 110 per cent of GDP, while RBS's assets are worth 122 per cent. Together the top ten banks have assets totalling 459 per cent of GDP, up from just 40 per cent in 1960.[1] So if total debt is 500 per cent of GDP, the banks' assets alone would just about cover it. But rather than ask for money from the banks, the government has given money to them. Since the 2008 bailout RBS, the bank with the largest assets, has been given most: a staggering £45.5 billion, the GDP of Kenya and Tanzania combined, of UK taxpayers' money has been used to prop up the Royal Bank of Scotland.[2] The British government, too, owns 84 per cent of RBS. But that didn't stop RBS paying out £1.3 million in bonuses in 2010 – and it plans to pay out more in 2011.[3] This year Stephen Hester, the state-appointed head of RBS, will take home an estimated £6.8 million in bonuses, salary and other payments.

The only proposal to come from the Coalition government is a £2 billion bank levy. But, as Neil Faulkner argues, 'At the same time, corporation tax is being cut, the bank levy is a pittance, and top salaries and bonuses have been restored to pre-crash levels. Oxfam has proposed that the bank levy should be £20 billion. Even the IMF thinks it should be £6 billion.'[4]

Can the corporations pay?

UK corporation tax is among the lowest in the industrialized world. Corporate tax rates between 1996 and 2001 were as follows: Canada 35.6 per cent; France 36.4 per cent; Germany 38.3 per cent; Italy 40.3 per cent; Japan 40.9 per cent; USA 39.3 per cent. The UK level of corporation tax was just 30 per cent, a full seven points below the average. New Labour cut corporation tax to 28 per cent, lower than under Margaret Thatcher. This year the Coalition government will lower corporation tax again to just 27 per cent – while the rest of us start to pay 20 per cent VAT.

It's not even the case that the profits of UK firms have taken a hammering during the recession.

1   *The Times*, 26 October 2010, p. 41.
2   World Development Movement, 'Take Action: Stop Taxpayers' Money Funding Climate Change', at www.wdm.org.uk.
3   BBC News online, 'Bank Bonuses "to run to billions in 2011"', at www.bbc.co.uk/news.
4   Neil Faulkner, 'Eleven Reasons to Fight the Con-Dem Cuts#6', at www.counterfire.org.

Of course there has been some decline in profits (about 10 per cent in the non-financial sector) but this is far less than the 26 per cent decline of the US. It's also far lower than the decline in profits of 20 per cent in the recession of the 1990s, and of 30 per cent in the 1980s. These, it must be stressed, are averages in the non-financial sector – so there are many firms out there still raking it in and paying lower corporation tax, while real wages are falling for the first time since the late 1970s.[5]

In the financial sector, profits were recovering by late 2009 when the Bank of England reported that over the past six months banks had been able to increase their profits, reduce concerns about future losses and raise further external capital.[6] The return of massive bonuses for bankers is just one sign of this profits revival.

Tax the rich?

So is 'tax the rich' just an emotionally appealing slogan for hard times, or would it work? The Public and Commercial Services (PCS) union has done research in association with the Tax Justice Network. Their findings show that if tax evasion (illegal non-payment of tax) and tax avoidance (finding legal loopholes so companies don't pay tax) were stopped, the whole of the national deficit could be paid for out of the increase in tax revenues.

The figures show that £25 billion is lost through tax avoidance and a further £70 billion is lost through tax evasion. So just the amount lost due to non-payment of tax is equal to three-quarters of the national deficit.[7]

As the PCS points out, 'Our personal tax system is currently highly regressive. The poorest fifth of the population pay 39.9 per cent of their income in tax, while the wealthiest fifth pays only 35.1 per cent. We need tax justice in personal taxation – which would mean higher income tax rates for the richest and cutting regressive taxes like VAT and council tax.' But the Coalition government has chosen to take the opposite course.

War and Trident: how much could we save?

The immediate costs of the Trident replacement system are estimated at £25 billion, or a bit less than 20 per cent of the whole national deficit. The same sum could fund 100,000 extra fire-fighters every year for the next ten years, or 60,000 newly qualified teachers every year for

---

5 RBS, 'UK Corporate Profits and Employment: Resilient – but can it last?, at www.royalbos.org.

6 BBC News online, 'UK Banking Sector "significantly more stable"', at www.bbc.co.uk/news.

7 Public and Commercial Services Union, 'There Is an Alternative: The Case Against Cuts in Public Spending', at www.pcs.org.uk.

the next twenty years, or 120,000 newly qualified nurses every year for the next ten years – or scrapping student top-up fees for the next ten years.[8]

In official figures released in mid-2010, the cost of the Afghan war was revealed to be much higher than previously thought. The cost to British taxpayers of fighting, diplomacy and reconstruction in Afghanistan and Iraq since the 9/11 attacks has passed £20 billion. This includes £18 billion for military operations on top of the normal defence budget, as well as hundreds of millions of pounds on aid and security for UK officials. But because the total does not cover expenses like troops' basic salaries or long-term care for the seriously wounded, so the final price is likely to be much higher.[9]

This revised figure, almost equal to the cost of Trident replacement, can be broken down in the following way: £190 for every person in Britain, enough to pay for twenty-three new hospitals, 60,000 new teachers, or 77,000 new nurses. Again, this money could be spent abolishing student fees for a decade.

Taken together, the cost of the Afghan War and Trident amounts to something approaching a third of the national deficit. If this money were poured into debt repayment, the national deficit would not be any greater than it has been for many years in the past. The entire 'emergency measures' justification for the government's cuts programme would vanish.

Ideology or necessity?
George Osborne announced the first round of cuts in the House of Commons in October 2010. When Labour's then Shadow Chancellor, Alan Johnson, rose to reply he drew attention to the fact the Tory backbenchers had cheered each cut as it was announced, and went on to claim that many cuts, though not all, were motivated by Tory ideology, not economic necessity. 'This spending review is not about economic necessity; it is about political choices', argued Johnson.[10] The Trades Union Congress (TUC) has adopted the same line. It opposes all 'unnecessary' cuts.

Yet, as we have seen, none of the cuts are 'necessary' in the sense that there is absolutely no other source from which the money could come. On the contrary, there are many other sources. So what the word 'necessary' means in this context is that the cuts are 'necessary' if one accepts the logic of the capitalist system. The Tories and the Liberal Democrats embrace this

---

8   CND, 'No to Trident Replacement Campaign Pack', at www.cnduk.org.
9   Stop the War Coalition, 'UK Cost of Afghan and Iraq Wars at least £20 billion', at http://stopwar.org.uk.
10   Hansard, 20 October 2010, at www.publications.parliament.uk.

logic absolutely and enthusiastically. They are keen to use the repayment of debt as a mechanism by which to alter the balance of class forces to the benefit of the banks and corporations. Rather like the boss of an individual firm faced with the necessity of making redundancies, they will try to sack the union rep first. Labour Party leaders, equally firm advocates of market values during their thirteen-year spell in office, now find it desirable to make an unconvincing case that they would only have made 'necessary' cuts.

But what is really necessary here is an opposition to government which bases itself on a rejection of the logic of capital. It was, after all, this logic which landed us in the crisis in the first place. We should recall that it was not just the banks that began the crisis, not just the 'casino economy' of the City and Wall Street. In fact, it was the interaction of the financial sector and the housing market. Sub-prime lending to house-buyers in the US began this crisis as banks and other lenders searched out ever more marginal and risky markets in which they could make those few extra dollars of profit. The deregulation of the banks spread this risk through the system thereby magnifying its effects, but the root of the default lay in lending to borrowers who could not repay the loans. And the loans were made because lending is a competitive market like every other: if Bank A doesn't do it, Bank B will. Debt repayment by governments involves the same competitive process: if Country A doesn't repay debt as fast as Country B, then credit agencies and international monetary institutions will, so to say, 'take their business' to Country B. This is the 'necessity' of which the politicians speak. Not the absolute necessity of being unable to find the money in any other way, but the absolute necessity of market-driven competition – in debt repayment as in everything else.

If the commonsense realization that there is in fact enough money in the system to pay the debt without making swingeing welfare cuts is to be sustained, it therefore has to be buttressed with the argument that we must break with the logic of capital. But this will never be a purely intellectual process. For the pro-marketeers the logic of the market will always be greater than the power of logic. So the power of logic will need the power of the streets, the unions and the workplaces to enforce it.

Power politics
There are many different ways in which power is won and lost in the streets.

In France in 1968, power was won by the students who fought the police and by the trade unionists who marched with them and then, inspired by their own daring, called a general strike. It was then lost in the electoral process which rescued De Gaulle's presidency. In Britain, power was won by the striking miners and trade unionists who defeated Edward Heath's government. And it was lost in the 'social contract' between the TUC and the Labour government that began to undermine union power and led to the first fall in real wages since the Second World War. That defeat led to the far greater catastrophe of Thatcherism.

The long arm-wrestle between the working people of Britain and Margaret Thatcher had its low point in the defeat of the miners in 1984–85 and its high point in the defeat of the poll tax in 1990. Eventually the social earthquake caused an electoral landslide and, in 1997, the Tories were thrown out of power for more than a decade. Oddly, though the Tories are back in government, the last election did not see a move to the right among the electorate. Most people voted left of centre – but they got a right-wing government because the Liberal Democrats chose to ally with the Tories. This is the root of the crisis of the Liberal Democrats: their increase in support was, to an important degree, a result of disillusion with Labour *from the left*. Many voted Lib Dem because of their opposition to the Iraq War, their opposition to Trident replacement, their opposition to the hike in student fees. Now the anger at their betrayal is producing not just single-digit poll ratings but a renewed crisis for the democratic system.

The student movement of 2010 was the first catalyst of this mood. Of course there have been important precursors. The student movement was prefigured by the anti-globalization movement born at the 1999 Seattle World Trade Organisation conference. For a decade, anti-corporate, anti-capitalist values and popular demonstrations which express these sentiments have been part of political life. They have left their mark on the attitudes and shaped the political participation of a generation of young people.

The anti-globalization movement, especially in Britain, fed into the anti-war movement as it arose after the attack on the World Trade Center in 2001. Mass anti-war demonstrations, large-scale political rallies, pickets and protests have provided a vehicle for political action for young people over this period.

Now all these elements have come together to pose one simple question: Can the government be broken? The Coalition's economic policy is as unpopular as the poll tax of 1990. The present government lacks democratic legitimacy in the same way that Blair's government lacked legitimacy when it invaded Iraq in the face of a hostile, mobilized public. The students have begun the fight, but they cannot win it alone. A movement has started, but its forces are, as yet, incomplete. Now the task, the challenge, is for others – pensioners, trade unionists, community groups, housing campaigners, disability activists, organizations representing women and blacks and Asians – to join them.

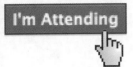

I'm Attending

WE WILL MARCH

'10.'11.'10

© Noel Douglas

👍 52,000 like this

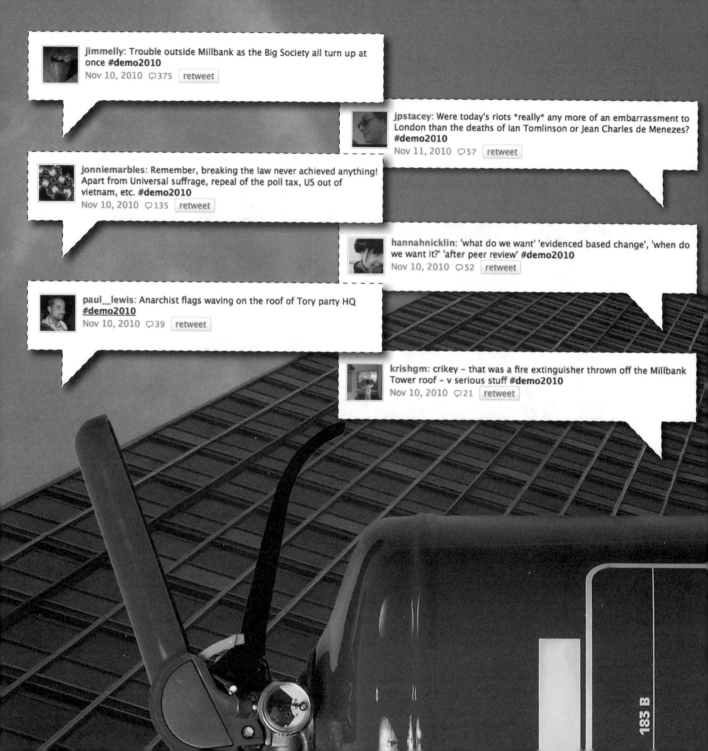

jackthorne: The story should be how many are here. FAR more than was predicted. Why? Because education is a right not a privilege **#demo2010**
Nov 10, 2010 ⬚75 [retweet]

tomtaylor91: "This shit wouldn't happen at hogwarts" best sign at **#demo2010**
Nov 10, 2010 ⬚150 [retweet]

chickpeajones: a few broken windows? thousands of broken futures. **#demo2010** #ema #hecuts #tuitionfees
Nov 10, 2010 ⬚15 [retweet]

chris_coltrane: Whitehall is utterly rammed for **#demo2010** – and people are still arriving! If we wanted to, we could definitely have a revolution today.
Nov 10, 2010 ⬚9 [retweet]

lynnjackson: Bet Tory HQ wish they could have got a moat on expenses **#demo2010**
Nov 10, 2010 ⬚14 [retweet]

aaronporter: Looking like this will be the biggest student demo in a generation. **#demo2010**
Nov 10, 2010 ⬚33 [retweet]

co11metpolice: We recognise your right to protest. If you are planning a demo in London we want to work with you. http://bit.ly /2HC9ZQ #dayX #demo2010

Nov 27, 2010 ♡13   retweet

DAY X
24:11:10

pennyred: Sitting with year 11s around a burning pile of paper. One hugs the other. 'I don't even know you but I love you' she says **#demo2010**
Nov 24, 2010 ♡35 [retweet]

lisaansell: You cannot tell students who grew up watching governments ignore protests and undermine unions– that peaceful protest works. **#demo2010**
Nov 24, 2010 ♡69 [retweet]

marshajane: @jonrogers1963 is with some angry parents outside the kettling – cops won't let them into kids or kids out to parents **#demo2010 #dayx**
Nov 24, 2010 ♡15 [retweet]

boycottbgbizsoc: Officers #CA950 & #U2128 reportedly assaulting children – let's get them trending **#demo2010 #dayx** #ukuncut
Nov 24, 2010 ♡69 [retweet]

drpetra: Politicians take note. For every student demonstrating there are parents and teachers who support them **#demo2010**
Nov 24, 2010 ♡41 [retweet]

jackieschneider: Hurray! Eldest son has made it home from **#demo2010** . Police behaviour has radicalised him far more than we have ever managed
Nov 24, 2010 ♡51 [retweet]

arg1985: Dear David Willetts, BBC, etc. protests are about CUTS as well as fees. And when will we see a "police assault children" headline? **#dayx**
Nov 24, 2010 💬33 [retweet]

arkadyrose: My 15-yr-old daughter is in the kettle right now. Phone goes straight to answerphone. V. worrying time for a parent. **#demo2010** #dayx
Nov 24, 2010 💬85 [retweet]

simoncollister: Just seen plain clothes cop get himself out of the kettle. Agent prov? **#demo2010**
Nov 24, 2010 💬28 [retweet]

darrylmason: Students chanting "Your Jobs Are Next!" at police. Ouch. #painfultruth **#DayX** #Demo2010
Nov 24, 2010 💬452 [retweet]

streets: Reports of mass clothes swapping inside kettle after police say kettle remains while they try to identify 'suspects'. #dayx **#demo2010**
Nov 24, 2010 💬26 [retweet]

andrewtindall: "the real story isn't a broken window, the real story is a broken public education system" #demo2010 **#dayx**
Nov 24, 2010 💬38 [retweet]

DAY X2
30:11:10

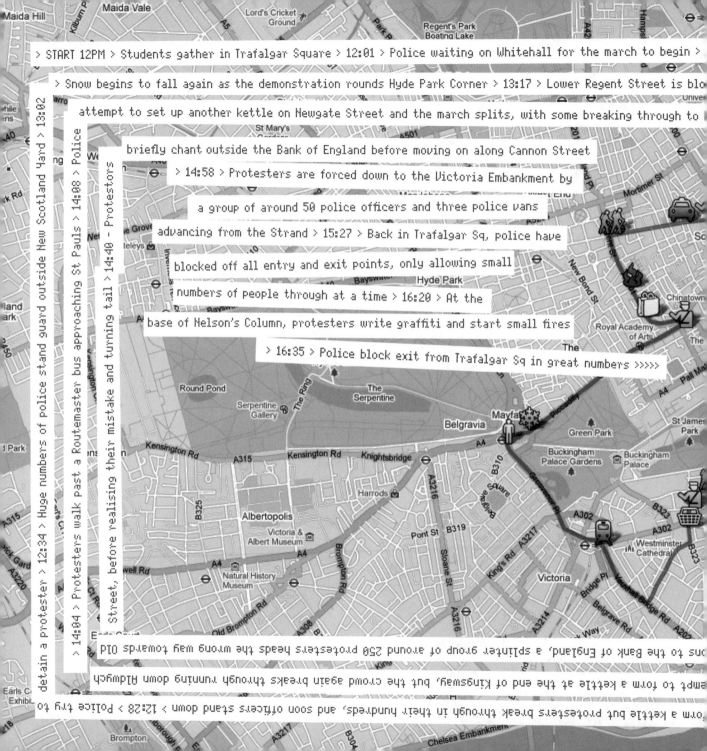

> START 12PM > Students gather in Trafalgar Square > 12:01 > Police waiting on Whitehall for the march to begin >

> Snow begins to fall again as the demonstration rounds Hyde Park Corner > 13:17 > Lower Regent Street is blo

attempt to set up another kettle on Newgate Street and the march splits, with some breaking through to

briefly chant outside the Bank of England before moving on along Cannon Street

> 14:58 > Protesters are forced down to the Victoria Embankment by

a group of around 50 police officers and three police vans

advancing from the Strand > 15:27 > Back in Trafalgar Sq, police have

blocked off all entry and exit points, only allowing small

numbers of people through at a time > 16:20 > At the

base of Nelson's Column, protesters write graffiti and start small fires

> 16:35 > Police block exit from Trafalgar Sq in great numbers >>>>>

13:02 > Police stand guard outside New Scotland Yard > Huge numbers of police stand guard outside New Scotland Yard > 13:02 >

> 14:08 > Police approaching St Pauls > 14:08 > Police

> 14:04 > Protesters walk past a Routemaster bus approaching St Pauls > 14:08 > Police

Street, before realising their mistake and turning tail > 14:40 – Protestors

detain a protester > 12:34 > Huge numbers of police stand guard outside New Scotland Yard >

ons to the Bank of England, a splinter group of around 250 protesters heads the wrong way towards Old

empt to form a kettle at the end of Kingsway, but the crowd again breaks through running down Aldwych

orm a kettle but protesters break through in their hundreds, and soon officers stand down > 12:28 > Police try to rotesters come up against a line of police on Whitehall and retreat > 12:13 > March diverts down The Mall > 12:17 >

by police, so the march heads down Regent Street > 13:20 > Shoppers look on as protesters stream down

Lane and others proceeding down Edward Street > 14:18 > In the tight back streets around St

Protesters, flanked by hundreds of police officers march alongside St James Park > 12:25 > Railings are

Regent Street > 13:28 > Two lines of police on either side of the street now flank the protesters as

Bartholomew's Hospital, the group find themselves squeezed into tighter and tighter

alleyways, until emerging by Barbican station > 14:40 > After someone asks a police officer for di

they pass through Oxford Circus > 13:36 > Police officers push over a number of protesters marching, Poli

bolted together in front of Parliament, so the group once again retreats from the police line > 12:27 > Police attem

A (possibly incomplete) map of student occupations that swept the UK at the tail end of 2010

Glasgow University
Edinburgh University
Newcastle University
York University
Sheffield University
Hull University
Nottingham University
Loughborough University
Warwick University
Cambridge University
University of East Anglia
Essex University

Strathclyde University
Durham University
Bradford University
Leeds University
Leeds Met University
Lancaster University
Manchester Met University
Manchester University
Birmingham University
Leominster University
Aberystwyth University
Oxford University
Dursley College
Cardiff University
University of West England
Bristol University
Bath Spa University
Exeter University
Plymouth University
University College Falmouth
Winchester University
Southampton University
Sussex University
Hastings College
Kent University

Goldsmiths University
University College London
Royal College of Art
Roehampton University
Camberwell College of Arts
London Metropolitan University
London Southbank University
Camden School for Girls
University of East London
London School of Economics
School of African and Oriental Studies
Slade School of Art
Birkbeck College
Royal Holloway

OCCUPATION
NATION!

DAY X3
09:12:10

omywow: Just had word that one of our Cambridge girls was crushed by a horse and has had her collar bone broken. **#dayX** #demo2010
Dec 9, 2010 💬115 [retweet]

carlmaxim: Police: "Protesters have failed to stick to the agreed route." To be fair, neither did the Lib Dems. **#dayx3** #solidarity #demo2010
Dec 9, 2010 💬1,289 [retweet]

queen_uk: Text from Prince Charles: "Hundreds of people tuned out to catch a glimpse of Camilla and me. They were excitedly banging on our car" **#dayx3**
Dec 9, 2010 💬518 [retweet]

unitonehifi: Police still kettling ppl on westminster bridge. Reports of ppl passing out. Pls retweet. The media aren't reporting it. **#dayx3** #ukuncut
Dec 9, 2010 💬216 [retweet]

00arika00: "Panic on the streets of London Panic on the streets Birmingham" Still a Smiths fan Cameron? **#demo2010**
Dec 9, 2010 💬27 [retweet]

studentactivism: Alfie Meadows "awake and speaking" after brain surgery for police beating at **#dayx3**. http://bit.ly/h3q97x #solidarity
Dec 10, 2010 💬23 [retweet]

jesshurd/reportdigital.co.uk

azkaahass: Gvt can afford to go to War in #Iraq, afford to bail out banks, afford to pay bonuses but can't afford education #disgusting #fees **#dayx3**
Dec 9, 2010 💬83 retweet

 paul_sagar: Horses prevented from entering Parliament sq by unbelievably brave Cambridge students forming human barrier **#dayx3**
Dec 9, 2010 💬88 retweet

 policestateuk: "Few of us stuck btwn horses & riot police– we all put our hands up–police responded by beating us to the floor" http://bit.ly /eJlh26 **#dayx3**
Dec 9, 2010 💬55 retweet

 bloggerheads: Jody McIntyre (@jodymcintyre) tipped out of his wheelchair by police + dragged off like baggage http://j.mp/dWtsBC **#dayx3**
Dec 13, 2010 💬21 retweet

 davidcameronesq: Thanks to all LibDem abstainers – without you, sitting on the fence, we would not have been able to shaft the students of tomorrow **#dayx3**
Dec 9, 2010 💬28 retweet

 **milesbarter:** Seeing police horses charge children has inspired me to join the protest after work. Who else is up for it? #dayx **#dayx3** #demo2010 #nocuts
Dec 9, 2010 💬43 retweet

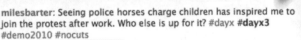

Flashback:

THE CHANGING ROLE OF THE BOURGEOIS UNIVERSITY[11]

Ernest Mandel

Furthermore, technocratic university reform, functionalization of the university – debasement of higher education to fragmented, overspecialized, and unintegrated professionalism – what the radical German students call *Fachidiotismus* ('Professional Cretinism') – has developed increasingly into organized incompetence.

One of the sharpest accusations that can be lodged against the existing social disorder is that in a period when scientific knowledge is expanding at explosive speed the level of university education is steadily declining instead of rising. Higher education is thus incapable of fully exploring the rich potential of scientific productive power. Moreover, it is producing incompetent labour power, not in the absolute sense, of course, but in comparison to the possibilities created by science.

Some neocapitalist spokesmen say openly what they want, like the authors of the West German university reform programme. It is in the order of things therefore for them to cynically assail the too liberal character of the old Humboldtian university. They admit that from their point of view, that is, from the standpoint of neocapitalism, the freedom of students to read, to study and to attend lectures as they choose must be curtailed.

Subordinating not production to human needs but human needs to production – that is the very essence of capitalism.

Self-management, therefore, is the key to full development of both scientific competence and the potential productive power of science. The future of the university and of society intersect here and finally converge. When it is said that many people are not suited to a university education, that is doubtless a truism . . . in the context of our present society. But this is not a matter of physiologically or genetically determined unsuitability but of a long process of preselection by the home and social environment.

---

11   From Trevor Pateman, ed., *Counter Course: A Handbook for Course Criticism* (Penguin, 1972), pp. 23–4.

When, however, we consider that a society that subordinates the development of men to the production of things stands the real hierarchy of values on its head, we can assume that, with the exception of marginal cases, there is nothing inevitable about this unsuitability.

When society is reorganized in such a way that it puts the education of people before the accumulation of things and pushes in the opposite direction from today's preselection and competition – that is, surrounds every less gifted child with so much care that he can overcome his 'natural handicap' – then the achievement of universal higher education does not seem impossible.

Thus, universal higher education, cutting the workday in half, and all-embracing self-management of the economy and society based on an abundance of consumer goods is the answer to the problem of the twentieth century – what shall the teachers teach? 'Who will watch the police?' Then social development would become a fundamental process of self-education for everyone. Then the word 'progress' will have real meaning – when humanity has the competence to determine its own social fate consciously and relying only on itself.

SOAS: SCHOOL OF ACTIVISM STUDIES

Elly Badcock

In 2009, at the height of the war on Gaza, students at the School of Oriental and African Studies (SOAS) were the first to occupy their university in protest at Israeli atrocities – and management failure to issue firm condemnation of Israel and build relations with Palestinian universities. Our action was a catalyst for occupations all over the country, from the London School of Economics to the BBC headquarters.

Just a year later, as students in Britain were looking up nervously at the butcher's knife of government spending cuts hanging precariously over them, we knew what to do. We were the first to occupy this time too – with demands ranging from the director circulating an open letter all the way up to passing a budget with no cuts or fee rises.

These occupations were different in a huge number of ways. The first lasted twenty-four hours; the second three painstaking but fantastic weeks. In 2009, we had a large but familiar group of activists; in 2010, students from dozens of different societies, courses, backgrounds and political persuasions were involved.

But the fundamental difference in 2010 was the open, inclusive nature of the decision to occupy. We presented a motion at our Union General Meeting, calling for occupation. The practicalities and the politics were debated with the whole student body, and our argument to occupy won – voted through in a packed-out common room. And once we occupied, that spirit of openness and mass democracy continued, with mass meetings of 200 staff and students deciding unanimously to remain in occupation until our demands were met.

That's not to say that we were wrong to take the decision to occupy in 2009 outside of the Student Union, with a smaller group of activists. The political climate was astoundingly different, and it was a decision that necessitated immediate action. The protest movement that existed, although large, angry, vibrant and fantastic, wasn't comparable to the hundreds of thousands of previously uninvolved students who demonstrated against tuition fee rises. In 2009, we acted as a spark; in 2010, we became a base of organization in the midst of a fiery and militant student movement.

Rather, our example shows us what's possible in mass movements like the recent student protests, and guides how we should organize in the future. Decisions, discussions and debates need to be had in the biggest possible forum, involving the largest number of people possible. We need to be explicit about what we want and how we're going to achieve it. In the midst of militancy, we need to be downright audacious – seizing the initiative and making it clear to the management of our schools, colleges and universities that we're in charge, and we're going to fight.

At SOAS, management looked on helplessly as we plastered the campuses with posters blaring 'OCCUPY NOW!' Although they brought a High Court injunction on the occupation, it was never acted upon because the strength, solidarity and passion of the anti-cuts movement on campus was so clear: tutors offered to stay awake all night on security; cleaning staff brought us sandwiches liberated from high-class catering events; and lecturers initiated teach-ins and radical seminars in our occupied space.

The broader anti-cuts movement has looked to the militancy and anger of the student protests, and drawn inspiration from them. As our struggles converge, and people up and down the country from all occupations and backgrounds join together, it's vital that the spirit of support and solidarity we've seen continues. Working alone, fighting sectional battles, we will fight, we will inspire – but we will ultimately fail; working together, we can bring down the government. Most of all, let's continue being militant and determined; as striking American Ford workers said forty years ago, 'We've got them by the balls – now squeeze!'

THE SIGNIFICANCE OF MILLBANK

James Haywood

The most incredible thing about the Millbank protest on 10 November 2010 is that it actually happened. The following day, many activists were saying to the media that it had 'not been part of the script'. Ten thousand students were supposed to turn up, march from A to B, then go home. Instead, triple the number that we expected showed up and took some of the most radical action we have seen in the UK since the miners' strike of 1984–85.

The Millbank protest broke the illusion of apathy. Students were supposed to be lazy and apolitical; Britain was supposed to be the home of moderation, politeness, peaceful action. Millbank shattered these ingrained myths.

I will never forget being on top of Millbank tower roof, looking down at a sea of thousands, bonfires dotted around. We had surrounded and occupied the headquarters of the party in government! Back in February 2003 two million people marched to protest the impending invasion of Iraq – and we were ignored. Millbank, however, was a protest that the government was unable to ignore. It proved that radical action can happen here, and that it can work. Those who thought that the smashed windows and rooftop occupation had distracted the media from the issue of fees couldn't have been more wrong. Fees became the focus for television, radio and print media, while the protest inspired other students to take a stand, as evidenced by the cross-country protests two weeks later that involved – at a conservative estimate – some 130,000 students.

But Millbank didn't just inspire more people to protest; it decisively changed the whole attitude to protest in the UK. What is noticeable now is how, especially among the younger students, demonstrations are being reclaimed: people march where they want to march, they break away from police kettles, they look for buildings to occupy. No-one waits for the unions or the organizers to give them orders. This is a new thing.

The impact of the protests has gone well beyond students or even education. This was the first serious fightback against the austerity measures of the coalition government, and has set the tone for future campaigns. Trade unionists were flooding students with support, many questioning their own leaders and demanding similar actions.

The impact has gone beyond the borders of the UK as well. A friend of mine from Palestine told of constant updates about the Millbank occupation on TV stations there. Another friend, from Belgium, saw pictures of us in his favourite magazine. Media interest came from all over the world: from Dubai to Paris, Greece to the United States. The significance of this was best summed up by a French student in London, who was in the SOAS occupation. He said that Europeans do not see Britain as being particularly radical, so when they heard the news of British students occupying government buildings, they knew something important was happening.

Millbank proved that even the most historically conservative of movements has the potential to break out and become a mass radical struggle – and all this despite the media witch-hunt, despite police violence and repression, and despite claims that our actions had lost us public support (the opposite was true). Millbank taught us that we can achieve our aims not by lobbying, not by polite protesting, but through action.

THE ART OF OCCUPATION

Jo Casserly

In the last few months, Britain's political landscape has been transformed. As we watched the windows at Tory HQ being smashed, we were bearing witness to the breaking of the Con-Dem cuts consensus. On 10 November 2010 we took to the streets in our thousands, occupying Millbank Tory HQ in the process. A couple of weeks later, a wave of occupations swept Britain's campuses.

Occupations are a tactic with a strong tradition in the student movement, from 1968 through to the present day. But for many of us, including myself, it was a totally new experience. We chose to occupy because we wanted to take direct action that could force the hand of both our university management and the government.

At UCL, as at many other universities, the management was complicit in the proposals to raise fees. In fact, it was UCL Provost Malcolm Grant who lobbied the Labour government to commission the Browne Review. It was becoming clear that our universities were being run by people interested more in their six-figure salaries, corporate branding and league tables than in education itself.

The people running our universities are not elected, and are not accountable to staff or students. And they have failed to defend our education and effectively oppose the cuts. It was time to take our campuses into our own hands.

The occupations drafted sets of demands, some aimed at the government and some at the university management. We demanded that university bosses release statements condemning cuts and fee rises, that they make no redundancies, and that they democratize university structures, opening them up to much greater student control.

Our successes on this front were mixed. Some universities – such as South Bank – won a number of their demands. Other universities, like UCL, issued statements opposing cuts, but refused to oppose higher fees. But it was testament to the power of our movement that we were nearly always taken seriously by management. We had become a force to be reckoned with.

One of the main achievements of the wave of occupations was the creation of organizing centres for the movement, both on and off campus. Workshops advised school and college students on walkouts and occupations; trade unionists visited to offer their solidarity and talk about the struggles in their workplaces. The occupations were also centres for creativity: in visually transforming our campuses, we showed how universities should not only be a place for formal education but also a place to learn to think critically and to protest. The impact of this should not be underestimated. Not only did we organize direct action, demonstrations and flash mobs, but we also created a solid network of activists, ready for further action. The experience of living and organizing together was exhausting but extraordinary, creating bonds of trust, respect and comradeship between students.

To have the biggest impact possible, our occupations needed to be well organized, with different teams or working groups dedicated to outreach to local communities, media and Twitter. Decisions were made in twice-daily general meetings which – though sometimes lasting into the night – were essential to organize the occupied space and to plan future actions.

The challenge of occupation is to create a space in which students with a wide range of opinions and experience can work together productively and in which everyone, from the seasoned occupier to the newcomer, can make equal contributions. We live in a society where those who 'do politics' are the elite: for the most part white men from privileged backgrounds. An occupation should create a space that is a counter-weight to this trend in society, and in which politics is for everyone.

But this will not happen automatically. It requires structures and procedures in place to promote participation. Some of the reflections on the occupations and the movement have praised it for being 'leaderless', 'structureless' and 'organic'. I'm sure we agree on what we *don't* want: a movement controlled undemocratically from the top, in which the participants have little control over the direction of the movement.

On the contrary, the movement we need today has to be radical and creative, has to establish deep roots in local organization, and has to come 'from the bottom up'. Most of all, we need a movement prepared to fight 'by any means necessary' to win. But my feeling is that those who praise the 'leaderless' nature of our movement are seeing what they want to see, and are often leaders themselves. Leaderships emerge in every mass movement, and ours is no different. In some occupations, a tendency arose for a handful of people to dominate meetings and activity, alienating less vocal occupiers, who would take a back seat in general meetings.

The question is therefore not whether or not we have leaders, but how we choose them: are they the people who shout the loudest, or are they elected and accountable? Let's get the structures in place to elect our representatives, and keep them accountable.

This means electing spokespeople for major media appearances and negotiations with management, collectively deciding on anti-cuts candidates for Student Union elections, and delegating tasks to individuals from the main group. These structures of democracy and accountability are essential and allow responsibility to be rotated. By not denying the reality of leadership, we can create democratic and 'bottom-up' structures. The alternative isn't 'leaderlessness', but unaccountable leadership.

On a national level, too, we need to be more, not less, organized. The last few months have shown the power of spontaneous anger and protest, especially from a generation of working-class school students. The question now is how to keep up momentum and step up the struggle in light of the vote. We cannot rely on spontaneity for this: we must be organized.

The challenges ahead of us are huge. Linking up with the trade unions and taking steps towards a general strike will require a rank-and-file organization that can take action with or without the trade union leaders. We will need organized self-defence, not just to defend demos against the police, but also picket lines, and communities against the English Defence League.

This kind of organization is something the movement has already started to develop, with central media hubs and twitpics of police lines during demos. In universities, occupations will continue to be a central part of the fight-back. Until now, occupations have been creating spaces for political debate and organizing. However, as the impact of the cuts starts to bite and there are redundancies at universities, our action will have to step up. On the continent, occupations block and shut down entire universities.

If we want to prevent pay cuts and redundancies among university staff, we will need to draw on these tactics ourselves and start taking more combative action, shutting down administration buildings and management offices and occupying whole departments, especially those threatened with closure. And when our lecturers take strike action, every student should be on the picket line, shutting down the campus.

Yes, this kind of action can be disruptive, but it's necessary to win. And the disruption of pickets and occupations pales in comparison to the havoc that the Con-Dems want to reek in higher education.

This kind of action would need to be coupled with huge efforts to get the message out to the entire student body and bring its support behind us. We will need a campaign of education, inspiring critical and anti-establishment thinking, challenging the logic of the cuts, looking at the alternatives and why direct action is the way forward to bring down this government.

There are huge challenges – but we are starting out from a position of strength few of us could have imagined possible just a few months ago.

To face these challenges, we will need to be organized and united. This means having unity in action around clear aims: opposing every cut, pushing for the scrapping of fees. Everyone fighting for this, whatever their wider political views and affiliations, should participate in the movement and have ownership over it. Unity in action does not mean depoliticization. Certainly, we must not set up ideological barriers to students and workers entering our movement, but we also must also not shy away from political debate.

Theory informs practice and vice versa. Occupying and maintaining a space is not an end in itself. Our aim is not to create a microcosm of socialism, functioning alongside the rest of society. Occupations are a tactic in a far wider struggle to change how our whole society works. Now is the time to be radical. For years, terms like 'solidarity', 'class' and 'revolution' have been considered out of touch, dirty words, even by parts of the left. We have proved that struggle is not something 'foreign' to the British and that we are not the post-ideological, apathetic generation we have so often been labelled as.

Anti-capitalist and socialist politics now have a new resonance among many young people. The post–Cold War, neo-liberal consensus is over, and the ideas of socialism are not dead – they are more alive than ever. Occupations provide a space to debate, and to ask questions about the society we live in. What is education for? What is real democracy? How can we change the system? Is another world possible?

It is clear that we have already learned important lessons from the past. Many of us first discovered direct action when we walked out of school at the time of the Iraq war. We joined two million people in London on 15 February 2003. The Stop the War movement had tremendous strengths. The scale of unity in action it achieved has yet to be matched by any mass movement since, not even in all the exuberance and radicalism of the student protests. It shifted public opinion and forced a political crisis that very nearly drove Tony Blair from office. What it lacked, however, was sustained industrial action by the labour movement. There was too much of a focus on the A-to-B march – not enough of a focus on strike action, on occupations, and other forms of direct action.

While the anti-cuts movement is also yet to achieve the coordinated industrial action that will be required to bring this government down, what we have seen already is a revival of more radical forms of social protest. The university occupations point the way to the kind of direct action that will be necessary in the very near future.

We can use occupations to discuss visions for another society and how to achieve revolutionary change, as was done back in the LSE occupation in 1968. But we must also learn from the failures of 1968 too. In May '68 in France, students celebrated their spontaneous action, occupying universities and fighting the police on the streets of the Latin Quarter. The protests of May '68 remain an inspiration to us all, but this spontaneous movement did not have the political direction and organization necessary to turn a mass uprising into a revolution and bring down the government.

We must not fall into this trap – far too much is at stake. Let's use the occupations to organize the student movement, to coordinate on a local and national level. With social-networking media such as Twitter, Facebook and blogs, we have at our disposal more tools to organize ourselves, more quickly, than ever before. Despite these great social changes in the world in which we are living, working and fighting, our movement is not separate and distinct from the history of class struggle that has gone before it – and we must profit, and learn, from this history.

To defeat these cuts, we will need a fight-back that reaches into every corner of society – not just students, but workers, the unemployed and pensioners. And let's be clear: defeating the cuts will mean bringing down the Coalition government.

This is where university occupations can play a crucial role as organizing centres for the movement. On every campus, those both with and without occupations, weekly, open and democratic assemblies of students and education workers are key. These can then link in to assemblies on a regional and national level. These assemblies can organize active solidarity for strikes, sending teams to picket lines and building the TUC march, as well as continuing to organize flash-mobs and further occupations. On the streets and on our campuses, we have already achieved a great deal. Now we need to build a movement that is organized, united, creative and radical – a movement that can win.

MY WHEELCHAIR IS THE BEGINNING

Jody McIntyre

Standing on the roof of the Conservative Party headquarters, with my wheelchair right beside me, I thought 10 November had changed my life. Little did I know at the time, it would be several demonstrations and a month later that I would be thrust onto a public platform.

It was a great demonstration. It was spontaneous and passionate. We had the police on their toes. None of which justifies a police officer to pushing a disabled man out of his wheelchair and dragging him across the road.

It had been referred to as 'Day X' – the day parliament would vote on tuition fees. After our experiences at Millbank and across the streets of London, we knew the momentum had to continue. When I first arrived in Parliament Square on 9 December, however, it seemed that the opposite had happened. It was good to see thousands of students packing out the Square as 'our' politicians sat cocooned in a bubble just across the road, but the lack of action was somewhat disheartening. You don't bring down governments by standing around and shuffling your feet.

I should have learnt not to underestimate this growing student movement. This was not a crowd of seasoned anti-war marchers; these were largely fourteen- and fifteen-year-olds who had never been to a demonstration before a few weeks previously. No boundaries had been set in their youthful minds, and they were out to make their voices heard.

In an instant, people began running towards the far end of Parliament Square, and my younger brother and I followed. As we got to the front of the crowd, it was clear that the police were desperate for violence.

Batons began to fly. One came landing straight onto my left shoulder, sending a sharp, shooting pain down my arm. Those standing around me were taking blows to the head and body;

children, women, men, all being brutalized by the police. Then the horses came, horses that could easily kill people. But we would not budge. We held our ground.

Suddenly, four policemen grabbed my shoulders and pulled me out of my wheelchair. My friends and younger brother struggled to pull me back, but were beaten away with batons. The police carried me away. Around five minutes later, my younger brother was also forced through, the wheelchair still in his hands.

I didn't know it at the time, but a photograph had been snapped of police trying to grab me out of the wheelchair, and had been posted on Twitter. Within minutes, the photograph had gone viral.

A crowd of around 200 had by now gathered on the other side of the police lines. We turned, and began marching, running, in the opposite direction. Morale was high. Anger at the government was even higher. Kicks and punches were thrown as we passed the Department of Education.

Eventually we found ourselves back at Parliament Square, this time approaching from the side of Millbank. Riot police came charging our way, but now they looked weak. Mounted police were just behind, waiting to charge.

Somehow, I and Finlay managed to weave our way through the police line. We found ourselves in a large no-mans-land, in between the riot police trying to stop the crowd and the police horses getting ready to charge. I turned in my wheelchair to face the police. 'Move out of the way!' one of the mounted police shouted at me. I shook my head. I did not feel comfortable with the idea of mounted police charging into the crowd, which included many children, standing behind us.

From the corner of my eye, I spotted one of the policemen from the earlier incident. He recognized me immediately and came charging towards me. Tipping the wheelchair to the side, he pushed me onto the concrete, before grabbing my arms and dragging me across the road.

Again, I had no idea at the time, but video footage of the incident was to be circulated online for weeks to come.

The real question to be asked in the aftermath of this event is not why the police officer pushed me out of my wheelchair, but why the public were so surprised. Is it really more shocking to see what happened to me than to see a police officer kicking a fifteen-year-old school girl in the stomach as she lay on the floor, or a police officer batoning a student in the head so that he is rushed to hospital for emergency surgery, within an inch of his life, thanks to internal bleeding to the brain?

To me, the actions of the police on 9 December did not come as a surprise; of course, it is the job of the police to protect the government. Nothing is a bigger threat to the government than the kind of scenes we saw on the student march of 30 November; thousands of students spontaneously marched across central London, without permission from the police, and not an ounce of violence followed. Such a demonstration was bound to draw huge public support against an unpopular governmental policy; thus, the demonstration was a direct threat to the government. So how do they combat such a threat? They send the police to attack us.

One justification the government used for police brutality at the demonstrations was that it was necessary to prevent violence on the part of the students. Not only does the example of 30 November prove this to be a pretence; it is also a hypocritical statement. Since when has the British government or the British state had any qualms about using violence to achieve its aims?

The British state had no problem with using violence when it backed the overthrow of Mohammed Mossadegh, Iran's first ever democratically elected leader, in 1953. The British government didn't mind using violence in forcefully evicting the 2,000 inhabitants of Diego Garcia from their homes to make way for an American military base.

More recently, we did not hesitate to use violence in our invasions of Afghanistan and Iraq. For political parties who supported these murderous invasions now to complain about the windows of the Conservative Party headquarters being smashed is beyond a joke.

It is the government that is smashing the future of our education system. It is the government that is wielding an axe against the poorest and most vulnerable sections of society. A broken window can be easily fixed, but an entire welfare state cannot. As long as the government continues to pursue its policy of a two-tier education system, and an ideology of inequality, we have every right to demonstrate, to resist, and to fight for an equal education for all.

Flashback:

Everywhere I hear the sound of
marching, charging feet boy

Cause summer's here and the time is right
for fighting in the street
— CHORUS   boy
So what can a poor boy do, cept to sing
For a rock n' roll band, cause in sleepy
London town there's no place for a
Street Fighting Man.

Hey said the time is right for a palace
revolution
But where I live the game to play is
compromise solution

CHORUS

Hey said my name is called disturbance
I'll shout and scream I'll KILL THE KING
I'll rail at all his servants
So what can a poor boy do cept to
sing for a rock n' roll band cause
in sleepy London town there's
no place for a
Street Fighting Man

Mick Jagger 1968

Mick Jagger's hand-written lyrics to 'Street Fighting Man' (*Black Dwarf*, 1968)

FURTHER EDUCATION

Joe Harvey, Kaity Squires, Stuart O'Reilly and Adam Toulmin

Adam Toulmin and Kaity Squires, both 17, are students at Havant College; Joe Harvey, 17, is a student at St John's College

The recent rises in student tuition fees and the devastating cuts implemented by the Con-Dem government has politicized a whole generation of young people, particularly school and FE students. We feel as if our future is being threatened, and that we aren't prepared just to lie down and accept it. We decided to act both on a national and local level, travelling to London to stand in solidarity with thousands of fellow young people, organizing local college walkouts and lobbying our local MPs.

In London, we were inspired to see so many people taking to the streets to help fight for a just cause. There was a strong feeling of solidarity, and that everyone was together. During the first demo, Demolition, everyone's spirits were high, and people were enjoying themselves. After Millbank, though, and as the vote on student fees approached, the policing became more and more heavy handed. The great majority of students who were there came away with the feeling that the police were there to protect the government and not the public.

Our main concern was the way the police were containing people in kettles for no apparent reason. They targeted innocent people. A small group of us managed to get out of one of the kettles early on, and as we were walking around we saw a man walking relatively far away from the police lines, talking on his phone. An officer shouted at him to 'get back'. He didn't hear, and the officer hit him on the head twice, knocking him to the ground. This violence and aggressive containment was obviously an intimidation tactic designed to try and scare people away from attending future protests.

We found opposition from our own college management too, although many of the teaching and support staff were encouraging and understanding about why we were walking out of classes. We believe the college should be supporting us, caring for the future of their own students, but instead we found them attempting to quash any action before it took place. We found our posters being torn down, and anyone seen to be involved with organization was called to meetings with vice principals. Anybody attending demonstrations found their EMA payments cancelled, and some faced disciplinary action from the college leadership.

The fightback against cuts and fee hikes isn't over, and we haven't given up. We hope that we can still change things and make sure that university isn't left as a luxury for just the elite and rich in society. We intend to keep organizing locally and keep attending national demonstrations, and won't give in to the pressure from above to stop. It's a cause that all young people should be fighting for, and it will affect us all.

Stuart O'Reilly, 16
Before the election I was Cameron's biggest fan. The Liberal-Conservative Coalition would dampen the more extreme views of the Conservative Party and create a near perfect government. I used to moan at people who said politicians were all liars and were all as bad as each other. I realize now how naive I was. Protesting against tuition fees has not only allowed me to express my opinion, it has allowed me to grow up.

CAMBRIDGE, DAY X ONE

Amy Gilligan

People probably don't immediately equate Cambridge with radical action, but the autumn of 2010 saw an upsurge in struggle here, as in much of the country. From the start of term Cambridge University students protested against the cuts and fee increases. As the protests developed we were joined by school and sixth-form students in their hundreds. 'Day X one' saw over a thousand people take to the streets and three hundred students on the lawn of Senate House.

Two days later we occupied the Senior Combination Room at the Old Schools site, the university's administrative heart. Lasting eleven days, the occupation brought together huge numbers of people – not just students – wanting to fight against the cuts, in education and the wider public sector. The demands of the occupation reflected this, among other things calling for the University to use its influence to oppose the spending review's threat to education, welfare, health and other public services. In practical terms, it meant that we went out from the occupation to union branch meetings and to leaflet at workplaces, as well as taking part in a flash occupation of the council chamber of the Guildhall.

The highlight of the occupation was the Cambridge General Assembly on the penultimate day, which drew over three hundred people. Called as an open forum to discuss the movement's next steps, it was a great success in building solidarity in the anti-cuts movement and bringing together members of a variety of trade unions. Representatives of trade councils and activists from the Cambridgeshire Against the Cuts campaign also came, along with Green Party and Labour Party councillors and other community activists. There were a significant number of Cambridge University academics, international students, parents, grandparents, pensioners, school and sixth-form students too.

While, predictably, the university management didn't respond well to students taking to the streets and taking control of part of the university, the response from academics was fantastic. Hundreds of them signed petitions in favour of the occupation, and many visited in full academic dress to show their support.

The key to the resistance in Cambridge, so far, has been the breadth of the involvement. The student protests have been a spark for wider action to fight the Con-Dem cuts; in turn, we in the student movement have much to learn from those who have been fighting for many years. Together, we can stop the government's plans and bring them down.

PROTESTS ON VIDEO

Kings College Students Union of the University of London makes a cracking video:
<http://tinyurl.com/KingsCollegeDemoPromo>

Clare Solomon is subjected to irrelevant questioning by Jeremy Paxman alongside NUS President Aaron Porter:
<http://tinyurl.com/ClareSolomonNewsnight>

David Cameron blames students for dragging a police officer off his horse and beating him. This is what really happened:
<http://tinyurl.com/WhatReallyHappened2010>

Second protest, Carnival of Resistance montage:
<http://tinyurl.com/CarnivalOfResistance>

And fifteen-year-old Barnaby Raine tells establishment to stick-it:
<http://tinyurl.com/15YearOldBarnabyRaine>

Book Bloc:
<http://tinyurl.com/BookBlocItaly>

Jody McIntyre is dragged from his wheelchair at the 9 December 2010 protest. Interviewer asks him 'Are you a revolutionary?' Watch his legendary response:
<http://tinyurl.com/JodyMcIntyreInterview>

University of the Arts claim Oxford Circus for their rendition of this classic:
<http://tinyurl.com/CantCutThis>

Paul Mason on the student occupations:
<http://tinyurl.com/NewsnightOccupations>

Press Conference for Alfie Meadows at ULU:
<http://tinyurl.com/AlfiePressConference>

A fantastic compilation of the lies and protests:
<http://tinyurl.com/StudentProtests2010>

Arts Against Cuts protest at the Turner Prize awards ceremony. The winner, Susan Philipsz, gives her support to the campaign against 100 per cent cuts to Arts funding:
http://tinyurl.com/TateTeach-in

Funny man Paul O'Grady surprises audiences with his revolutionary rousings:
http://tinyurl.com/PaulOGrady and http://tinyurl.com/PaulOGrady2

2

ITALY

THE FACTORY OF PRECARIOUS WORKERS[1]

Giulio Calella

Reducing labour costs: Tremonti, Gelmini and the 3+2

Bill number 133, 2008, in opposition to which the new movement in Italian universities was born, isn't just Tremonti and Gelmini's perfidious invention.

On the contrary, it represents the deepening of a process – which hasn't been without its problems and contradictions – that began almost twenty years ago and has been accelerated all over Europe by the so-called 'Bologna Process', which in Italy brought about the 3+2 reform signed by Berlinguer and Zecchino.

This is a process in line with an old idea of capitalism: privatizing profits and socializing losses.

After all, ever since the Gui reform of 1968 the Italian ruling class has been thinking of pretty much the same kind of reform. Right from the beginning of the era of mass access to higher education, they started thinking that it would be easier and more useful to make the university serve their interests than to close its doors.

Once they moved beyond the idea of simply reducing access to universities, the problem became how to make universities operate for a profit – i.e. how to use universities for private ends, as opposed to privatizing them. The Italian ruling class much prefers the state to continue to pay. But the state must only pay as much as they need: not least because – today more than ever – cutting university funding and financial aid for students may free up liquid assets for unscrupulous bankers: that is to say, to pay for the crisis.

It matters little if, according to the OSCE data, Italy's expenditure on higher education in relation to GDP is half the average of OSCE countries (in 2005, it was 1.6 per cent, compared

---

1   From *L'onda anomala: Alla ricerca dell'autopolitica* (Rome: Edizioni Alegre, 2008).

to a 3 per cent average among OSCE nations); and if expenditure per student is among the lowest in the industrial nations, it's just above that of Hungary, Korea, the Czech Republic, Slovakia, Mexico, Greece and Poland alone.

In fact, a recent successful book by Roberto Perotti titled *L'università truccata* ['The Rigged University'] – which represents the position of Confindustria [General Confederation of Italian Industry] on university politics – invents a new method to massage the data: 'If a university spends 10 euros and has 2 students enrolled, only one of which is a full-time student, the total university expenditure is de facto directed towards the full-time student, so that the average cost per full-time student is not 5, but 10 euros.'[2] All you need to do is not count part-time students, and there you are: Italy's expenditure becomes the fourth among OSCE countries and is therefore above the average, which means that it needs to be reduced.

In addition, the 3+2 reform must also ensure the high rate of exploitation of future graduate workers: that is, it must build, cheaply, a factory that cuts labour costs.

The 'Bologna Process': building the factory

It is with the Ruberti reform of 1990 that we have the first qualitative change. The organization and financial autonomy it provided for universities, which were pushed to activate contracts and conventions, establish consortia and obtain 'contributions' from private citizens, began to incentivize university corporatization and competition. Its goal was to create a two-tier system that would select students and channel them into the top- and bottom-ranking institutions.

But the definitive deathblow arrived ten years later, with the Zecchino reform: it was represented by the introduction of pedagogical autonomy, in addition to financial autonomy, of individual universities, and by the two 'laurea' degree levels.

On 19 June 1999, the ministries of education from thirty countries belonging to the European Union and the former Soviet bloc ratified an agreement that established the harmonization of higher education in Europe. They thus gave birth to what has been termed the 'Bologna Process'. The first decade of the new millennium was the designated period for the creation of a homogeneous higher education system based on two cycles, and in November 1999 the Zecchino reform – i.e. the 3+2 – was approved by decree.

This model was sponsored by the centre-left government, which argued that it would strengthen universities' financial and didactic productivity, and that by increasing the number

---

2 Roberto Perotti, *L'università truccata* (Turin: Einaudi, 2008), pp. 37–8.

of graduates it would bring the number of Italian graduates in line with the European average: it was argued that the reform would solve the problem of university students who don't finish their studies in the prescribed time; that it would offer students a greater variety of study options; that it would help universities to prepare graduates to meet labour market needs by granting them more didactic autonomy – in other words, that it would transform the university into a location for so-called *permanent training*. All of this was to be achieved by also adjusting students' workloads to meet their ability to assimilate through the introduction of the credit system,[3] and by promoting competition among universities in order to put pressure on lecturers to increase productivity. On the other hand, in line with the culturally hegemonic neo-liberal view, it was asserted that schools and universities were not functioning because they were not conceived as enterprises competing with each other to sell a product or a commodity. Principals were to become managers, university councils were to become boards of directors, and each outcome had to be evaluated and measured in terms of productivity and of the relationship between input and output.

According to the myth that customer satisfaction is what the market is all about and that the customer is king, this approach obviously involves finding a customer.

But with the enterprise university we have two customers: the student is the immediate customer, who in order to get used to the new system needs to pay higher fees – the buyer always has to pay.

But the final customer is private capital. The main sponsor of this university reform is in fact Confindustria, which hopes that it will produce a qualified and malleable workforce.

The factory's raw material: student masses

If one of the goals was to align the university with the requirements of the job market, it would clearly have been foolish, in a mode of production shaken by constant technical and organizational innovations, to think that it would be possible to plan for the specific, 'specialized' requirements of the labour market years in advance. In fact, what is needed in this context is probably an even more comprehensive formation, which would be able to manage complex and flexible situations. On the contrary, the 3+2 was devised to introduce specialization right from the beginning of the degree course.

---

3   Each credit corresponds to twenty-five hours of work: 180 hours are needed to obtain a first-level degree and 300 hours are needed for a second-level degree.

In the end, this has resulted in a massive increase in the number of first degree courses: from 2,444 in 2000 to 5,517 in 2007, including 'Linguistic mediation science for television and cinema dialogist translators' in Turin, and 'Dog and cat breeding, wellbeing and hygiene' in Bari.[4]

All of this would seem absurd – unless the goal was to create an army of precarious workers, a qualified but malleable workforce that is willing to accept any job opportunity.

Yes, an army. This is the reason mass access to higher education is maintained and even expanded.

With the introduction of the three-year *laurea* degree course, the number of university students has in fact grown. According to the data of the Italian Ministry of Higher Education, in 2005/06 there were 1,823,886 students enrolled – i.e. almost 200,000 students more than in 2001/02 (when the Zecchino reform was put into practice). The total number of graduates per year has also doubled: from 175,386 in 2001 to 301,298 in 2005. Admittedly, the number of students is inflated, in that many students have moved from the old to the new courses looking for credit validation. But the point is that we have two very different degrees – the new first-level *laurea* degree course and the old single-cycle *laurea* degree.

This of course does not mean that today the university is open and accessible to everybody. There is still class selection in access to education. But this selection process has become more complex and diversified.

Still, according to the data of the Ministry, since the reform was put into practice, the percentage of matriculants who enrol at universities has grown from 65 per cent to 75 per cent. Consequently, the percentage of nineteen-year-olds who enrol at universities has grown from 46 per cent to 56 per cent.

This also means that 44 per cent of Italian nineteen-year-olds still don't go to university, and that there is a class selection that operates within the secondary school system: almost 100 per cent of the students who attend a senior high school [*liceo*] enrol at a university; but among those who attend a polytechnic school the percentage is 55 per cent, and among those who attend a vocational school the percentage is only 27.6 per cent. In addition, 25 to 30 per cent of Italian students still leave school before they graduate.

Moreover, less than 50 per cent of the students who enrol at universities manage to complete the first-level degree, and 20 per cent of students drop out of university during the first year.

---

4   See Perotti, *L'Università truccata*, p. 135.

It is therefore wrong to argue – as do some political areas within the student movement – that there is an absolute growth in student enrolments: to the extent that the right to education is no longer seen as an issue, the struggles for 'simple' inclusiveness and for quality education are placed in opposition.[5] This argument is also wrong, because in the last few years we have seen the introduction of 'channelling' and 'diversified inclusion' mechanisms that have been used to try to strengthen and render more flexible the classic methods used to deny the right to education: differentiation in student fees not only in competing universities, but also for different degrees; restricted entry in some *laurea* degree courses; different criteria used to assign bursaries between the first and second levels, and so on.

On the other hand, even though in the last forty years Italy has had some of the biggest and longest-lasting student movements in Europe, it stands out as one of the worst OSCE countries in terms of the right to education, with only 15.9 per cent of total university spending devoted to interventions in support of the right to education – compared to an average of 17 per cent in OSCE countries. And still today, at the national level 27 per cent of eligible students fail to secure a bursary due to lack of funds (which produces the unconstitutional figure of the individual student who is 'eligible but not successful'). Likewise, available accommodation at student residences caters to only 2 per cent of residential students – compared to between 7 and 10 per cent in France and Germany, and 20 per cent in Denmark and Sweden.

But in any case, the logic of 3+2 is not to restrict access to higher education, but to increase and differentiate it.

After all, if the university is a factory that produces precarious workers, raw materials are obviously urgently needed.

Twenty-first-century university students are therefore very different, in terms of social composition, from students in the 1960s and 1970s, or even from the students in 'la Pantera' [the Panther] movement [of 1990]. They come from a much more diverse social background, and the percentage of students coming from a bourgeois milieu is much smaller.

This social diversification doesn't just affect the student body as a whole. Students coming from the most exploited classes are also much more prominent than they were in the past in the most militant sectors of the movement. The jokes about rich lefty students are old-fashioned, tired clichés – i.e. pretty much what you'd expect from those who make them. These people either have bad faith or don't understand the institution that endows them with power.

---

5   See Edufactory, 'Tutto il potere all'autoformazione', in *L'Università globale* (Rome: Manifestolibri, 2008).

The great majority of today's students, of the 'Onda' ['wave'] movement students, don't have family or personal resources to support their education. The university is no longer the prerequisite for an easy, successful career.

The great majority of bourgeois youth and of the offspring of the Italian ruling class desert public universities and choose to go abroad or, in some cases, to private universities. Students from the middle and upper classes look for mechanisms of self-promotion parallel or completely external to the university. And the loss of quality in the new university for the masses will increasingly influence them in this direction – at least until some of kind of diversification of academic paths or an Italian version of Ivy League institutions is introduced.

Those who enrol, or will enrol, at the 3+2 public university, go and will still be going to university because they are looking for a better future – or at least for a decent future.[6]

Factory products: precarious workers

According to the data of the Almalaurea survey,[7] new first-level graduates earn lower salaries and have more precarious jobs than graduates in possession of the old one-cycle *laurea* degree.

In 2000, one year after graduating, 45.7 per cent of graduates with the old degree had secured stable employment (through a permanent contract or freelancing), while 54.3 per cent had a precarious contract (an atypical or temporary contract of employment, or no contract). Universities were already producing precarious workers, but the 3+2 has accelerated this process: in 2006, one year after graduating, only 39 per cent of first-level graduates had secured stable employment, while the percentage of precarious workers had gone up to 61 per cent.

Moreover, the average salary of a first-level graduate one year after graduating is 993 euros – and among those who had not worked before getting their degree, it went down to 881 euros. In some disciplinary groups, such as literary studies, the figure was below 800 euros per month. And even three years after graduating, the average salary was well below that of a metalworker.

Here, too, if we compare these data with those of the graduates with the old *laurea* degree, we perceive an acceleration of the same process: in 2001, one year after graduating, graduates with the old *laurea* degree on average earned 1,015 euros per month. And Almalaurea also adds that 'obviously a more accurate analysis must refer to real wages corrected for inflation over the

---

6 For a broader analysis of the nature of the new student body, see *Sstudiare con lentezza* (Rome: Edizioni Alegre, 2006).
7 Almalaurea, *Condizione occupazionale dei laureati. Indagine 2007*, at www.almalaurea.it.

last few years. It thus turns out that in 2007 a new graduate earns less than a colleague did five years before!'[8]

So, here we are beginning to see the function assigned to the 3+2 enterprise university. The pompous neo-liberal ideology that saturated the statements about the function of the university disguised a cynically pragmatic approach: as we have seen, the university has continued to produce a growing percentage of precarious workers, and has managed to lower the expectations of graduates regarding the use of their acquired competences in the labour market, their career paths and their income.

Ultimately, in addition to cutting funds, the university reforms dictated by Confindustria in the last few years have aimed at ensuring that private companies could get the mental workers required by the new productive techniques – which often ensure high profits – while keeping their salaries low.

The 3+2 has no doubt been effective in ensuring that students lose any hope of becoming intellectuals, or at least professionals. The slogan of the old university's professor, according to which anyone who entered the university was a 'scholar, not a student', has been buried under the super-professional labels of the new laurea degree courses; the frantic pace imposed on full-time students; continuous assessments; bibliographies made of textbooks; and a de facto trimester system which impedes any attempt by the student to familiarize himself or herself with the subject, and therefore to develop any kind of critical approach to it. This is a deskilled and devalued pedagogy, the engine of a factory that produces precarious workers and fragments knowledge-production by amplifying its specialized and partial character. As the Zecchino reform itself says, 'credits can become obsolete'.

What's happening all over Europe with the so-called 'Bologna Process' is in fact what the student movements of the 1970s had already foreseen, and what has become a concrete reality: a proletarianization – and precarization – of graduates, on the basis of which, on the one hand, graduates increasingly tend to get the jobs that were previously reserved for matriculants, or even for workers with no formal education, which in turn results, on the other hand, in a process of growing alienation of graduates in terms of their control over their working conditions. This way, the mental labour market becomes similar to the manual labour market: contrary to what is presumed in traditional economic theory, individuals with the same level of formal education end up not only doing a wide range of jobs, but also earning a wide range of salaries.

Certainly, in this case the Ministry's statistics office is happy to highlight OSCE data that are on other occasions put aside. According to these data, in addition to greater ease in finding

---

8   Ibid., p. 82.

work compared to the average of the population, graduates also have an income differential with matriculants of 43 per cent – a percentage that is still inferior to the average of OSCE countries, where that differential reaches 75 per cent in the US, 71 per cent in the UK, 50 per cent in Germany and 48 per cent in France.

But it takes time to achieve these things. One must be patient.

Even the unemployment rate is lower among matriculants between twenty-five and twenty-nine: 10.1 per cent, compared to 21.9 per cent among graduates. But as soon as you move to thirty-four-year-olds, the unemployment rate among graduates goes down to 8.7 per cent. So, the Ministry's document concludes, 'even though the increase of 12 per cent in the rate of unemployment among graduates compared to matriculants of the same age group is in effect very high, there are clearly long-term benefits in carrying on with your studies'.[9]

Leaving aside the fact that – to quote Keynes – 'in the long run we are all dead', this is still an assumption used to keep graduates quiet: an assumption used as a sleeping pill to be given to qualified workers ready to be exploited, and who are going to be paid badly: sooner or later, your salary will grow.

Certainly, it might well be that one will have to continue studying, either by taking unpaid internships or by enrolling on very expensive Masters degrees. But this is part of what they call 'permanent training', by which they mean precarization (permanent, of course).

In reality, as has been rightly noted by Zenezini, in the present context an academic degree

> continues to be important, but not so much as a qualification and therefore to ensure that one gets a status-adequate job placement: rather – in line with the argument put forward by Spence a quarter of a century ago – it is an instrument for the differentiation of labour power. We are talking of workplace competition mechanisms, as a result of which academic qualifications increasingly tend to be used not so much for the competences they certify, but rather to promote one's position in job seekers' queues, and therefore as a dispositif to displace towards the bottom those with lower qualification levels.[10]

It is therefore clear that students should not be expelled from the university en masse: they are a useful differentiation tool in a downward trend within the workforce, and they are also well equipped consumers of new technological products.

---

9 Miur statistics office, *L'Università in cifre 2007*, p. 80, at www.miur.it.
10 Maurizio Zenezini, 'Il cavallo non beve', in *La rivista del manifesto*, no. 23 (December 2001).

It is also clear why it is not convenient for the ruling class to privatize the university, which is an institution full of micro-powers and petty interests that are difficult and expensive to manage – it is more than enough to use it for private ends as a disposable tool. This is what the 'autonomy' of the university has been planned for: to allow local companies to manage the 'factories of precarious workers' according to their specific needs.

Through the private trusts established by bill number 133, private companies will in fact be able to directly enter public institutions without being forced to fork out any money. This idea of private trusts, which comes from the Berlusconi government, is in fact the exact opposite of the kind of intervention devised to bail out big banks and save them from the crisis: Berlusconi – with Veltroni's support – is ready to give billions of euros to the banks without asking for any right over their management. Private companies, on the contrary, will be able to join universities' boards of directors and therefore decide which professional figures should be trained, what kinds of internships these trainees should take, or what kind of research universities should do – again, all without forking out a single euro. Still the same idea: privatizing profits and socializing losses.

This way, universities tend to become public labour precarization agencies. Moreover, through the introduction of internships (which in many cases are considered a prerequisite to getting course credits) they have created a new permanent army of workers, who are not just precarious and poorly paid but completely 'cost-free'. In this way, whole sectors of workers – think of proofreaders in publishing companies – are replaced by an army of unwaged workers. This is how they concretely intervene to lower labour costs.

Workers or factory-produced commodities?

There is a debate in the 'Onda anomala' movement, which is the same debate taking place among all the student movements in the last few years.

Are students as such already precarious workers in the knowledge factory, or are they a commodity produced by this factory – that is, precarious workers in the making?

The first thesis corresponds to the theory that we have witnessed the emergence of a 'new post-industrial configuration of capitalism: cognitive capitalism, that is, an accumulation system in which the productivity of intellectual and scientific labour becomes dominant, while the central element of capital valorization is directly related to the control of knowledge and its transformation into a fictitious commodity'. In this new configuration of capital, it is 'no longer possible to consider the constitution of labour power (supposedly in the making) through the old lens of Fordism, thinking of the student as an inactive and non-productive figure, unworthy of remuneration. The figure of the student and that of the waged worker, or of a poor worker, tend to blur.'[11]

This approach gives absolute priority to the so-called knowledge workers and argues that today innovation and creativity – that is to say, knowledge – determine added value, and that as producers of creativity our knowledge and brain have become the main means of production. It follows that Marx's labour theory of value (which posits value as deriving from human labour and not from exchange operations) has become obsolete, and that the real problem is no longer exploitation but knowledge control.[12] According to this approach, copyright and patents represent the principal forms of knowledge control and division that should be left behind in order to free production and creativity, and to produce an 'exodus' from the system.

Even though there is no doubt that the emerging forms of labour in most advanced economies on average require higher levels of qualification, which are needed to manage the technological processes involved in production, at the same time the basic mechanisms of production have not radically changed: they continue to be either material or immaterial. And often when we talk about knowledge workers, we are not dealing with workers who perform jobs requiring high qualifications – and much less creative jobs. This is the reason we prefer to talk about mental workers. As Bartorello points out:

> Freedom and creativity are not always the characteristics of knowledge-related production: often this production requires an amount of mechanization of movements and such a degree of routinization that the tasks performed in front of the computer are comparable, in terms of alienation, to the tasks performed in Fordist production. The activity of writing and programming, which is such a big part of these new jobs, is more and more frequently paid on the basis of the number of characters produced and not on the basis of its qualitative level. New ways of measuring labour have been introduced on the basis of the logic of cost accounting (number of employees, hours, characters per page), as if we were still talking of mass production or piecework.[13]

---

11   Carlo Vercellone, 'Capitalismo cognitivo e modelli di regolazione del rapporto salariale', in *L'Università globale*, p. 121.

12   Michael Hardt and Antonio Negri, *Empire* (Cambridge, Mass.: Harvard University Press, 1999).

13   Marco Bartorello, *Un nuovo movimento operaio* (Rome: Edizioni Alegre, 2004), p. 40.

And it is thanks to such a devaluing of mental labour that today we have a system such as the 3+2.

In addition, we continue to think that Marx's theory of value remains correct, and we continue to find his third argument meaningful:[14] we are talking here of the indirect argument about a capitalist society without labour exploitation. If there were a society in which production was completely automated, and where, as a result, human labour disappeared, capitalist society, which is based on commercial exchange and income, would no longer exist: limitless production would not generate the incomes needed for consumption – there would be no consumers left. This is the reason we are witnessing the constant creation of new kinds of exploited labour, in which workers use language rather than a hammer.

The elimination of copyright and patents would lead to the overcoming of some devastating monopoly situations – think of anti-retrovirals or Microsoft – and would also lower the cost of many products, thereby accelerating what Marx calls the 'tendency of the rate of profit to fall'. But it would not, in itself, eliminate the social structure of capitalism, which is based on exploitation.

Students are therefore already precarious workers, but not simply because they produce knowledge. They are exploited as zero-cost labour in compulsory internships and in precarious jobs with no rights that they are forced to accept as a result of cuts in higher education funding.

But above all they are a commodity in the making, a particular kind of commodity. This is how precarious workers, ready to be exploited in the mental labour market, are produced and trained: with the new *laurea* degrees that offer fragmented knowledge for a precarious future, with the fast-paced study paths imposed by the 3+2, which train students to lose control of their lives and to be ready to accept *any* job.

And that is how – as if by magic – the student is turned from customer into commodity. So that, if he is unsatisfied with his study path, he 'can still rejoice at being considered a "product" to be released *just-in-time* to the local productive fabric'.[15]

---

14 As regards the other two arguments, the first consists in splitting the price of each commodity into its constitutive elements, demonstrating that if we go to the root of each of them all we find is abstract human labour. The second argument begins with the observation that if we realize an infinite exchange of commodities – i.e. exchangeable and comparable commodities – these must have at least one quality in common; that is to say, human labour.

15 Riccardo Bellofiore, 'Ai confini della docenza', in *Inchiesta*, July–September 2005.

The crisis of the factory: the barons

But there is a problem that has been recognized by all the ideologues of the 3+2 – namely, that too often 3+2 in effect equals 5.

Today about 70 per cent of those who obtain the first-level *laurea* degree decide to enrol in the second-level, specialized *laurea* degree. This phenomenon illustrates an attitude of self-defence among students, who, in order to avoid becoming precarious workers, decide to study two years more in the hope that they will thereby receive a broader, more general and critical training. This is a vain hope, because the devaluing and deskilling of senior high schools and of the first-level *laurea* degree also produce a de facto devaluing and deskilling of the specialized laurea degree.

In short, there is something wrong with the original project and, in the end, with a reform that was meant to shorten study time at university but has ended up lengthening it. As a result, there are no places to train the future ruling class. In the absence of a strong tradition of private universities, today's ruling class doesn't know where to send its sons and daughters to study.

In 2005, Minister Moratti had already attempted to find an answer to this problem. This was the so-called Y system: all students had to be enrolled in basic courses for a minimum of sixty credits, and then merit criteria would establish which arm of the Y they should follow. No longer the 3+2 (*laurea* degree and specialist *laurea* degree) but 1+2 *or* 1+2+2, and in the first year the students would have gambled their opportunities to get into a low- or high-ranking degree course (with little chance of getting into the latter).

The mobilizations that took place in 2005 eventually induced the centre-left government to revise this measure, but even the new centre-left minister, Mussi, who took office in 2006, was addressing the same problem, and thus proposed tighter barriers between the first and second level.

Now Confindustria has found the culprit, which up to this point had been, and to tell the truth still is, its accomplice: the barons.

The above-mentioned book by Perotti, which inspired the anti-baron propaganda during the student movement, points the finger at them: they are considered – not without reason, given their representation in parliament – the real culprits in the 'distortions' of the 3+2.

It was they who produced the exponential increase in *laurea* degree courses, and they who caused each university to enter the race to grab specialized courses, which in the original plan should have been the prerogative of top universities only. It is not easy to introduce entrepreneurial logic when management still think and act in feudal terms. Hence the entirely justified denunciation – finally with some names and surnames attached – of rigged competitions, exchanges of favours, and so on.

But this justified attack in reality hides a new offensive: we can't just rely on private trusts, we must turn the university into an enterprise once and for all.

Therefore, public funding must not only be cut, but also exclusively linked to 'merit' – of a purely quantitative kind – with the introduction of the evaluation of research productivity through bibliometric criteria (citation numbers for publications) and peer review (evaluation by a panel of recognized experts). Secondly, according to this argument, faculty wages must also be liberalized so as to encourage universities to compete to grab the best academics. And that's still not enough.

Perotti insists on students financially contributing to the university: first of all by the liberalization of university tuition fees, which should provide more than the current 20 per cent of total funding. If students pay dearly for their university education, they will demand a better service, and at the same time universities will have to provide better quality, or ask for less money. In fact, people have failed to notice that since the Ciampi government's financial bill in 1993 – which modified the rules for university funding, recognizing, among other things, the autonomy of universities in establishing tuition fees, on the proviso that they could not be more than 20 per cent of state funding – there has been a constant increase in fees. The percentage of student contributions to the total funding of the university has increased from 3 per cent to 11 per cent – all of which has failed to produce results in terms of quality. On the contrary: there are European countries such as Germany, Denmark, Sweden and Greece that have universities that are certainly no worse than ours, and to which access is completely free.

But let's move on. According to this approach, restricted entry to degree courses must be extended and liberalized, while bursaries must be replaced with student loans. Yet again, what is proposed is not exclusion, but a preventive attack on the future salary, with savings for the state: if one gets into debt, after all, one is more motivated to study than if one received the money as a gift through a bursary. At the end of the day, if the average expenditure per student is 7,000 euros per year, 'with an interest rate of 3 per cent, after 5 years a student will have accumulated a debt of 37,000 euros': small change. Once he gets his degree, he has to give back just 8 per cent of his salary. So, 'an individual who earns 20,000 euros before taxes [about 1,000 euros per month after taxes] in thirty years would repay about thirty per cent of his debt', but 'with a salary of 40,000 euros before taxes he would be able to repay the entire debt'.[16] Considering the data regarding graduates' salaries that we have just seen, forty years would not be enough to relieve oneself of this burden.

And then there is the proposal to abolish the degree's legal value in order to formally sanction the existence of top- and low-ranking universities. Perotti has the merit of being straightforward. He stresses that 'the idea that all universities should be the same and offer the same didactic level is a typical myth of government-controlled societies'.[17] This argument highlights the bankruptcy of the centre-left rhetoric that seasoned the Zecchino reform, according to which competition would have levelled universities towards the top, and not towards the bottom: here differentiation is invoked explicitly.

The worrying thing is that, after the uncontainable 'Onda' movement, many of these proposals are reiterated by the government in its 'Guidelines for the Government of the University', which was written on 6 November 2008 in response to the movement. And so it is with these proposals that we will have to deal in the near future.

The strikes of precarious workers in the making: unhinge the 3+2, stop precariousness

In this context, with such a project on the doorstep, the 'precarious workers in the making' must find their own ways of striking. *They must try to halt their own production as precarious workers in the making.*

But doing this cannot just be a matter of having a bit of self-training recognized as credits. We cannot find a way out in the folds of Autonomia. Unfortunately, as Adorno had it, 'Wrong life cannot be lived rightly.' In the most positive hypothesis, we may end up creating some interesting experiences. But these are practically irrelevant among the additional fifteen annual modules.

Blocking the production of precarious workers, on the contrary, entails a radical questioning of the 3+2 and its unhinging; it entails a fight against the mechanisms of negation of the right to education that produce the channelling of students; it entails a struggle against the abolition of degrees' legal value and against the mechanisms that aim to create competition among universities and inequalities at all levels. Yes to the demand for excellence, but for everybody. In this way, it is the official degree programmes that need to be questioned – not just by introducing

---

16   Perotti, *L'Università truccata*, pp. 104–5.
17   Ibid., p. 120.

self-managed seminars, but also by demanding participation in discussion and decision-making regarding degree programmes and prescribed texts. In the same way, students must also participate in their evaluation, which must be based on social, rather than quantitative, criteria.

We must abolish the timetables of the 3+2, we must change the clock, we must reappropriate the possibility of 'slow studying'. It is therefore fundamental to struggle against compulsory attendance, against all barriers, to merge exams and to abolish exams worth just two or three credits.

But that is still not enough. The alliance with workers must be conceived as a necessary alliance against paying for the crisis. The future precariousness of students is the key to this alliance – an alliance between subjects which does not contemplate the figure of the student-intellectual who leads the working class. But it also should not contemplate the figure of the student as a supposedly central figure within cognitive capitalism. If it was ever useful in the past, looking for a central social subject today has no meaning. Productive diversifications, de-localizations, and differing contractual conditions have fragmented workers. The capitalist logic can therefore only be understood by looking at the totality of its relations. The challenge is thus to come up with unifying demands.

The abolition of atypical contracts, the 1,300-euro minimum wage for all sectors, the social wage for precarious workers and the unemployed: all of these could provide the content on the basis of which we might relaunch concretely, rather than ideologically, the modern alliance between students and workers.

This is something like what happened in France with the mobilization against the CPE (First Job Contract) – but this time on the offensive: refusing to pay a single euro for their crisis.

A Map of Occupations

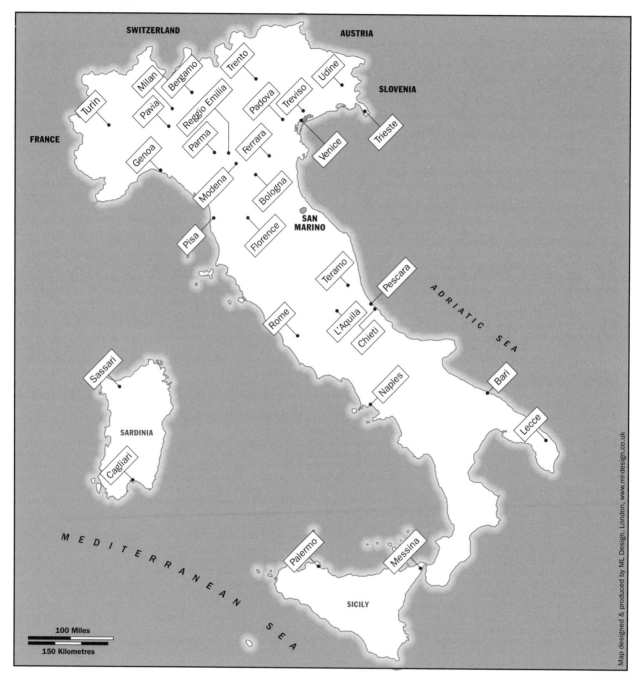

SWITZERLAND

AUSTRIA

SLOVENIA

FRANCE

Turin
Milan
Bergamo
Trento
Pavia
Reggio Emilia
Padova
Treviso
Udine
Parma
Ferrara
Venice
Trieste
Genoa
Modena
Bologna
Pisa
Florence
SAN MARINO
Teramo
Pescara
ADRIATIC SEA
Rome
L'Aquila
Chieti
Sassari
Naples
Bari
SARDINIA
Lecce
Cagliari
Palermo
Messina
MEDITERRANEAN SEA
SICILY

100 Miles
150 Kilometres

Bari	Students block traffic swarming through the city: "If they block our future, we block the city"
Bergamo	Banners and dung in front of Minister of Education Maria Stella Gelmini's house
Bologna	Universities occupied. 700 students go to Rome for anti-Gelmini protest
Cagliari	Student demonstrations in front of the Regional Council
Chieti	The protest goes on, thousands demonstrate
Ferrara	Students occupy the Faculty of Architecture
Florence	Students and researchers occupy the Chancellor's Office
Genoa	Attack on the city council: "Freedom for the arrested"
L'Aquila	"No to education reform, yes to reconstruction"
Lecce	Roman amphitheatre occupied
Milan	Milan Stock Exchange occupied
Messina	Students and precarious education workers join in a demonstration
Modena	Violent clashes. Students charged with batons
Naples	Occupation and sit-ins in high schools
Padova	The protest amongst high schools and universities sets off again
Palermo	Demonstrations, sit-ins and road blocks
Parma	Mobilization around the confidence vote
Pavia	Six high schools occupied
Pescara	Funeral procession for the death of the university
Pisa	Students invade the Leaning Tower and picket the prefecture
Reggio Emilia	Loud and peaceful protest
Rome	Education D-Day, Parliament besieged
Sassari	Researchers abseil from the Chancellor's Office
Teramo	University radio station occupied
Trento	Sociology Department of the University of Trento occupied
Treviso	Anti-Gelmini students' demonstration
Trieste	University on the streets against education reform
Turin	Five thousand students march against the government
Udine	Railway station blocked
Venice	Students invade the city

THERE IS SOMETHING NEW IN THE AIR[1]

Marco Bascetta and Benedetto Vecchi

The intensification and extension of junior faculty and student mobilizations in the last few days has no equal in recent times, not even in the conflict high-points of the last twenty years. Today, for the first time in a long time, a long period of sedimentation of analysis, practices and experiences coalesces into a manifestly and directly political passage that succeeds in communicating with society as a whole and making itself understood, puts pressure on political forces and institutions, affects the social climate, and challenges the commonplaces and ideological taboos that for many years have determined the order of discourse and the horizon of what's possible all across the political spectrum. There is definitely something new in the air. Why is the question of the university and education so crucially important in this new phase? Firstly, because it is on this terrain that the ideology and practice of neo-liberalism – and related disciplinary dispositifs – have set up a laboratory for programming the future, have devised techniques and processes for control of the new forms of labour (or labour power), and have theorized and put into practice precariousness as a blackmail tool disguised by the rhetoric of efficiency, meritocracy and international competition. Precarious work and the forms of dependency that characterize it, and that today threaten labour and force it to go on the defensive, have imposed their model starting precisely with the education system and cognitive labour. To checkmate neo-liberal ideology and its selection mechanisms within the university is nothing less than to checkmate it *tout court*. Without imposing 'unconditional availability' within the school and the university, it would not be possible to impose it on the workers of Pomigliano d'Arco either: the latter are in fact as sociologically and culturally different from the workers' vanguards of the 1960s and 1970s

---

1   From *Il manifesto*, 11 December 2010.

as they are close, in terms of aspirations and lifestyles, to both the students who are part of the movement and to precarious youth.

Taking a close look at big and medium-sized factories would in fact show how precariousness doesn't just affect young people who enter the labour market. Today, it is the pivotal principle guiding the relationship between capital and labour, including where there is a permanent contractual relationship. However, it would be wrong to interpret the 'unity against the crisis' – which energized the great metalworkers trade union (FIOM) demonstration of 16 October and now casts its shadow over the next one on 14 December – in the classic terms of an alliance between industrial workers and students, or between permanent and precarious workers, or between different generations – which would then beg the question as to who will hegemonize the movement and which social subject will be endowed with the power of becoming the 'engine of history'. Things are not the way they used to be. Neither students, nor industrial workers, nor, more broadly, the exploited masses are what they were forty years ago. Today, static social identities, with their related forms of consciousness and 'alliance politics', are at odds both with subjective perceptions and with the nature of production processes. But what is most relevant here is that, much as it manifests itself in individual bargaining as each person's individual destiny, this labour mobility and precariousness is in fact a collective phenomenon: it has become part of our social fabric. The labour market is based on rules and power relations that leave no room for individual aspirations, while, at the same time, it uses these aspirations against collective action. But what is happening now is that we are starting to become aware of this collective element, of the connections between our different positions in society. And this means that we are beginning to see through the endless flow of bollocks about 'human capital' and 'self-enterprise' that for many years has poisoned the social climate and distorted people's perceptions of their prospects. The classic theme of 'class recomposition', or of the coming class, must be rethought in terms of recognition: not of similarity, but of difference; not of the identity of a social group, but of identity of interests – economic, social and cultural. This recomposition is not going to happen on an ethical or solidaristic basis, but rather on the basis of the recognition of how the negativity of our social position is linked to the negativity of the other's social position, and therefore of how overturning all these negativities is also interconnected. In all of this, the recognition of migrant labour represents the decisive test.

The minister of education, Maristella Gelmini, is horrified when she sees students and pensioners demonstrating together. But there is no precarious worker who is not aware that the parent's pension supplements his or her meagre income, much as there is no pensioner who wouldn't want to be relieved of this burden – not to mention their compromised autonomy. What we are talking about is the recomposition of complex subjectivities, which cannot be reduced to the basic and stereotypical traits of their (temporary) social position. This is a recomposition that immediately assumes the form of political reasoning.

Finally, the Gelmini bill is cursed: it comes at the end of a cycle. Gelmini is less fortunate than her predecessors, the left reformers who paved the way for the bill and its ideological legitimation. Unlike them, she can't just talk until she is proved wrong: her project has already failed. It's already buried under the ruins of the failed relationship between the university and the enterprise system, between education and private interests: a relation that is supposed to be its *raison d'être*. Entrepreneurs are bankrupt, top students have no opportunities; the crisis is triggering a war for resources, which is disguised as measures to relaunch the economy, and which in reality is just a desperate attempt to offload costs and protect profits and positions of privilege. The neo-liberal, competitive university, in which all that is invested is student and junior faculty debts, finds itself in the midst of the still-worsening economic crisis, in a world indebted up to its eyeballs. All it can do is to fraudulently pass off cuts as necessary and rationalization. This is a miserable argument, to say the least: an argument that does not succeed in mitigating either the crisis's rough reality or the failure of the measures with which its makers pretend to overcome it. It's time to ask the university 'reformers' who have followed one another – each of them with his or her own failed experiment, but all following the same path – to foot the bill.

There is also a brand new, decisive element that is clearly at variance with the context in which past movements emerged – including the powerful movement that experienced the glory days of the clashes in Genoa, the flourishing of social forums and the anti-war mobilizations. This is the complete destabilization of Italy's political landscape (in the context of political destabilization on a global scale). The troubled passage of the bill on higher education is itself a sign of how political forces that are uncertain about their future – and lack political and cultural tools other than those that have already been worn down by the crisis and by popular impatience – find themselves wrong-footed, confused and frightened by the growing wave of movements. It is a sign of how a political culture (or lack of culture) is beginning to crumble: of how the art of compromise and the attempt to build political alliances came up against real conflicts; of how trying to find the lowest common denominator among parliamentary forces diverges from the increasingly popular idea of a different kind of common (see, for instance, the extraordinary success of the public water campaign). When the crisis of representation produces disaffection only among sulky, marginalized and disillusioned critics, the political class can pretend that nothing happened. But when demonstrators exercise their right to veto in the streets, and when popular assemblies assert a right to put forward proposals, that's when the political class is forced to face its own insubstantiality and begins to fear that its self-reproduction might be compromised. The point then is to stop this type of 'class recomposition': that is, to prevent power elites, after the toppling of Berlusoni, from regrouping under the banner of 'antiberlusconismo' in order to ensure the continuity of neo-liberal policies and reinstate social control and exploitation mechanisms. This is what is at stakes in the universities, in the factories, in the different territorial realities.

The demonstration that will take place on 14 December isn't just to get rid of Berlusconi and the most sinister figures in his court. It doesn't just aim to re-establish the innocuous rules of democratic etiquette. It also aims to prevent a new pact among bosses. It aims to start finding a path through the crisis that will not leave power relations unchanged. As the opposition movement knows very well, stopping this university reform also means putting into question everything behind it.

GENEALOGY OF THE BOOK BLOC

23 November: Book Bloc hits the streets of Rome

24 November: Book Bloc gets its name

On 24 November, a few hours after students clashed with the police in Rome carrying padded shields styled as books, Wu Ming reports:

> Our novel *Q* clashes with the Italian police. Students and teachers on the war path. Riots and demonstrations all over the country. High schools and universities occupied by the students. Violent clashes with the police in front of the Senate. Berlusconi's education reform is encountering blatant opposition, and the fact that the government is in crisis makes the movement raise its multifarious head even more. This afternoon, in Rome, students confronted the cops while carrying shields with book titles on them. The meaning was: it is culture itself that's resisting the cuts; books themselves are fighting the police. It was in this incendiary midst that our novel *Q* showed up, and in good company to boot: *Moby Dick*, *Don Quixote*, Plato's *Republic*, *A Thousand Plateaus* . . . These pictures appeared on the websites of the most important daily papers. It goes without saying that, whatever will happen, we're proud of what our novel is doing in the streets. Omnia sunt communia!

A comment on this entry is the first record of the 'Book Bloc' on the internet.

28 November: a new narrative for the battle

Interviewed by the daily paper *Il Fatto Quotidiano*, Wu Ming invites us to look closely at the classics the students chose to put on their shields.

> Let's look at the frontline.
>
> Boccaccio's *Decameron*, which is about people sharing stories while waiting for the plague to end.
>
> Asimov's *The Naked Sun*, which is the description of a world where humans no longer touch each other.
>
> Melville's *Moby Dick*, which is an epic tale of obsession.
>
> Cervantes' *Don Quixote*, the story of a proud, noble man led astray by an obsolete ideology (the chivalrous one).
>
> Petronius's *Satyricon*, the description of a greedy, decadent power.
>
> Henry Miller's *Tropic of Cancer*, a piece of 'auto-fiction', a scandalous mix of autobiography and fiction.
>
> Lenin's *What Is To Be Done?*, which deals with the problem of organization.
>
> Deleuze and Guattari's *A Thousand Plateaus*, on the theme of nomadism, the nomadic war machine.
>
> Shall we summarize? [. . .]

Our world is infected by the plague (*Decameron*). The plague is the atomization of social relationships (*The Naked Sun*). Those who refuse this state of things are often prey to an obsession that cripples their initiatives (*Moby Dick*), that is to say: the obsession with 'Him', Silvio the Malignant Whale, this 'berluscocentrism' affecting the public discourse. This obsession becomes an ideological barrier and causes us to attack windmills that are put in front of us as baits (*Don Quixote*). The risk is to be mesmerized by the scene of an outraged, sex-addicted, ever-carousing power (*Satyricon*). We will avoid such risk only if we find a new story, a narrative of ourselves that will break into this world as a real scandal (*Tropic of Cancer*), as opposed to all the fake scandals we see in the media. The emergence of a new, unified, conflict-bearing subjectivity would be the only truly intolerable scandal. 'For it must needs be that scandals come', says the old maxim [Matthew, 18:7]. Hence the problem of organization (*What Is To Be Done?*) and, perhaps, the need to re-read Lenin, rejecting what is to be rejected, revamping what can be revamped.

Of course, today the process of organization can no longer aim at building the party of the proletariat as in the twentieth century: organization must take into account the enemy's superior mobility; it must make us able to fight in an ever-changing situation, a scenario of constant deterritorialization (*A Thousand Plateaus*). However, without a narrative, without stories to be told in the night around the campfire, any guerrilla warfare in the desert is doomed to failure. And so we return to the first book, the *Decameron*: it is thanks to the stories we tell one another that we can prevent the spreading of the plague [. . .]

Well, *Q* is the only book in the 'Book Bloc' whose authors are still living. Should they have chosen only dead writers? We might say that *Q* represents the 'here and now' of the struggle, the need to act now.[1]

7 December: Book Bloc comes to London

Inspired by, and in solidarity with, the Italians and their demonstration against Berlusconi's education reforms, an assemblage of life-size books are constructed for the 9 December national demonstration against austerity measures. With arts and humanities a particular target for UK cuts, this is a literal display of literary resistance.

---

1 Translated excerpts from an interview with the daily paper *Il Fatto quotidiano*, 28 November 2010.

8 December: the democratic library

Uniriot.org – Network of Rebel Faculties – put out a survey to decide collectively which books will feature in the Book Bloc on 14 December. The results were:

The Will to Knowledge – History of Sexuality, vol. 1, by Michel Foucault
1984, by George Orwell
The Nonexistent Knight, by Italo Calvino
The Origin of Species, by Charles Darwin
Noi Saremo Tutto, by Valerio Evangelisti
Ethics, by Benedict de Spinoza
Fahrenheit 451, by Ray Bradbury
Fight Club, by Chuck Palahniuk
Doctor Zhivago, by Boris Leonidovich Pasternak
Without a Glimmer of Remorse, by Pino Cacucci
The Divine Comedy, by Dante Alighieri
Q, by Luther Blisset
What a Body Can Do, by Gilles Deleuze
Cyborg Manifesto, by Donna Haraway
Total Chaos, by Jean-Claude Izzo
The Odyssey, by Homer
The Tempest, by William Shakespeare
The Shock Doctrine, by Naomi Klein
Comedians, Frightened Warriors, by Stefano Benni
The Possessed, by Fyodor Dostoevsky

9 December: Italian press takes credit on behalf of nation

The Book Bloc – foam books/shields invented at La Sapienza University of Rome – now marches on London too.

– Antonio Castaldo, *Corriere della Sera*

9 December: Book Bloc London press release

The Book Bloc joins the student and public sector workers' protest to affirm and defend what is under attack: our universities and public libraries, literacy, thought, culture and jobs. In the past few weeks our attempts to do so peacefully have been met by police with batons, riot shields and horses. These are not isolated incidents of brutality but part of a system of institutional violence. By bringing books into the streets we are drawing attention to the violence at the heart of the neo-liberal ideology of the Con-Dem government.

When the police kettle us, baton us or charge us we will not only see police violence against individuals but the state's violence against free thought, expression and education.

Books are our tools – we teach with them, we learn with them, we play with them, we create with them, we make love with them and, sometimes, we must fight with them.

– A declaration of intentions by Arts Against Cuts

9 December: Book Bloc stands firm in Britain

Indymedia reports:

> The Book Bloc did well during today's demo at Parliament Square and beyond (as did all the other brilliant fighters in the masses). Here Guy Debord's great text *The Society of The Spectacle* resists police attacks.

9 December: The Book Bloc recognizes itself

Europe Calling: This is just the beginning!

[. . .] Within the Book Bloc a new generation recognized and found itself in the protest. Today in many cities the Italian student movement is showing something more than just solidarity. This is because your struggle is our struggle. All around Europe students are against the increase of fees, the privatization of university[ies], and the education cuts. You are not alone in [the] UK: a European movement, a new generation do not want to give up. We have the force of those who want to change the world and we have the intelligence to do it. It is just the beginning!

– Anomalia Sapienza, Uniriot Rome

10 December: corporate media read the books

Radical writing is often described as being at the intellectual barricades, but here at the protest, metaphor became reality. The books were not only at the barricades, they were the barricades, behind which the students could both take shelter and push forward; could 'transgress' across the police lines while the truncheons fell on the books, not the demonstrators. The scene embodied something profound: ideas do shield people, and those who dislike the status quo can find protection in words of subversion.

– Jay Griffiths, *Guardian*

12 December: Book Bloc shows up in Genoa

12 December: Wu Ming examines the titles

In the public representation of movements, never had books been given such importance. One book, of course, had already been in the squares, the 'Little Red Book', by Mao Zedong. But it was *one* book, and always the same, waved around as a sacred text. Today, the metaphor 'books as weapons' has become concrete, in a way that is unprecedented, through a *multiplicity* of references, dense with meanings. Seeing a cop hammer away at a classic . . . well . . . it's priceless!

Wu Ming

14 December: Book Bloc reaches the age of majority in its home town

While Silvio Berlusconi is confirmed as Life Emperor of Italy, books are seen all around the riots and clashes being heavily repressed by police and clumsily depicted by corporate media.

A group of demonstrators, dubbed the 'book bloc', brought giant polystyrene shields to the protest, each covered and painted to look like a famous work of philosophy, political theory or literature. Alongside titles by Hegel, Derrida, Adorno, Badiou, Debord and Orwell was *Just William*, ironically understating the ensuing conflict between the civil disobedience of the young and the full weight of the Metropolitan police. When the two sides clashed on Whitehall, the book bloc's attempts to counter police force with thought created images that were both powerfully symbolic and disarmingly tongue-in-cheek (even in footage released by the police). They certainly give the lie to the popular conception that those involved in police violence are mindless thugs.

Adam Harper, *Guardian*

14 December: also in Milan

22 December: and Palermo

23 December: cover feature in Spain
Diagonal, Spain's most-read underground periodical, reports: "La dictadura de los mercados sacude Europa", illustrated with books from Rome.

24 December: Recipe for a savoury book

AN AFTERNOON OF GUERRILLA ACTIVITY[1]

Giacomo Russo Spena

Rome: 'Someone give me a lemon, I can't see anymore!' The Book Bloc *One, One Hundred, One Hundred Thousand* by Luigi Pirandello lies on the floor, crushed in the general stampede. The police charge and don't economize on the use of tear gas: his eyes are inflamed and swollen, half closed by the stinging pain. It is shortly after 1 p.m. when the students try to break the police block and reach Montecitorio, the Italian Chamber of Deputies. 'We demand the resignation of that puppet', shouts a youngster from a megaphone. On the frontline, university students and their book-shields – the imagination of these titles knows no limits; behind them, primary school students.

They walk towards Corso Rinascimento, where they find a roadblock of three armoured vehicles parked across the road. They start throwing vegetables first, then firecrackers. A similar scene had unfolded half an hour earlier in Piazza Venezia, when they were trying to reach Palazzo Grazioli, the noble Roman residence of the puppet. But this time around the students are showing more resolve: the police charge heavily to push them back to Corso Vittorio Emanuele, and here they cause the first casualties and make arrests. It's all over, so I think. Now there will be a peaceful march all the way to Piazza del Popolo. But I am quickly proved wrong.

On the way, banks are targeted and 'sanctioned', shop windows smashed, and cash machines set on fire. This is only the start of what would happen in the centre an hour later. It is hotting is up. A rumour goes around that Berlusconi has just lost the confidence vote in parliament. Exultation. Roars of jubilation. A minute later, the cold shower: the real news comes. The reaction: 'Shame on you! Shame on you!' The demonstration continues: luxury cars are smashed and

---

1 Extract from MicroMega online, 14 December 2010.

some people start filling their rucksacks with empty bottles and stones. Road signs are diverted. When someone, covered from head to toe, throws a stone at the Ara Pacis, he is attacked by a sort of internal police service: 'It's a monument, not a bank, you idiot!' I laugh, but then turn serious when an officer from the Municipal Police decides to ride through the demonstration on a motorbike and just misses a demonstrator. He is literally assaulted and lynched by the mob, but miraculously manages to escape. In the meantime, we reach Piazza del Popolo. There are several thousand people there, a good turnout. Marching together, students and others 'United against the crisis' – that is, the union FIOM, parties from the radical Left, committees from Terzigno and L'Aquila and sections from the Purple People. Here the fates of these different souls diverge: some decide to try to reach Montecitorio again and clash with the police block in Via del Corso. FIOM, the parties and the Purple People leave the square, though they do not dissociate themselves from what would happen from 3 p.m. onwards in the centre of the capital. That is, a revolt – an urban guerrilla in which, by pure chance, nobody dies, because an officer of the Finance Police, surrounded by protesters, takes his gun out of its hoster. But, luckily, he does not shoot. These kinds of clashes have not been seen since the G8 in Genoa, 2001. On one side there are the police, and it is legitimate to ask who is on the other side. The Black Block? Perhaps this would be reductive. In the square, there are still many young people under thirty; many from Campania, maybe Terzigno. There are people from all over Italy. But do they add up to 10,000? Because as many as that took part in the riots of Piazza del Popolo. I really don't think so. On those streets, there was a new generation of young people, tired of Berlusconi and his policies. 'Today we take back our future', screams one with a helmet on his head and a club in his hand. Some lines behind, another chants: 'Our motion of no confidence comes from below: let's seize the palace of power!' Police officers fire tear gas and more tear gas, it's impossible to breathe: people are vomiting and panicking all around. But the square is seized. People resist and don't back down. They're attacked by a police van that catches fire. And here I return to Genoa. The police are charged by thousands of people who throw objects and have no fear of physical confrontation. Officers get beaten up. The dynamics are similar to those of football stadiums; I cannot believe my eyes. Protesters don't seem to want to go home. The words 'Free Rome, Free Rome' resound, alongside 'Revolt' and 'London'. The harsh confrontations first occur in Via del Corso, then repeatedly in Piazza del Popolo. Officers manage to clear the road only by means of armoured van charges. And it is still not over. In Piazzale Flaminio there are more beatings. The march splits in all directions. At Muro Torto there is another confrontation with the Finance Police. Along the Tiber a patrol car is set alight. Bins are overturned and in flames. Rome is paralyzed. Black smoke in the sky. Ambulance and fire brigade sirens all around. The hunt for protesters starts; they hide in the courtyards of palazzi. The balance for the day? Almost one hundred injured, forty-one arrests, destruction everywhere, much fear, and one certainty: today, in the square, I did not see the Black Block.

OCCUPIED DEPARTMENT OF LITERATURE, LA SAPIENZA UNIVERSITY, ROME

FROM THE UNIVERSITY IN REVOLT: A STUDENT'S LETTER TO BERLUSCONI

Elisa Albanesi

2 December 2010

Dear Prime Minister,

We are writing to you because we feel the urge and duty, as students and citizens, to explain what happened yesterday. You will grant us, we hope, this as a premise: many students at the demonstration not only have never set foot in a social centre, they also have above-average grades. We could show you many of our transcripts, but we won't, because we know who we are and this is enough for us.

But now, to return to the purpose of this letter, we want to answer a question that you must have asked yourself on many occasions: Why do so many people – students, workers, artists, etc. – demonstrate? Usually the answer is that revolts are 'rebellions of the belly', motivated by hunger, due to the global economic crisis. This is the case, certainly. But let us illustrate another point of view through the words of the historian Edward Palmer Thompson, who, in the essay 'The Moral Economy of the English Crowd in the Eighteenth Century', reflects on the uprisings of the English people:

It is of course true that riots were triggered off by soaring prices, by malpractices among dealers, or by hunger. But these grievances operated within a popular consensus as to what were legitimate and what were illegitimate practices in marketing, milling, baking, etc. This in its turn was grounded upon a consistent traditional view of social norms and obligations, of the proper economic functions of several parties within the community, which, taken together, can be said to constitute the moral economy of the poor. An outrage to these moral assumptions, quite as much as actual deprivation, was the usual occasion for direct action.

We quote, finally, a slogan-accusation of the eighteenth-century peasants to the miller, the 'evil' of the time: 'For ther-bifom he stal but curteisly, but now he was a thief outrageously'.

Do not misunderstand us. We are not accusing your government of outrageous thievery; we are accusing the whole country of it. Italy now thieves dreams, hopes and truth. We even accuse our mothers and fathers, who keep defending us from the world, the internet and Facebook, but still don't understand that the real danger of our times is them, their inability to criticize, to will.

We condemn indifference because we believe that the quality of a society is inversely proportional to the quantity of its indifference.

And thus we condemn ourselves, for not being clever enough to make it more evident and clear. The evidence is this: we are the future generation of precarious workers; or, rather, we will fill the lines of what we might call 'the precarious class'. As the Industrial Revolution produced the working class, revolutionary *par excellence*, so this system of speculation-turned-exploitation has caused the emergence of a new revolutionary class, whose members do not form 'structures', but are linked by relations and a shared human condition.

You taught us that one man can change a country. Luckily, there are thousands, maybe millions of us.

Perhaps you are coming to understand what we are saying. We will give you a hint. What you must fear the most is public happiness – that feeling as ancient as the French Revolution, which goes more or less like this: a human understands herself as such only when she is in movement, and in this discovers the fun and sheer pleasure of being together. Public happiness. The rest is guilty silence and a disquieting sense of tedium. Yesterday, for the first time, she came back. It was not folly that you saw: it was happiness. Collective happiness. And on this, we know for sure, you won't be able to understand us.

Cordially,

  Elisa Albanesi
  Assembly of the Occupied Department of Literature
  La Sapienza University, Rome

WHO IS THE BLACK BLOCK? WHERE IS THE BLACK BLOCK?

Autonomous University Collective

On the day after the Rome protests, this was the question in every newspaper, and it deserves an answer: Do you want to see the faces behind the scarves, helmets, balaclavas?

They are the same faces that pay you rent for derelict houses; the faces you look at when asking them to sign work contracts of 500 euros a month with the chance of employment after one month of trial and a switch to full-time for 800 euros. They are the faces that submit dissertation proposals and who you force to mention your boring texts; the faces of the kids from out of town that you slap when you catch them with a bit of smoke.

They are the ones who cook your tender sirloin steak at the fancy chic eatery, and do it for 50 euros a night, undeclared; they make your cappuccino with froth. They answer your phone saying: "892424; how can I help?", and buy vegetables at Lidl because the supermarkets are too expensive. They entertain you on your 450-euro package holiday, and set up the market stalls where you buy your fresh fruit.

They are the ones whose life-blood is being sapped by precariousness, whose lives are shit, and they are tired of putting up with it.

We belong to a generation who, for one day, stopped accumulating cirrhosis from the neurosis of a life-long training in precariousness; we supported the revolt. We are the future you should listen to: the only healthy part of a country plagued with metastases. The events of 14 December 2010 were epochal in their nature: when an armoured police van caught fire the whole of Piazza del Popolo exploded in a liberating roar. That roar is our existence, the existence of those who could not believe that such a government could sustain itself on four (or rather three) miserable people – and finally many of us, thousands of us, managed to scream:

'Together, we inspire fear!' A roar of joy and anger exploded on the right side, while the wrong side was shut inside parliament.

The Black Block strikes again. Careful: rumour has it that you might meet them at the lecture, in the library, by the bar's coffee machines, in the pub, at the beach, or even in the tram.

POSTCARDS FROM OCCUPIED ITALY

Rome

Milan

Pisa

Turin

Venice

Palermo

Flashback:

THE STRUGGLE AGAINST CAPITALISM IN ITALY: A POLITICAL MANIFESTO[1]

Vittorio Rieser

In distinguishing possible objectives of the movement, one must view the student movement on an international level. On a Western European level at least, it is not too idealistic to hope for coordinating action towards analogous objectives. If one looks for extra-university objectives on a purely national scale, one forfeits what is possibly the movement's greatest long-term advantage: the fact that its roots lie in objective conditions which tend to be similar in the various European countries, and it therefore assumes some analogous political characteristics in the various countries *even before* any political coordination is organized.

By distinguishing traits which are common, or tend to be common, to the various European student struggles, one can suggest a series of possible objectives or 'lines of action' which on the one hand are 'too one-sided' with regard to the universal contestative force of the movement, and on the other 'too general' with regard to the specifically student stamp of the movement, but which nevertheless roughly correspond to its current stage of political development.

Authoritarianism
The struggle with authoritarianism is the general context of the student movement. At the present moment it can, however, be translated into various specific objectives. On the level of Western European society, one of these could be the fight against the various 'authoritarian laws' which flourish continually: emergency laws in Germany, restriction of the right to strike

---

1 Vittorio Rieser, 'The Struggle Against Capitalism in Italy: A Political Manifesto', in Tariq Ali, ed., *New Revolutionaries: Left Opposition* (London: Owen, 1969).

in England, laws of public security in Italy. The student movement can act as an incentive and a guide in the struggle against these laws, thus removing this struggle from the influence of the prospects and methods of orthodox Communist or similar parties (wherever it runs the risk of being monopolized by these forces or channelled into a jaded prospect of 'democratic alliance').

The problem of information

The student movement appears to be the best equipped to organize 'counter-initiatives' against the capitalist monopoly of mass-means of communication: whether by counter-attacks and direct polemic or by the creation of new ways and means of information, concentrated upon political subjects chosen by it. The field of information seen as a central element in any labour or political formation seems to be that in which the student movement could, in the most practical and permanent way, take political initiative, even on subjects of international politics (such as Vietnam and anti-imperialist wars in general), and partly also in relationships with the working classes.

Relationships with working-class struggles

Here, too, there are analogous phenomena in the various European countries: on the one hand, a capitalist policy of integration (at the moment largely unopposed) which weighs more and more on the working-class organizations; on the other, a working-class reaction, which sometimes finds no organized means of outlet but at other times finds them within the trade-union organizations themselves (in which the integration process, politically accepted at the summit, is rendered more contradictory and difficult by the lack of opposition and by the consequent risk of loss of any basic agreement). Some experiences of the SDS, and some indications of the Italian situation, show that the student movement can have a function in this context: by providing, through example and direct communication, a stimulus to fight; by promoting specific forms of information and political debate, within the trade unions or outside them; by acting informally as an element of international communication (severely lacking in the current stage).

It remains to be seen what the long-term outcome of this action will be: that is, if it will be purely transitory, if the student movement as such will assume a permanent function in this field, or if it will contribute to the formation of new organized forces on a working-class level. Working along the lines indicated above does not imply an a priori choice of one or other prospect.

Political formation of technicians and 'other intermediate groups'

This problem is linked with that of the 'transitoriness' of the student stage. The movement can overcome this transitoriness either by becoming a political movement which extends beyond scholastic limits, or by forming people politically so that their influence will be transmitted to the next stage. At the moment it is perfectly possible to follow the first alternative (that is, not merely on the level of individual political formation), which is obviously the more interesting; but it still remains necessary to take action at the same time in accordance with the second alternative – the more so, since the nucleus of the current movement is made up of people from the humanities departments, with the risk that people from the polytechnic (in other words, those who are in fact going to end up in production) will remain on the fringe of the movement.

It is therefore necessary to concentrate the work of political formation in these sectors of education, so as to create groups of technicians capable of reacting to the 'antagonistic stimuli' produced by the factory structure and of acting methodically in their professional destination. (This is a field in which one could usefully cooperate with the trade unions.) Even in the humanities departments there is a problem of 'orientation and political control' with regard to professional deployment, in the form of preparation and political organization of future teachers (so as vastly to exceed the limits within which the majority of left-wing teachers move at present).

Some concluding considerations

In the more advanced stages of struggle of the student movement, there exists, or there is a risk of, a growing divergence between the practical development of the conflict (more and more radical, and with a more and more general and political counterpart) and the development of the discussion and political organization of the movement (which often stagnates 'due to *force majeure*', in that all the power of discussion and organization is expended in the day-to-day organization of the conflict).

This divergence was, and is, partly inevitable: but it must be recognized as a negative element and one to be combated. Instead, however, the tendency seems to be to accentuate it: in other words, after every forward step in the practical conflict, to elaborate a new and 'more advanced' theorization of the movement, a theorization elaborated by a small handful of people and in general passively accepted by the ranks.

The strategic development of the movement thus takes place in the minds of the leaders, who attribute this or that significance to this or that conflict.

Now, however, a strong effort at political elaboration must be made by the *rank and file*, if the movement is to survive. If the political consciousness of the *whole* movement does not take a 'leap forward', the movement runs a double risk of disintegration: either the risk of progressive diminution of the number of those capable of enduring prolonged conflict, or the more probable one of disintegration as soon as there is any slowing down of or pause in the immediate conflict.

It is therefore necessary that, generally speaking, there should be homogeneity on a national level in the choice of central *methods* and *subjects* for this 'politicization' of the movement.

3

OCCUPIED CALIFORNIA

fall
2009
OCCUPIED
california
CLASHES, MOBILIZATIONS,
DEMONSTRATIONS, &
OCCUPATIONS

locked down occupation
open occupation and/or sit-ins
march and/or rally
blockade

prison $

East Bay
UC Berkeley
Berkeley City College

"Sacramento"

Davis
UC Davis

San Francisco
SF State
SF City College

Turlock
CSU Stanislaus

Santa Cruz
UC Santa Cruz

PACIFIC
OCEAN

Fresno
CSU Fresno

NEVADA
CALIFORNIA

N
W   E
S

MAP
OF
CALIFORNIA

CAMPUS LOCATIONS,
PRISONS, TOPOGRAPHY,
& OTHER POINTS OF INTEREST

Los Angeles
UCLA

Fullerton
CSU Fullerton

Irvine
UC Irvine

USA
MEXICO

INTRODUCTION

Evan Calder Williams

From the fall of 2009 through the spring of 2010, the struggle in California to 'defend public education' became something very different. On 24 September 2009, thousands of students, staff, workers and faculty across the University of California (UC) system walked out in protest of fee hikes, layoffs, furloughs and cuts to departments and services. At the end of that day, a group of students and teachers entered the Graduate Student Commons building at UC Santa Cruz and occupied it for a week. The months to come saw a sequence of direct actions up and down the state, too many to detail here. Later in September and October, there were study-ins, sit-ins, and open occupations at libraries in the UC and California State University (CSU) system. In November, while the UC Regents met at UCLA to discuss – and ultimately approve – a 32 percent fee hike, along with further cuts and layoffs, campuses erupted across the state, setting off an intense three-day wave of occupations, marches, sit-ins, blockades, demonstrations, arrests and shut-downs in Davis, Los Angeles, Santa Cruz, Berkeley, Fresno and San Francisco. They held assemblies and argued about what to do and how to do it, dropped banners that declared *WE ARE THE CRISIS*, angered some, impelled others. They threw dance parties in common spaces and wore masks to hide their faces. They wrote anonymous texts and built analyses together. They made demands they knew wouldn't be met, and they refused to make demands. Afar, there were solidarity marches in New York City and Vienna, two cities where university occupations before and during this period furthered the sense both of a shared crisis and an explicitly anti-capitalist response that exceeded the particular 'budget squeeze' of California.

In December, students at San Francisco State University occupied the business building and renamed it Oscar Grant Memorial Hall after a young black man murdered by police a year before. The 'Live Week' at Berkeley, where Wheeler Hall was held open during the 'dead week' before finals, ended when police came in the early morning and arrested the occupiers. That night, a mob with torches attacked the chancellor's mansion. In the new year: library sit-ins at Davis, arrests and police confrontations at a benefit party for prior arrestees in San Francisco, a street party and riot in Berkeley following an occupation, and tireless planning for the long-anticipated state-wide strike on 4 March and week of actions. The 4th was a day of massive marches, rallies, demonstrations and occupations as students blocked entrances to their schools, made it possible for workers to join the picket lines, brought businesses to a halt, and spilled from their campuses into their cities and, in Oakland and Davis, onto the freeways.

The texts which follow – a thin slice of the mass of writing across the state during those months – speak for themselves. However, two guiding points should be made to help situate them alongside texts and analyses from other struggles in other parts of the world.

First, one will notice the particular emphasis throughout on *occupations* and on *barricades*, of seizing buildings and blocking entrance to them. This should not be taken as a mere rhetorical deployment or theoretical figure, as the practice of *occupation* means something quite distinct in the American context – a meaning elaborated in the texts that follow. Unlike occupations of university buildings in England, Austria, Germany, and elsewhere, where students are often allowed to remain undisturbed for extended periods of time without an invasive police presence, the events in California, like those in New York the previous spring, showed again and again that those taking the space have a very limited period of time before police will attempt to enter the building. To speak of barricades is therefore not, first and foremost, a hearkening back to a language of street-fighting and revolutionary situations. It is a practical issue: if the doors are not blocked and controlled by those inside, occupiers will – and did – shortly find themselves forcibly removed, beaten and arrested.

Second, many of the texts included here were ascribed to, and helped develop the theoretical direction of, what was variously called the *adventurist, insurrectionary, anarchist, communist, ultra-left,* or *anti-capitalist* tendency within the 'movement'. I cannot clarify the murkier questions of what that tendency looked like 'as a whole' or its degree of internal cohesion. Instead, I will add only a qualification that may not be immediately apparent in the texts themselves. One of the more striking aspects of this sequence of struggle was that, however significant the divisions may have been between the desired ends, relations to the university system, and declared political stances of those involved, the genuine moments of advance and rupture were the instances, however fleeting, when these divisions proved irrelevant in the face of tactical considerations and the fact of coming together not in abstract solidarity, but in acts. An anecdote from Santa Cruz may help to clarify this. Before one of the state-wide days of action in the spring, it became evident that many of the unionized service workers who had faced the nastiest effects of the cuts would be legally unable to join the mass of students, faculty, workers and those who didn't fit cleanly into one of those three positions – legally unable and subject to punishment, that is, unless they could 'get safely' onto campus. On the morning of the action, every point of access to the campus was blocked with rows of bodies, including many of those 'anarchists in black' designated as anti-union, or with material barricades. Consequently, those workers had to be given the day off, and they joined with everyone gathered outside the shut-down campus. That is to say: there is no solidarity that is not a doing – nothing other than a recognition of what is *not* held in common, the distances separating where we begin apart from each other, and, above all, what it takes to come together against the order of the day.

Flashback:

SAN FRANCISCO – REAGAN PLANS HIS FUTURE[1]

Governor Ronald Reagan's hard-line new appointee as president of San Francisco State College, Dr S.I. Hayakawa, declares total war on the students who have been on strike since November 6th.

San Francisco State College, with a student body of some 26,000, principally drawn from the working classes, is one of the largest ethnically mixed colleges in the United States. Local student leaders have been inconspicuously using student funds to address broader social and political issues since the middle of the decade. In 1965 they had established an experimental college where students could design their own courses and hire their own teachers: a microcosm of the society they wanted to create in the world outside.

By November 1968 the campus is rife with different radical factions. The Black Students Union (BSU) is a student front of the Black Panthers, the Chicano activists have created the Third World Liberation Front (TWLF), and a group of Maoists dominate the local SDS. All are agreed that San Francisco State College needs a Black Studies Program. The faculty, backed by Governor Reagan, vetoes the idea. On November 6th the BSU, supported by other groups, call a strike on the issue. The college president, Robert Smith, who favors a compromise, is unceremoniously sacked by Reagan.

Reagan and the hawks on the Faculty Board are set on defeating these uppity niggers and their Chicano and white friends. On December 1st Hayakawa declares a 'state of emergency' and orders students to return to their classes by the following day. The BSU and TWLF mount pickets on the campus to persuade their fellow students not to attend. An overwhelming majority of students continue to back the strike. Leo McClackley, chairman of the academic Senate,

---

1   Extract from Tariq Ali and Susan Watkins, *1968: Marching in the Streets* (New York: Free Press, 1998), ff. 204.

speaks out against Hayakawa's decision and calls for a negotiated settlement, declaring that 'Professors would not teach under the shadow of violence.'

It is all strangely analogous to the bigger war going on in Vietnam. The hawks want more bombs. The doves want a negotiated settlement. Hayakawa is a bomber. He now decides to embark on a policy of naked repression. The police are invited on to the campus, where, in a symbolic show of strength, they parade their hardware outside the library.

Throughout December there are constant skirmishes, marches and demonstrations around the campus. The city as a whole is divided, but shows a surprising degree of support for the college students. Just before the Christmas break the TWLF call for a Third World community day march to the campus. The response is impressive: blacks, Chicanos, Latinos and representatives of the Chinese, Filipino and Japanese communities announce their intentions to join the march. Hayakawa panics and closes the college. The students march to the City Hall, to be joined by several thousand supporters, including striking oil workers.

Ultimately, the student strike is crushed by repression and mass arrests – 450 students are charged with a series of offences.

Nevertheless, it has reforged an interracial unity on the streets of California, where thousands of students (90 percent of whom were white) have fought together. In the months that lie ahead divisions will arise, encouraged by police provocateurs who seek to fan racial tensions. But the memory of those December days will not fade.

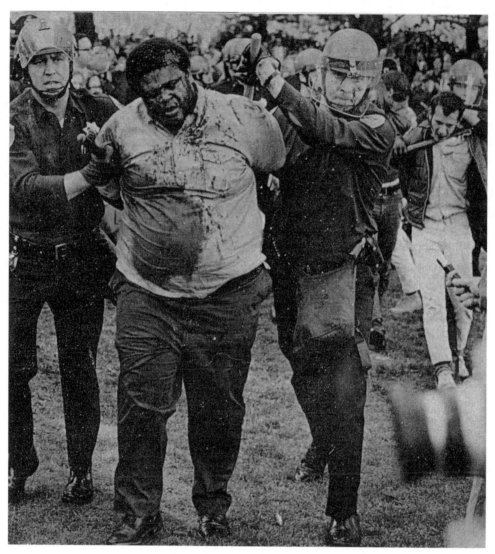

San Francisco State College 1968

TIMELINE

2009

24 September: Students at UC Santa Cruz occupy the Graduate Student Commons. The occupation ends a week later.

9 October: Study-in at UC Berkeley anthropology library.

15 October: Students at UC Santa Cruz occupy the Humanities 2 buildings for a period of several hours. They leave without police knowledge. One student is arrested and another is also on trial.

13 November: Students at UC Santa Cruz hold a study-in at the science and engineering library.

18 November: Students at UC Santa Cruz occupy the Kresge Town Hall to create an organizing space against budget cuts. Fourteen students arrested at UCLA, some involved in a sit-in disrupting the Regent's Meeting.

19 November: Students at UCLA occupy Campbell Hall and rename it Carter-Huggins Hall. Two are arrested at UCLA. Students at UC Santa Cruz occupy the main administrative building, Kerr Hall. This occupation ends four days later on November 22nd. Students at UC Davis occupy Mrak Hall (UCD main administration building); fifty-two students are arrested.

20 November: Students at UC Berkeley occupy Wheeler Hall for twelve hours, heavy police brutality ensues (forty-one students arrested, then cited and released). Another three students arrested earlier that day. Students at UCD enter Dutton Hall to hold a sit-in but are later dispersed. Students at CSU Fresno hold another library sit-in that lasts until the next morning.

22 November: Kerr Hall occupation ends. Students at UCD call for daily study-ins at Mrak Hall.

23 November: Between 100 and 150 students enter the UC office of the president and hold a sit-in. The sit-in ends around 6 p.m. with no arrests.

24 November: Students at UC Irvine surround Aldrich Hall en masse (approximately 700 to 1,000). One student is arrested at UCI.

5 December: In response to a publicly announced library occupation at UC Irvine, the administrators leave the doors open twenty-four hours a day.

7 December: Students at UC Berkeley enter Wheeler Hall and occupy it for Live Week. The doors are unlocked.

9 December: Between thirty and forty students at San Francisco State University occupy the business building at 5 a.m.

10 December: Students occupying the SFSU business building and some outside are arrested at 4 a.m. Twenty-three occupiers and ten outside protesters are arrested. Protesters block traffic on Highway 1/19th Avenue in San Francisco, demanding that the arrested individuals are cited and released. Their demands are met.

11 December: Sixty-six or more individuals inside Wheeler Hall (UCB) during Live Week are awoken and arrested without any dispersal warnings by the police. The dean of students was inside the building directing the police. Later in the evening, after a concert, a small riot ensues, leading to property destruction at the Chancellor's Mansion on UC Berkeley campus. Eight people are arrested while leaving the scene.

2010

15 January: Eviction of the California Valley Miwok Tribe delayed for another thirty days.

20 January: Attempted occupation by university students of Hibernia National Bank building in San Francisco, CA.

30 January: Benefit party for occupation arrestees ends with eleven people arrested.

5 February: Students at UC Davis hold a weekend-long study-in at the Shields Library. A few days after the event announcement, the administrators respond similarly to UCI's library study-in in December, and they leave the library open twenty-four hours a day for the weekend.

11 February: Students at City College of San Francisco hold a study-in, extending library opening by three hours.

25 February: A dance party at UC Berkeley moves to and occupies Durant Hall. After an hour, the dance party descends downtown. It turns into riot as Berkeley police arrive and batter protesters.

26 February: A sit-in at the UCSD chancellor's office lasts for several hours, in response to a noose being found in the library the night before amidst racial tensions from the previous week.

3 March: Students take over multi-story Humanities building at CSU Fullerton, barricading it from inside. But police infiltrate the building through underground tunnels. Occupiers cited and released.

4 March: Massive student walkouts/strikes throughout US. CSU Fresno occupies the main administration building for several hours. UCLA holds a sit-in. UC Santa Cruz shuts down the entire campus for more than twelve hours.

14 April: Occupation attempt at SFSU results in two arrests. Fifty or more students sit-in at UCD Mrak Hall.

1 May: May Day marchers in San Francisco attempt to occupy a closed high school; some are arrested.

9 July: The verdict for Johannes Mehserle, the police officer who executed Oscar Grant, is released. Thousands take to the streets in downtown Oakland, and later in the evening a riot breaks out.

The selection here is limited due to lack of space, but there are two online sources that more fully document the range of writings, analyses, and events taking place:

After the Fall: Communiqués from Occupied California, a winter 2010 publication that includes important writings from 2009, a timeline and links, as well as significant new texts written specifically for this platform. As the tagline reads: 'This isn't a newspaper, this is dynamite.' See http://afterthefallcommuniques.info

Occupy California is the preeminent site documenting struggles throughout the state and elsewhere, carrying innumerable links, photos, communiqués and articles. It played an important role in disseminating information without requiring any centralized organization. See http://occupyca.wordpress.com

COMMUNIQUÉ FROM AN ABSENT FUTURE:
ON THE TERMINUS OF STUDENT LIFE

We live as a dead civilization. We can no longer imagine the good life except as a series of spectacles preselected for our bemusement: a shimmering menu of illusions. Both the fulfilled life and our own imaginations have been systematically replaced by a set of images more lavish and inhumane than anything we ourselves would conceive, and equally beyond reach. *No one believes in such outcomes anymore.*

I

Like the society to which it has played the faithful servant, the university is bankrupt. This bankruptcy is not only financial. It is the index of a more fundamental insolvency, one both political and economic, which has been a long time in the making. No one knows what the university is *for* anymore. We feel this intuitively. Gone is the old project of creating a cultured and educated citizenry; gone, too, the special advantage the degree-holder once held on the job market. These are now fantasies, spectral residues that cling to the poorly maintained halls.

Incongruous architecture, the ghosts of vanished ideals, the vista of a dead future: these are the remains of the university. Among these remains, most of us are little more than a collection of querulous habits and duties. We go through the motions of our tests and assignments with a kind of thoughtless and immutable obedience propped up by subvocalized resentments. Nothing is interesting, nothing can make itself felt. The world-historical with its pageant of catastrophe is no more real than the windows in which it appears.

For those whose adolescence was poisoned by the nationalist hysteria following 9/11, public speech is nothing but a series of lies, and public space a place where things might explode (though they never do). Afflicted by the vague desire for *something to happen* – without ever imagining we could make it happen ourselves – we were rescued by the bland homogeneity of the internet, finding refuge among friends we never see, whose entire existence is a series of exclamations and silly pictures, whose only discourse is the gossip of commodities. Safety and comfort, then, have been our watchwords. We slide through the flesh world without being touched or moved. We shepherd our emptiness from place to place.

But we can be grateful for our destitution: demystification is now a condition, not a project. University life finally *appears* as just what it has always *been*: a machine for producing compliant producers and consumers. Even leisure is a form of job training. The idiot crew of the frat houses drink themselves into a stupor with all the dedication of lawyers working late at the office. Kids who smoked weed and cut class in high school now pop Adderall and get to work. We power the diploma factory on the treadmills in the gym. We run tirelessly in circles.

It makes little sense, then, to think of the university as an ivory tower in Arcadia, as either idyllic or idle. 'Work hard, play hard' has been the over-eager motto of a generation in training for . . . what? Drawing hearts in cappuccino foam or plugging names and numbers into databases. The gleaming techno-future of American capitalism was long ago packed up and sold to China for a few more years of borrowed junk. A university diploma is now worth no more than a share in General Motors.

We work and we borrow in order to work and to borrow. And the jobs we work towards are the jobs we already have. Close to three-quarters of students work while in school, many full-time; for most, the level of employment we obtain while students is the same that awaits us after graduation. Meanwhile, what we acquire isn't education; it's debt. We work to make money we have already spent, and our future labor has already been sold on the worst market around. Average student loan debt rose 20 percent in the first five years of the twenty-first century – 80 to 100 percent for students of color. Student loan volume – a figure inversely proportional to state funding for education – rose by nearly 800 percent from 1977 to 2003. What our borrowed tuition buys is the privilege of making monthly payments for the rest of our lives. What we learn is the choreography of credit: you can't walk to class without being offered another piece of plastic charging 20 percent interest. Yesterday's finance majors buy their summer homes with the bleak futures of today's humanities majors.

This is the prospect for which we have been preparing since grade-school. Those of us who came here to have our privilege notarized surrendered our youth to a barrage of tutors, a battery of psychological tests, obligatory public service ops – the cynical compilation of half-truths towards a well-rounded application profile. No wonder we set about destroying ourselves the second we escape the cattle prod of parental admonition. On the other hand, those of us who came here to transcend the economic and social disadvantages of our families know that for every one of us who 'makes it', ten more take our place – that the logic here is zero-sum. And anyway, socio-economic status remains the best predictor of student achievement. Those of us the demographics call 'immigrants', 'minorities', and 'people of color' have been told to believe in the aristocracy of merit. But we know we are hated not despite our achievements, but precisely *because* of them. And we know that the circuits through which we might free ourselves from the violence of our origins only reproduce the misery of the past in the present *for others*, elsewhere.

If the university teaches us primarily how to be in debt, how to waste our labor power, how to fall prey to petty anxieties, it thereby teaches us how to be consumers. Education is a commodity like everything else that we want without caring for. It is a thing, and it makes its purchasers into things. One's future position in the system, one's relation to others, is purchased first with money and then with the demonstration of obedience. First we pay, then we 'work hard'. And there is the split: one is both the commander and the commanded, consumer and consumed. It is the system itself which one obeys, the cold buildings that enforce subservience. Those who teach are treated with all the respect of an automated messaging system. Only the logic of customer satisfaction obtains here: Was the course easy? Was the teacher hot? Could any stupid asshole get an A? What's the point of acquiring knowledge when it can be called up with a few keystokes? Who needs memory when we have the internet? A training in thought? You can't be serious. A moral preparation? There are anti-depressants for that.

Meanwhile the graduate students, supposedly the most politically enlightened among us, are also the most obedient. The 'vocation' for which they labor is nothing other than a fantasy of falling off the grid, or out of the labor market. Every grad student is a would-be Robinson Crusoe, dreaming of an island economy subtracted from the exigencies of the market. But this fantasy is itself sustained through an unremitting submission to the market. There is no longer the least felt contradiction in teaching a totalizing critique of capitalism by day and polishing one's job talk by night. That our pleasure is our labor only makes our symptoms more manageable. Aesthetics and politics collapse courtesy of the substitution of ideology for history: booze and beaux arts and another seminar on the question of being, the steady blur of typeface, each pixel paid for by somebody somewhere, some not-me, not-here, where all that appears is good and all goods appear attainable by credit.

Graduate school is simply the faded remnant of a feudal system adapted to the logic of capitalism – from the commanding heights of the star professors to the serried ranks of teaching assistants and adjuncts paid mostly in bad faith. A kind of monasticism predominates here, with all the Gothic rituals of a Benedictine abbey, and all the strange theological claims for the nobility of this work, its essential altruism. The underlings are only too happy to play apprentice to the masters, unable to do the math indicating that nine-tenths of us will teach four courses every semester to pad the paychecks of the one-tenth who sustain the fiction that we can all be the one. Of course *I* will be the star, *I* will get the tenure-track job in a large city and move into a newly gentrified neighborhood.

We end up *interpreting* Marx's 11th thesis on Feuerbach: 'The philosophers have only interpreted the world in various ways; the point is to change it.' At best, we learn the phoenix-like skill of coming to the very limits of critique and perishing there, only to begin again at the seemingly ineradicable root. We admire the first part of this performance: it lights our way. But we want the tools to break through that point of suicidal thought, its hinge in practice.

The same people who practice 'critique' are also the most susceptible to cynicism. But if cynicism is simply the inverted form of enthusiasm, then beneath every frustrated leftist academic is a latent radical. The shoulder shrug, the dulled face, the squirm of embarrassment when discussing the fact that the US murdered a million Iraqis between 2003 and 2006, that every last dime squeezed from America's poorest citizens is fed to the banking industry, that the seas will rise, billions will die and there's *nothing* we can do about it – this discomfited posture comes from feeling oneself pulled between the *is* and the *ought* of current left thought. One feels that there is no alternative, and yet, on the other hand, that another world is possible.

We will not be so petulant. The synthesis of these positions is right in front of us: another world is not possible; it is necessary. The *ought* and the *is* are one. The collapse of the global economy is here and now.

II

The university has no history of its own; its history is the history of capital. Its essential function is the reproduction of the relationship between capital and labor. Though not a proper corporation that can be bought and sold, that pays revenue to its investors, the public university nonetheless carries out this function as efficiently as possible by approximating ever more closely the corporate form of its bedfellows. What we are witnessing now is the endgame of this process, whereby the façade of the educational institution gives way altogether to corporate streamlining.

Even in the golden age of capitalism that followed after the Second World War and lasted until the late 1960s, the liberal university was already subordinated to capital. At the apex of public funding for higher education, in the 1950s, the university was already being redesigned to produce technocrats with the skill-sets necessary to defeat 'communism' and sustain US hegemony. Its role during the Cold War was to legitimate liberal democracy and to reproduce an imaginary society of free and equal citizens – *precisely because no one was free and no one was equal*.

But if this ideological function of the public university was at least well-funded after the Second World War, that situation changed irreversibly in the 1960s, and no amount of social-democratic heel-clicking will bring back the dead world of the post-war boom. Between 1965 and 1980 profit rates began to fall, first in the US, then in the rest of the industrializing world. Capitalism, it turned out, could not sustain the good life it made possible. For capital, abundance appears as overproduction, freedom from work as unemployment. Beginning in the 1970s, capitalism entered into a terminal downturn in which permanent work was casualized and working-class wages stagnated, while those at the top were temporarily rewarded for their obscure financial necromancy, which has itself proved unsustainable.

For public education, the long downturn meant the decline of tax revenues due to both declining rates of economic growth and the prioritization of tax-breaks for beleaguered corporations. The raiding of the public purse struck California and the rest of the nation in the 1970s. It has continued to strike with each downward declension of the business cycle. Though it is not directly beholden to the market, the university and its corollaries are subject to the same cost-cutting logic as other industries: declining tax revenues have made inevitable the casualization of work. Retiring professors make way not for tenure-track jobs but for precariously employed teaching assistants, adjuncts and lecturers who do the same work for much less pay. Tuition fee increases compensate for cuts while the jobs students pay to be trained for evaporate.

In the midst of the current crisis, which will be deep and protracted, many on the left want to return to the golden age of public education. They naively imagine that the crisis of the present is an opportunity to demand the return of the past. But social programs that depended upon high profit rates and vigorous economic growth are gone. We cannot be tempted to make futile grabs at the irretrievable while ignoring the obvious fact that there can be no autonomous 'public university' in a capitalist society. The university is *subject* to the real crisis of capitalism, and capital does not require liberal education programs. The function of the university has always been to reproduce the working class by training future workers according to the changing needs of capital. *The crisis of the university today is the crisis of the reproduction of the working class, the crisis of a period in which capital no longer needs us as workers.*

We cannot free the university from the exigencies of the market by calling for the return of the public education system. We live out the terminus of the very market logic upon which that system was founded. The only autonomy we can hope to attain exists *beyond capitalism.*

What this means for our struggle is that we can't go backward. The old student struggles are the relics of a vanished world. In the 1960s, as the post-war boom was just beginning to unravel, radicals within the confines of the university understood that another world was possible. Fed up with technocratic management, wanting to break the chains of a conformist society, and rejecting alienated work as unnecessary in an age of abundance, students tried to align themselves with radical sections of the working class. But their mode of radicalization, too tenuously connected to the economic logic of capitalism, prevented that alignment from taking hold. Because their resistance to the Vietnam war focalized critique upon capitalism as a colonial war-machine, but insufficiently upon its exploitation of domestic labor, students were easily split off from a working class facing different problems. In the twilight era of the post-war boom, the university was not subsumed by capital to the degree that it is now, and students were not as intensively proletarianized by debt and a devastated labor market.

That is why our struggle is fundamentally different. The poverty of student life has become terminal: there is no promised exit. If the economic crisis of the 1970s emerged to break the back of the political crisis of the 1960s, the fact that today the economic crisis precedes the coming political uprising means we may finally supersede the cooptation and neutralization of those past struggles. There will be no return to normal.

III

We seek to push the university struggle to its limits. Though we denounce the privatization of the university and its authoritarian system of governance, we do not seek structural reforms. We demand not a free university but a free society. A free university in the midst of a capitalist society is like a reading room in a prison; it serves only as a distraction from the misery of daily life. Instead we seek to channel the anger of the dispossessed students and workers into a declaration of war.

We must begin by preventing the university from functioning. We must interrupt the normal flow of bodies and things and bring work and class to a halt. We will blockade, occupy, and take what's ours. Rather than viewing such disruptions as obstacles to dialogue and mutual understanding, we see them as *what we have to say, as how we are to be understood*. This is the only meaningful position to take when crises lay bare the opposing interests at the foundation of society. Calls for unity are fundamentally empty. There is no common ground between those who uphold the status quo and those who seek to destroy it.

The university struggle is one among many, one sector where a new cycle of refusal and insurrection has begun – in workplaces, neighborhoods and slums. All of our futures are linked, and so our movement will have to join with these others, breaching the walls of the university compounds and spilling into the streets. In recent weeks Bay Area public school teachers, BART employees and unemployed have threatened demonstrations and strikes. Each of these movements responds to a different facet of capitalism's reinvigorated attack on the working class in a moment of crisis. Viewed separately, each appears small, near-sighted, without hope of success. Taken together, however, they suggest the possibility of widespread refusal and resistance. Our task is to make plain the common conditions that, like a hidden water table, feed each struggle.

We have seen this kind of upsurge in the recent past – a rebellion that starts in the classrooms and radiates outward to encompass the whole of society. Just two years ago the anti-CPE movement in France, combating a new law that enabled employers to fire young workers without cause, brought huge numbers into the streets. High school and university students, teachers, parents, rank-and-file union members and unemployed youth from the *banlieues* found themselves together on the same side of the barricades. (This solidarity was often fragile, however. The riots of immigrant youth in the suburbs and university students in the city centers never merged, and at times tensions flared between the two groups.) French students saw through the illusion of the university as a place of refuge and enlightenment and acknowledged that they were merely being trained to work. They took to the streets as workers, protesting their precarious futures. Their position tore down the partitions between the schools and the workplaces and immediately elicited the support of many wage workers and unemployed people in a mass gesture of proletarian refusal.

As the movement developed, it manifested a growing tension between revolution and reform. Its form was more radical than its content. While the rhetoric of the student leaders focused merely on a return to the status quo, the actions of the youth – the riots, the cars overturned and set on fire, the blockades of roads and railways, and the waves of occupations that shut down high schools and universities – announced the extent of the new generation's disillusionment and rage. Despite all of this, however, the movement quickly disintegrated when the CPE law was eventually dropped. While the most radical segment of the movement sought to expand the rebellion into a general revolt against capitalism, they could not secure significant support and the demonstrations, occupations and blockades dwindled and soon died. Ultimately the movement was unable to transcend the limitations of reformism.

The Greek uprising of December 2008 broke through many of these limitations and marked the beginning of a new cycle of class struggle. Initiated by students in response to the murder of an Athens youth by police, the uprising consisted of weeks of rioting, looting and occupations of universities, union offices and television stations. Entire financial and shopping districts burned, and what the movement lacked in numbers it made up in its geographical breadth, spreading from city to city to encompass the whole of Greece. As in France it was an uprising of youth, for whom the economic crisis represented a total negation of the future. Students, precarious workers and immigrants were the protagonists, and they were able to achieve a level of unity that far surpassed the fragile solidarities of the anti-CPE movement.

Just as significantly, they made almost no demands. While of course some demonstrators sought to reform the police system or to critique specific government policies, in general they asked for nothing at all from the government, the university, the workplaces, or the police. Not because they considered this a better strategy, but because they wanted nothing that any of these institutions could offer. Here content aligned with form; whereas the optimistic slogans that appeared everywhere in French demonstrations jarred with the images of burning cars and broken glass, in Greece the rioting was the obvious means to begin to enact the destruction of an entire political and economic system. Ultimately the dynamics that created the uprising also established its limit. It was made possible by the existence of a sizeable radical infrastructure in urban areas, in particular the Exarchia neighborhood in Athens. The squats, bars, cafés and social centers, frequented by students and immigrant youth, created the milieu out of which the uprising emerged. However, this milieu was alien to most middle-aged wage workers, who did not see the struggle as their own. Though many expressed solidarity with the rioting youth, they perceived it as a movement of entrants – that is, of that portion of the proletariat that sought entrance to the labor market but was not formally employed in full-time jobs. The uprising, strong in the schools and the immigrant suburbs, did not spread to the workplaces.

Our task in the current struggle will be to make clear the contradiction between form and content and to create the conditions for the transcendence of reformist demands and the implementation of a truly communist content. As the unions and student and faculty groups push their various 'issues', we must increase the tension until it is clear that we want something else entirely. We must constantly expose the incoherence of demands for democratization and transparency. What good is it to have the right to see how intolerable things are, or to elect those who will screw us over? We must leave behind the culture of student activism, with its moralistic mantras of non-violence and its fixation on single-issue causes. The only success with which we can be content is the abolition of the capitalist mode of production and the certain immiseration and death which it promises for the twenty-first century. All of our actions must push us towards communization; that is, the reorganization of society according to a logic of free giving and receiving, and the immediate abolition of the wage, the value-form, compulsory labor, and exchange.

Occupation will be a critical tactic in our struggle, but we must resist the tendency to use it in a reformist way. The different strategic uses of occupation became clear this past January when students occupied a building at the New School in New York. A group of friends, mostly graduate students, decided to take over the Student Center and claim it as a liberated space for students and the public. Soon others joined in, but many of them preferred to use the action as leverage to win reforms, in particular to oust the school's president. These differences came to a head as the occupation unfolded. While the student reformers were focused on leaving the building with a tangible concession from the administration, others shunned demands entirely. They saw the point of occupation as the creation of a momentary opening in capitalist time and space, a rearrangement that sketched the contours of a new society. We side with this anti-reformist position. While we know these free zones will be partial and transitory, the tensions they expose between the real and the possible can push the struggle in a more radical direction.

We intend to employ this tactic until it becomes generalized. In 2001 the first Argentine *piqueteros* suggested the form the people's struggle there should take: road blockades which brought to a halt the circulation of goods from place to place. Within months this tactic spread across the country without any formal coordination between groups. In the same way repetition can establish occupation as an instinctive and immediate method of revolt taken up both inside and outside the university. We have seen a new wave of takeovers in the US over the last year, both at universities and workplaces: New School and NYU, as well as the workers at Republic Windows Factory in Chicago, who fought the closure of their factory by taking it over. Now it is our turn.

To accomplish our goals we cannot rely on those groups which position themselves as our representatives. We are willing to work with unions and student associations when we find it useful, but we do not recognize their authority. We must act on our own behalf directly, without mediation. We must break with any groups that seek to limit the struggle by telling us to go back to work or class, to negotiate, to reconcile. This was also the case in France. The original calls for protest were made by the national high school and university student associations and by some of the trade unions. Eventually, as the representative groups urged calm, others forged ahead. And in Greece the unions revealed their counter-revolutionary character by canceling strikes and calling for restraint.

As an alternative to being herded by representatives, we call on students and workers to organize themselves across trade lines. We urge undergraduates, teaching assistants, lecturers, faculty, service workers, and staff to begin meeting together to discuss their situation. The more we begin talking to one another and finding our common interests, the more difficult it becomes for the administration to pit us against each other in a hopeless competition for dwindling resources. The recent struggles at NYU and the New School suffered from the absence of these deep bonds, and if there is a lesson to be learned from them it is that we must build dense networks of solidarity based upon the recognition of a shared enemy. These networks not only make us resistant to recuperation and neutralization, but also allow us to establish new kinds of collective bonds. These bonds are the real basis of our struggle.

We'll see you at the barricades.

OCCUPY CALIFORNIA: STATEMENT FROM THE OCCUPATION OF GRADUATE STUDENT COMMONS, UC SANTA CRUZ

We are occupying this building at the University of California, Santa Cruz, because the current situation has become untenable. Across the state, people are losing their jobs and getting evicted, while social services are slashed. California's leaders from state officials to university presidents have demonstrated how they will deal with this crisis: everything and everyone is subordinated to the budget. They insulate themselves from the consequences of their own fiscal mismanagement, while those who can least afford it are left shouldering the burden. Every solution on offer only accelerates the decay of the State of California. It remains for the people to seize what is theirs.

The current attack on public education – under the guise of a fiscal emergency – is merely the culmination of a long-term trend. California's regressive tax structure has undermined the 1960 Master Plan for free education. In this climate, the quality of K-12 education and the performance of its students have declined by every metric. Due to cuts to classes in community Colleges, over 50,000 California youth have been turned away from the doors of higher education. California State University will reduce its enrollment by 40,000 students system-wide for 2010–11. We stand in solidarity with students across the state because the same things are happening to us. At the University of California, the administration will raise student fees to an unprecedented $10,300, a 32 percent increase in one year. Graduate students and lecturers return from summer vacation to find that their jobs have been cut; faculty and staff are forced to take furloughs. Entire departments are being gutted. Classes for undergraduates and graduates are harder to get into, while students pay more. The university is being run like a corporation.

Let's be frank: the promise of a financially secure life at the end of a university education is fast becoming an illusion. The jobs we are working towards will be no better than the jobs we already have to pay our way through school. Close to three-quarters of students work, many full-time. Even with these jobs, student loan volume rose 800 percent from 1977 to 2003. There is a direct connection between these deteriorating conditions and those impacting workers and families throughout California. Two million people are now unemployed across the state; 1.5 million more are underemployed out of a workforce of 20 million. As formerly secure, middle-class workers lose their homes to foreclosure, Depression-era shantytowns are cropping up across the state. The crisis is severe and widespread, yet the proposed solutions – the governor and state assembly organizing a bake sale to close the budget gap – are completely absurd.

We must face the fact that the time for pointless negotiations is over. Appeals to the UC administration and Sacramento are futile; instead, we appeal to each other, to the people with whom we are struggling, and not to those whom we struggle against. A single day of action at the university is not enough because we cannot afford to return to business as usual. We seek to form a unified movement with the people of California. Time and again, factional demands are turned against us by our leaders and used to divide social workers against teachers, nurses against students, librarians against park rangers, in a competition for resources they tell us are increasingly scarce. This crisis is general, and the revolt must be generalized. Escalation is absolutely necessary. We have no other option.

Occupation is a tactic for escalating struggles, a tactic recently used at the Chicago Windows and Doors factory and at the New School in New York City. It can happen throughout California too. As undergraduates, graduate students, faculty and staff, we call on everyone at the UC to support this occupation by continuing the walkouts and strikes into tomorrow, the next day, and for the indefinite future. We call on the people of California to occupy and escalate.

THE BEATINGS WILL CONTINUE[2]

Should you make a move from protest to resistance, you will be brutalized, arrested, destroyed.

That is the message sent by the police attack upon two students outside the second UCSC occupation on 15 October. Carrying a picnic table towards a building with the best intentions – *to wedge a stick into the maw of capital* – they were pepper-sprayed without warning. One of them, cuffed, arrested and thrown in a cruiser, now faces suspension.

What could be less surprising? *There is no difference* between the treatment of these students by the cops and the treatment of all students by the administration, an assault on lives in deference to already-falsified expenses. Our lives are permanently under attack, and the beatings will continue until we convert the crisis we are in into the generalized revolt we must become.

Why have students begun to barricade the doors of buildings that we claim as our own? To carve out material spaces of resistance and emancipation. To do so requires us to make explicit the state of siege under which we live, to exteriorize the locks and chains by which it compels assent. This teaches us that these emancipated spaces can only exist *outside the law, inside the barricades*. The students inside the building evaded arrest; the students outside the building were attacked and detained. *The spaces in which we are free are those that we take and hold by force.* That is the hard lesson we all have to learn.

Some of us are learning it more quickly than others. Let there be no end of generosity towards comrades who are punished for their courage rather than for their complacency. Our

---

2   Issued on 18 October 2009, following the occupation of UCSC Humanities II.

support for those willing to act will be material, immediate and unyielding. Networks of mutual aid will be essential.

Though we have no interest in theatrical protests intended to court police crackdowns, we know that as the movement becomes more militant the brutality of the police and the punitive character of the administration will not cease to make itself evident. In the confrontation between property and people, the police are agents of property, poorly paid to protect the rights of things. As long as they refuse to act in solidarity with other exploited workers, they can only protect the sanctity of walls, dumpsters and picnic tables while attacking anyone who might challenge the logic of their own exploitation. We must sustain our militancy in the face of their attacks, and our support for those targeted.

This arrest is the first aimed at student resistance on UC campuses this year. We know there will be more. How could it be otherwise, so long as the absolute antagonism between oppression and resistance continues to clarify itself?

For the soldiers of property: nothing but contempt.

Demand nothing. Occupy everything.

Research and destroy!

ANTI-CAPITAL PROJECTS: Q&A

Why occupation?

Why occupation? Why barricades? Why would an emancipatory movement, one which seeks to unchain people from debt and compulsory labor, chain the doors of a building? Why would a group of people who deplore a university increasingly barricaded against would-be entrants itself erect barricades? This is the paradox: the space of UC Berkeley, open at multiple points, traversed by flows of students and teachers and workers, is open in appearance only. At root, as a social form, it is closed: closed to the majority of young people in this country by merit of the logic of class and race and citizenship; closed to the underpaid workers who enter only to clean the floors or serve meals in the dining commons; closed, as politics, to those who question its exclusions or answer with more than idle protest.

To occupy a building, to lock it down against the police, is therefore to subtract ourselves, as much as possible, from the protocols and rules and property relations which govern us, which determine who goes where, and when, and how. To close it down means to open it up – to annul its administration by a cruel and indifferent set of powers, in order that those of us inside (and those who join us) can determine, freely and of our own volition, how and for whom it is to be used. *The university is already occupied – occupied by capital and the state and its autocratic regime of 'emergency powers'.* Of course, taking over a building is simply the first step, since our real target is not this or that edifice but a system of social relations. If possible, once this space has been fully emancipated, once we successfully defend ourselves against the police and administrators who themselves defend, mercilessly, the inegalitarian protocols of the university, the rule of the budget and its calculated exclusions, then we can open the doors to all who wish to join us, we can come and go freely and let others take our place in determining how the space is used. But we stand no chance of doing so under police watch, having sat down in the building with the doors open, ready to get dragged out five or six hours or a day later. Once our numbers are sufficient to hold a space indefinitely, then we can dispense with locks.

Our goal is straightforward: to broadcast from this space the simple truth that, *yes, it is possible* to take what was never yours; *yes, it is possible* for workers to take over their workplaces in the face of mass layoffs; for communities where two-thirds of the houses stand empty, foreclosed by banks swollen with government largesse, to take over those houses and give them to all who need a place to live. It is not just possible; as the current arrangement of things becomes ever more incapable of providing for us, it is necessary. We are guided by a simple maxim: *omnia sunt communia*, everything belongs to everybody, as a famous heretic once said. This is the only property of things which we respect.

If possible, we will use this space as a staging ground for the generalization of this principle, here and elsewhere – a staging ground for the occupation of another building, and another, and another, for the continuation of the strike and its extension beyond the university. Then we can decide not *what we want* but *what we will do*. If we fail this time, if we fall short, so be it. The call will remain.

Why now?

It is true that the upcoming vote at the Regents meeting – an almost certain ratification of the 32 percent fee increase proposed by Mark Yudof and the UC Office of the President – is merely the latest in a long litany of insults and injuries. But it is also the moment where the truth of the UC is undeniable, where its ostensible difference from the violence of the larger society vanishes. The hijacking of student fee money for construction bonds tells, in capsule form, the larger story of our enchainment to debt: credit card and mortgage debt, student loans we will spend our lifetime paying off.

We want students to see this increase for what it is: a form of exploitation, a pay cut from future wages at a time when widespread unemployment already puts those wages in jeopardy. Let's be honest: aside from all its decorations, university study is a form of job training. We pay now in order to attain a better wage in the future. It is *an investment*. But the crisis of the university and the crisis of employment means that, for many, the amount they pay for a degree will far exceed the benefits accrued. We could, at the very least, conclude that it is *a bad investment*.

But stepping back for a minute, what would it mean to restore the public university to its former glory as an engine of class mobility, as a sound investment in the future? It would mean the restoration of a system which, while ensuring that some individuals, here and there, ascend the rungs, also ensures that the rungs themselves remain immovable. The best we can hope for is that *different people will get fucked next time*. There is no escape from this fact. The university can't be made accessible to all without the absolute devaluation of a university degree. To save the university means to save poverty, pure and simple. *It means to save a system in which some people study and some people clean the floors . . .* The same goes for the entirety of the education system – there is no way to reduce the inequality in K-12 education without a total transformation of society. The schools are designed to produce this inequality. If they were equally funded and equally administered and we still lived in a class society, then the education received there would be meaningless as a claim on future livelihood. *There has to be an underclass*. This is the truth of education. And it is the one thing we are supposed never to learn in school – the one thing which, despite all the gestures of solidarity, divides the campus student movement from the most exploited university workers.

This is why we must seize these spaces – spaces that were never ours – and put them to new uses. If there is any value to the university it is its centrality as a point of transmission, an instrument of contagion, in which struggle is broadcast, amplified and communicated to the society at large. If we achieve this or that reform along the way – save wages and salaries, lower fees – this will make us happy. We understand how meaningful such achievements are for the people who work and study here. But we also understand how meaningless they are for the society at large. Sometimes saving the university is a stop on the way to destroying it. There is no insoluble contradiction, then, between us and the larger movement. We are one face of it.

Why no demands?
First, because anything we might win now would be too insignificant. Countless times past student struggles have worked months and years – striking and occupying buildings and mobilizing thousands upon thousands of people – only to win back half of what they had already lost, a half that was again taken away one or two years later. But in any case, we are as yet far too small to win anything on a scale remotely close to the mildest of demands – a reduction or freeze of student fees, an end to the layoffs and furloughs. Even these demands would mean only a return to the status quo of last year or the year before – inadequate by any but the most cowardly measure. If we set our horizons higher – free education, a maximum salary differential of, for instance, three or five, a university managed by faculty and students and workers – then we must realize, immediately, that nothing short of full-scale insurrection could ever achieve

this. And if we were strong enough to bring the existing order tumbling down around us, why would we stop short and settle for the foregoing list?

The process of negotiation – the settlement of demands – is a dangerous one for a movement. It often signals its death. We have no illusions about this. We understand that, if we were to become powerful enough, and if we remained steadfast in our refusal of all negotiation or settlement, someone, some group, would step in and begin negotiating for us. There is no avoiding that. Once we become a threat, then the bargaining will begin. If the first or second set of demands seems a worthy terminus, then we have a piece of advice. Become a threat first. You just might win something. But you'll never become a threat by determining to fight over the crumbs.

The whole theory of demands as it currently exists seems to rest upon a fundamental misconception. The demand is never really addressed to the existing powers. They can't hear us – everyone knows that. And, in any case, they've never responded to petitions or requests, only force. The real addressee of the demand is on our side, not theirs. A demand defines those who utter it; it sets the limits of the struggle, determining who is and who is not in solidarity with a given fight. And such demands are, invariably, bound to exclude some party or group. We recognize, of course, that they can be useful in this respect – useful as a means to constitute and unify a body in struggle, but this body can only be partial, fragmentary, divided from further support. Some groups attempt to get around this problem by making their demands an eclectic laundry-list, but such solutions always end in absurdity. This is why we make no demands. Because we want to be in solidarity with all who are oppressed and exploited. We will not say who they are in advance. They will define themselves by rising up and standing with us.

Why this building?

Well, it's perfect, isn't it? As the UC levies students with ever-steeper fees and drives workers further into poverty in order to continue with its inglorious expansion – football stadiums, high-tech research centers, new administrative buildings, $1.35 billion in new construction during a supposed crisis – we can see no better target than one of the nerve centers of this strategy of accumulation, one of the routing points of this logic which privileges buildings over people. *Capital Projects* indeed. Even if the university is not, in a strict sense, profit-seeking like a capitalist corporation, the leveraged transformation of ever-greater levels of personal debt into new buildings, the congealing of our living activity into dead matter designed to react back upon us, to become the newest labyrinth of our unfreedom, is nothing less than a little blazon of the *project of capital* itself: capital which is nothing if it is not growth, expansion, multiplication, investment, and which continues along this path without the slightest regard for human needs. This is no less true of the UC, which will grow and build at any cost. Any growth is good growth, as the front page of the *Wall Street Journal* tells us. Gross Domestic Product knows no qualities. A pile of guns is the same, to it, as a pile of anti-malarial drugs. It is a system which *must grow or die*, which requires more and more resources and energy, more and more workers, regardless of what this work is doing. This is why no patchwork of reforms and technology and consumer morality could ever address the growing ecological crisis – a crisis, at base, of a system which knows no limits. And so we take our stand here, at the Office of Sustainability, Real Estate Services, Capital Projects. We will not create more of what people do not need. Not today. Here, in this building which coordinates the acquisition of property and the optimization of real estate assets, we refuse to be subordinate to the logic of accumulation. And we call upon all of those in solidarity with us to take over other spaces on campus, in their communities, to take over their workplaces, to refuse the rule of things, the rule of dead matter. It is easy enough. Countless buildings lie ready for the taking. We can, all together, chant *Whose university? Our university!* And we can really mean it.

18 November 2009, Berkeley

STATEMENT FROM THE OCCUPATION
OF CAMPBELL HALL, UCLA

On November 19 at approximately 12.30 a.m. students occupied Campbell Hall at UCLA. The time has come for us to make a statement and issue our demands. In response to this injunction we say: we ask nothing. We demand nothing. We will take, we will occupy. We have to learn not to tip-toe through a space which ought by right to belong to everyone.

We are under no illusions. The UC Regents will vote the budget cuts and raise student fees. The profoundly undemocratic nature of their decision-making process, and their indifference to the plight of those who struggle to afford an education or keep their jobs, can come as no surprise.

We know the crisis is systemic – and that it reaches beyond the Regents, beyond the criminal budget cuts in Sacramento, beyond the economic crisis, to the very foundations of our society. But we also know that the enormity of the problem is just as often an excuse for doing nothing.

We choose to fight back, to resist, where we find ourselves, the place where we live and work, our university.

We therefore ask that those who share in our struggle lend us not only their sympathy but their active support. To those students who work two or three jobs while going to school; to those parents for whom the violation of the UC charter means the prospect of affordable education remains out of reach; to laid off teachers, lecturers; to students turned away; to workers who've seen the value of their diplomas evaporate in an economy that 'grows' without producing jobs – to all these people and more besides, we say that our struggle is your struggle, that an alternative is possible if you have the courage to seize it.

We are determined that the struggle should spread. That is the condition in which the realization of our demands becomes possible.

To our peaceful demonstration, to our occupation of our own university, we know the university will respond with the full force of the police at its command. We hear the helicopters circle above us. We intend to learn and to teach through our occupation, humbly but with determination. We are not afraid. We are not going anywhere.

19 November 2009, Los Angeles

BACK TO MRAK: AN ASSESSMENT

One might have imagined that 'negotiations' and 'continued constructive dialogue' were merely a means of deferring, defusing, displacing the university struggle. They are certainly that. But it was clear last night in Mrak Hall that these are also a direct extension of police intimidation, of the immediately repressive apparatus of the administration.

This was the case, first, because our negotiations focused primarily upon the role of the police in last week's occupation, thus turning our attention away from our collective bond in the present, and away from the future of the university, towards a retroactive struggle against an injustice done to our friends and comrades. That struggle is, of course, a crucial aspect of our solidarity, and it is no small thing that it was at least partially won last night. But, as one impassioned student pointed out as the negotiations were concluding, she didn't get fucking arrested in order for her fucking charges to be dropped. Presumably, she got arrested due to the immediate urgency of a total demand: an end to the destruction of our lives and our universities by the neo-liberal agenda of state legislators and opportunistic administrators.

But the directly repressive role of dialogue was perhaps most evident in the fact that negotiations could not proceed without the presence of the police. It was during our first encounter with Vice Chancellor Janet Gong that the cops arrived on campus, called in before the negotiations began and establishing their positions under their cover. These were not riot cops, the chief of police informed us, but 'police with tactical equipment'. While we were talking, these police with tactical equipment began closing down the doors of Mrak Hall, as they had on Thursday 19th. We should note the simple structural fact that students were able to guard those doors because they stopped talking to the administration. They rushed away from an endlessly circular conversation and into tactical positions; they had to remove themselves from the essentially performative scenario of dialogue in order to carry out the concrete task of defending their preferred configuration of the building against the police. Successfully defending those doors against closure last night was perhaps a greater victory than any eventual concession to our demands.

Unable to close the doors, the cops then closed off access to the washrooms. And this, too, occurred in a breach of good faith with the spirit of 'negotiations' – one which only served to confirm their true function. Having expressed their emotional distress at the police presence – after having seen their friend violently arrested last week and videos of police brutality on the Berkeley campus – students demanded that the cops be sent off campus. Agreeing to 'consider' this possibility for three to five minutes, administrators and the chief of police left the building – only to send in two columns of armed and helmeted officers while they were gone, striding through the crowd in order to check doors and to establish positions in a side hallway and at the top of the steps. Thereafter, all access to the washrooms was prohibited: an obvious tactic both to disperse occupiers from the building and to pressure negotiations towards a favorable outcome for the administration. The Vice Chancellor, the chief of police, and an armed police guard then returned to the building no sooner than thirty minutes later to resume the 'conversation'.

It should be a clear and unyielding principle of any future occupations at UC Davis that there can be no discussion with the administration whatsoever while tactical police forces are on the campus. As long as the administration has already called the cops to arrest us whenever necessary, negotiations are a total sham, and must be treated as such. There can be no 'discussion' with administrators once they have already called in repressive forces to coerce and intimidate their interlocutors. What happened at UCLA, UCD, UCB and UCSC between 18 and 22 November will not soon be forgotten: police deployments by the administration effectively militarized our campuses; students and faculty were arrested en masse; a UCSC professor fell from a second-story patio and was carried from the scene on a stretcher; students at UCLA were tasered; a student at UC Davis was repeatedly slammed against the hood of a car; students at UC Berkeley were beaten and maimed by punitive riot cops. The nightstick, the taser, the riot shield became an extension of the bureaucratic violence of the administration. All this because students occupied buildings in order to refuse the privatization of their universities, as do students in Europe for weeks, without any police response whatsoever. The sequence of events that unfolded last week – and the UC administration's accountability for the brutality that ensued – is a fact that has consequences. We will certainly continue to resist and to struggle collectively; but we should not enter in dialogue with administrators who have proved themselves to have no respect whatsoever for our collective well-being, until they prove otherwise by refusing to deploy police forces that have demonstrated their malice and incompetence.

But there is also a different story to tell about Mrak on 24 November, which was, after all, a victory of sorts. There are different modalities of victory. And if there was a victory yesterday afternoon and last night, it was not just that certain demands were met by administrators. It was a victory of the intellect sharpened by praxis. The day was a sequence of remarkably precise articulations from a multiplicity of perspectives and positions. When we spoke among ourselves, we showed that in the context of collective struggle we can cut through issues that all too often confuse and divide the movement. We did so with no facilitator, no stack. When we spoke to the administration and the police, we felt the clear superiority of our goals, our motives, and our collective intelligence over their own. We understood, immediately, the legitimacy and integrity of our action. We felt the power of our being-correct.

There are no 'students', 'faculty', 'staff' any longer, among those who manifest themselves at Mrak. There is collective determination breeding active reason, measuring the strength of its consequences.

24 November, Davis

FROM HANOI TO THE MAGIC KINGDOM, AND BACK AGAIN: UPR STRIKE, DAY 27

José Laguarta

As the sun rose on Wednesday, 21 April 2010, two hundred students, mostly masked, some brandishing makeshift shields of wood and plastic traffic drums, approached the main vehicular access gate to the University of Puerto Rico's historic Río Piedras campus, and chained it shut.

Thus began the ongoing campus occupation, which has now spread to all eleven campuses of the UPR system, becoming the first ever system-wide public university strike in Puerto Rico. It is also the longest-lasting strike action of any kind in this US island colony since the Río Piedras student strike of 2005 (which lasted twenty-nine days). With no end in sight, the UPR strike of 2010 will soon boast the longest campus occupation in Puerto Rico's history.

The students' three main demands are: repeal Certification 98, which opens the door to eliminating tuition waivers for honor students, athletes and employees and their families; stop summer term tuition hikes; and fiscal transparency.

Río Piedras strikers have humorously dubbed their internal two-line struggle as 'Vietnam and Disney', with the front gates controlled by radical humanities and social science students as the former, and the gates at the back of the campus controlled by more moderate law and natural science students, as the latter. The comparison apparently was overheard early on from a cop who had been assigned to both gates at different times.

In terms of negotiations (the usual caveats about generalization and simplification apply): 'Vietnam' sees the strike as part of a broader struggle for social change, and tends to favor a hardball approach, seeking concrete successes and guarantees upon which to build a long-term movement. 'Disney', on the other hand, tends to conceive the strike as a necessary evil in the

search for a more just, inclusive coexistence with university authorities, and would rather secure the successes at hand over risking them by pushing for more.

During the first two weeks of the strike, administrators refused to even recognize the legitimacy of the students' sixteen-member Negotiating Committee (it includes representatives of 'base committees' from different campus colleges and constituencies), and later did so grudgingly and dragging their feet. All the while, a number of deans and administrative assistants have been provoking confrontations with students by entering the campus through the one gate that students have been unable to barricade, and which has remained under control of UPR security. Students and professors have maintained a picket line, but constant police presence has precluded any hope of enforcing it effectively. Fortunately, scabbing by students and professors has been negligible.

The Board of Trustees initially designated a five-member committee of its own to 'study' the students' demands. UPR President José Ramón de la Torre finally met the Negotiating Committee only after mediation by the Civil Rights Committee, a publicly funded legal NGO, even though he had already publicly met with and congratulated the 'Silent Majority', a small group of students opposed to the strike. This group later revealed, however, that although it opposed the strike, it held the administration responsible for resolving the situation by negotiating.

No progress came until the Board of Trustees as a whole declared its intent to meet with the students. Several days of expectation, however, resulted in deadlock.

As of this writing, Chancellor Ana Guadalupe has declared an administrative lockout of the Río Piedras campus until July 31, in response to a massive student assembly held last Thursday, 13 May, which ratified the strike by near unanimity.

That assembly was called by the Río Piedras Student Council in concert with the administration, outside the campus, on the administration s terms, in hopes that students opposed to the strike, eager to graduate, or simply worn out by over three weeks of uncertainty and tension, would assist in droves and vote to end or at least temporarily suspend the strike. The plan backfired when the overwhelming majority of the more than 3,000 students in attendance voted to keep the strike going.

Following their unexpected victory, the assembled students then marched to the Capitol building, to underscore the fact that the policies they are protesting respond to broader budget cuts that result from the current government's neo-liberal 'austerity measures'. The notorious Law 7, which has authorized the sacking of tens of thousands of public employees, also removes several key sources from the UPR's constitutionally mandated funding, thereby draining resources even further.

Other campuses have not held assemblies so far to determine the future of the strike. It is believed that other campuses largely depend on Río Piedras for momentum, due to the sheer size of its student body (18,000) and its history of militant struggle. However, it is undeniable that all of the campuses have developed their own leadership and particular demands in the course of this struggle. The Mayagüez and Humacao campuses, in addition to Río Piedras, have even created their own digital radio stations.

The broad, sytstem-wide appeal of the strike movement was demonstrated on Friday, 6 May, when thousands of students and supporters from all eleven campuses marched together to the Presidential Offices, where the Board of Trustees and the Río Piedras Negotiating Committee were deliberating. Police blocked the entrance to the grounds, forcing protesters to form a massive picket in an important intersection in the middle of rush hour, partially holding up traffic for several hours.

Following complaints by other campuses that they were being left out of the negotiation process, a National Coordinating Committee was formed, with representatives from every campus, which will now lead attempts to pull the administration back to the table.

Negotiations between the UPR Board of Trustees and the Río Piedras Negotiating Committee broke down when the administration rejected the students' proposal to repeal Cert. 98. Instead, it submitted an alternate agreement that in theory made important concessions, but contained a poisonous clause that eliminated waivers for students receiving Federal Pell Grants. This possibly illegal and unconstitutional measure would brazenly discriminate against poorer students who receive federally funded need-based aid, making them ineligible for merit-based waivers.

A carefully orchestrated corporate media campaign then began, which proclaimed that the end of the strike was at hand and that the ball was now in the students' court. The administration appears to have hoped the grant-waiver tradeoff, which would be unacceptable to 'Vietnam', would divide the Negotiating Committee, delegitimizing and isolating the radicals.

That attempt proved a catastrophic failure when the striking students' participative process of deliberation produced an overwhelming support for continuing the strike, encouraging 'Disney' to close ranks.

It was then that the Board of Trustees decided that the 'democratic' thing to do was to put the question to the entire student body, spending several million dollars (despite the fiscal crisis that produced the very cuts students are protesting) on an off-campus venue and several newspaper ads that falsified preliminary understandings signed by student negotiators, passing them off as 'agreements'.

That didn't go well.

The historic 13 May assembly turned the tide in favor of the students once again. The following day, however, strikers and supporters had a rude awakening, as the notorious police riot squad cordoned off the perimeter of the one-mile-radius Río Piedras campus.

A father attempting to pass food and water to his striking son inside the campus was beaten and arrested. Police Superintendent José Figueroa Sancha later confirmed that he had personally given the order to cut off food and water deliveries, and anyone with a problem should try the courts. The administration also announced it would request that water and electricity service to campus facilities be shut off as well. Later in the day, a physically disabled graduate student who had exited the campus momentarily was beaten unconscious, dragged into a squad car, and arrested. Police pepper-sprayed onlookers who attempted to aid him. The student was treated at a nearby clinic and released without charges late into the night.

This re-escalation of repressive force, however, also resulted in a massive display of public support. The blockade of food and water, which the police have maintained despite a series of confusing court orders, was effectively broken early on when hundreds of supporters tossed bags of food and bottles of water over the fence and over the heads of police officers in front of the television cameras. This method of delivery has continued, with occasional scuffles, as police continue to deny free access. Thousands of people arrived at the scene throughout the day, with huge picket lines forming at gates located on opposite sides of the campus. At one point in the afternoon, Ponce de León Avenue, which straddles the main entrance to the campus, was flooded with supporters, and had to be closed to traffic. At this point, the crowd became too large for police to control students entering the campus by simply jumping the fence. Demonstrations extended well into the night.

The following day, public presence ebbed and flowed, with police heavy-handedness fluctuating likewise. At one point, a well-known doctor tried to enter the campus in order to treat students reporting high fevers, and was forcefully pushed back by police. Eventually, however, he was allowed access. The ebbing, tense situation is ongoing at the time of this writing.

The newly constituted National Negotiating Committee has renewed overtures to the Board of Trustees, to no avail as of yet. Public solidarity and morale among students remains high, but at this point, the iron intransigence of the capitalist moguls pulling the strings of both the UPR administration and the government can only be broken by a massive people's movement that brings the island to a standstill.

A coalition of labor unions has called for a twenty-four-hour labor stoppage next Tuesday, 18 May, but it remains to be seen what they are willing and able to pull off. Many of these unions, grouped primarily in the US internationals ALF-CIO and Change-to-Win, have lost much credibility and drawing power among their base as a result of past capitulations. Among other things, they have sided with past governments from both dominant parties (pro-statehood and pro-status quo) by supporting the notorious public service unionization law that bans strikes, a regressive and highly unpopular sales tax, and attempts to crush the militant, rank-and-file, independent teachers' union. Many also believed they squandered the opportunity to build a mass movement against layoffs and privatizations after the 'national strike' of 15 October last year.

Meanwhile, more consistently militant or genuinely rank-and-file unions have yet to announce their plans. Some speculate the delay may be due more to sectarian squabbling than anything else, although it is fair to note that unlike the business-model 'internationals', rank-and-file unions actually have to consult their base before taking crucial decisions.

The struggle has thus entered a crucial stage that depends on ordinary workers' and people's capacity and willingness to act and flood the streets on 18 May and beyond, independently of their leadership. International displays of solidarity, whether financial or by way of action, are needed more than ever.

17 May 2010

4

FRANCE AGAIN

FRENCH LESSONS: THE STRUGGLE GOES ON[1]

Sebastian Budgen

In contrast to Northern Europe and the Anglophone world, where they are largely considered with bemusement or barely concealed contempt, in Southern Europe youth rebellions generally and student movements more particularly are treated with greater seriousness as genuine political actors, and the repression they encounter is sometimes duly proportionate. France, at least since May 1968, is an extreme case, inasmuch as mobilizations of school students, university students and youth from the *banlieues* have been a constant threat to governments of both Left and Right (but particularly of the Right) over the last forty years, and in the last five years have been peculiarly rich both in frequency and in changing forms. Student and school student movements in France can, of course, be confined to purely sectoral struggles with little wider impact; but they can also take the shape of relatively autonomous processes that detonate other sectors in parallel explosions, as in '68, or they can converge with and echo broader concerns in the working population regarding 'flexploitation' [*précarité*] (as we will see with the 2006 struggle against the CPE, below), or indeed they can play a radicalizing, catalytic role within much broader fronts (such as during the 2010 anti-pension reform movement). The nervousness of France's rulers when *la jeunesse est dans la rue* stems from its recognition of this protean nature.

The period opened up by '68 – the so-called 'red years' – which stretched out throughout the 1970s, was marked by a high level of activism, unionism and radical political debate in the universities, and this simmering also 'contaminated' the school student sector. Many

1 This article is heavily dependent on the highly recommended piece by Robi Morder, 'Jeunesse étudiante, précarité et mobilization anti-CPE', *Critique communiste* 181 (2006). Thanks also to Stathis Kouvelakis for his comments.

contemporary trade union and political activists – including current leading figures of the Socialist Party – were politicized by and preserve a memory of these tumultuous years. As with other social movements, the early 1980s – with the intoxication of the Left's victory in 1981 rapidly replaced by a head-splitting hangover marked by austerity and the gallop rightwards of the Socialists combined with the emergence of the Front National – saw a decline in activism in the *facs*. However, the newly elected right-wing government led by Jacques Chirac, attempting to ape the Reagan-Thatcher turn in the Gallic context, soon stoked up the fires with the higher education reforms of 1986 (the 'Devaquet reforms', named after the hapless minister Alain Devaquet). In November and December – fateful months for any 'reforming' right-wing government in France – a large-scale protest movement erupted, led by the student *coordination* resting on sovereign general assemblies in all the campuses concerned and supported by the student union UNEF-ID, which drew in hundreds of thousands and was also marked by a tragedy that was burned into the political consciousness of many of that generation: on 6 December, a twenty-two-year-old student, Malik Oussekine, walked out of a jazz club in the Latin Quarter into the tail-end of a demonstration in which students attempting to build a barricade confronted the police. Chased by baton-wielding police on motorcycles, Oussekine sought refuge in the hall of a neighbouring building but was followed and beaten to death by the forces of order. An estimated 400,000 people attended the funeral four days later at the Père Lachaise cemetery in Paris (and many participated in silent demonstrations throughout the country). The student *coordination* had called on the trade unions to declare a general strike – indeed there were spontaneous work stoppages and almost half the contingents on the funeral march were from unions. Not coincidentally, Devaquet resigned and Chirac announced that the reforms were to be promptly binned.

The second ray of sunlight to pierce the leaden skies of the neo-liberal consensus of the 1980s and early '90s was the youth revolt of 1994 – arguably, a herald of the turning point movement led by the railway and public sector workers a year later. Now under the prime-ministerial leadership of the neo-liberal Édouard Balladur, the right-wing government tried to slide through in February the creation of the 'Contrat d'insertion professionnelle' (CIP) which, in a supposed attempt to tackle youth unemployment, constituted a short-term job contract (from six months to a year) remunerated at 80 per cent of the minimum wage for under-twenty-six-year-olds. Three weeks of intense and sometimes violent protest were ignited between 3 and 25 March, drawing in layers of previously relatively passive working-class students in technical colleges and suburban youth. Three hundred demonstrations of between 700,000 and a million protestors in total took place in 130 cities, with major clashes with the police in Nantes and Lyons. Once again, the government backed down and withdrew its project.

Between 1995 – when the student protest movement, largely focused on financing issues and concentrated in the poorer, provincial universities, preceded the public sector strikes (indeed, the government conceded quickly to head off any convergence between the two) – and 2002, various student contestations emerged, but generally on a smaller scale, although this period saw also the 're-unification' of the major student union, the UNEF. Perhaps most significantly, the school students' rebellion against the neo-liberal reforms of the Socialist minister of education, Claude Allègre, in 1998 claimed his scalp, thereby simultaneously demonstrating that, although rare, political victories were possible even under a Left government, as well as highlighting the growing cleavage between the Lionel Jospin government and both teachers and youth – the two categories in which he was to suffer the biggest electoral losses four years later.

The failure of Jospin to get through to the second round of the presidential election in April 2002, and his replacement by the gargoyled figure of Jean-Marie Le Pen in the run-off with Jacques Chirac, sparked enormous demonstrations that pulled in many young and very young participants. While the 'union sacrée' formed around Chirac during these feverish weeks in April and May was politically highly dubious and fuelled by delirious panic-mongering (Le Pen's presence was more an arithmetical symptom of the collapse of the Socialist vote and the multiplication of candidates representing participants in the previous 'plural left' government than the sign of any major increase in the racist or pro-fascist electorate), and while the consciousness of many demonstrators was characterized by extreme naivety and ingenuousness, it would be wrong to deny that, despite the manipulation involved, this mobilization was an expression of a healthy anti-racist instinct for tens of thousands of young people, and it served as a first politicizing experience for very many.

Of course, the morning after had a bitter taste, especially when the large-scale protests at the first wave of pension reforms in 2003 were defeated, undermined by the lack of unity between union confederations. The social movements fell into a slump over the next year, but 2005 was branded by three distinct but highly significant events. First, the reforms to the *lycée* system proposed by François Fillon (currently prime minister, then minister of education) were contested, from December 2004 through to April 2005, initially by the teachers' unions and then by an impressive school students' movement. On 6 January 2005, searches were conducted by police across 1,200 supposedly 'troublesome' schools, which can only have helped stoke the tension. Demonstrations of school students, led by school student unions but also by newly created *coordinations* – a highly democratic form of self organization that had first been seen in the 1986 student struggles and then spread to nurses' and railway workers' strikes between '86 and '88 – started at the beginning of February, and by 10 February these had swelled to 100,000 across France, growing again to 150,000 by 15 February. Despite some concessions by the government, the national *coordination* maintained its maximum demands, including total withdrawal of the Fillon reforms, and on 8 March 200,000 demonstrators (165,000 according to the police) poured onto the streets. On 10 March, trade unions called a day of action around the rising cost of living, which resulted in strikes and demonstrations by a million across the country.

Unfortunately, the movement was only partially successful in causing the withdrawal of the part of the government's proposals concerning the *baccalauréat*. Moreover, the demonstration of 8 March was sullied by some clashes between protestors and other youths (numbering, supposedly, between 700 and 1,000) who – rather like the 'steamer gangs' accused of being active during the Notting Hill Carnival in London – ran through the ranks and engaged in robbery of mobile phones, money and so forth from some and in the roughing up of others. Such incidents were expressive of real social, spatial and ethnicized divisions within French 'youth', which is clearly not a homogeneous or harmonious body, but they were blown out of all proportion by certain media commentators who, with the help of *Le Monde*, Hachomer Hatzaïr and Radio Shalom, spread a hysterical notion of rampant 'anti-white racism', resulting in an appeal against 'anti-white *ratonnades* [close to the term 'lynchings']' which was signed by such luminaries as Alain Finkielkraut, Jacques Julliard, Bernard Kouchner and, scourge of the 'Judeophobia' of the radical and pro-Palestinian Left, Pierre-André Taguieff.

The second event which helped cleanse the political atmosphere was the surprising victory of the 'No' campaign in the referendum on the European Constitutional Treaty in May 2005. Against all odds, and, more importantly, against the consensus of all the establishment parties and almost all of the media in favour of the Treaty, a genuinely bottom-up mobilization of citizens and campaigning organizations had succeeded in creating a broad front, on a progressive, nonnationalist and anti-neo-liberal basis, that had defied all expectations and served as a flagrant slap in the face for the country's elites at all levels.

Finally, October and November 2005 saw the longest ever period of urban rioting in France's history, resulting in the installation of a state of emergency and even calls by some (such as the hard-right Philippe de Villiers) for the use of troops and tanks. On 27 October in Clichy-sous-Bois (Seine Saint-Denis), chased by police on suspicion of theft from a building site, three youths, Bouna Traoré (fifteen), Zyed Benna (seventeen), and Muhittin Altun (seventeen), took refuge in an electricity generator. Traoré and Benna died from electrocution and Altun escaped with severe burns. The whitewashing of police responsibility for the accident began immediately, with Nicolas Sarkozy, then minister of the interior, in the front rank (and, indeed, the two officers have never been convicted). Rioting began that very evening in Clichy-sous-Bois, with claims of live rounds being fired at a riot police vehicle, and then the launching of a tear gas canister into the local mosque. The clashes soon spread into what the Renseignements généraux (which could be described as the French FBI, specializing in 'political intelligence') called 'a form of unorganized insurrection' over three weeks, which by 7 November embraced 274 *communes* or districts, and had resulted in over 9,000 burnt cars, dozens of burnt public buildings, shops and so forth, 4,770 arrests and over a hundred injured police. As might be expected given the location of the clashes, and judging from the profiles of those arrested, the majority of those involved were from families of immigrant origin, and from those layers most affected by dropping out of school, unemployment or highly precarious jobs and pauperization. It would misleading, however, as some would like to do, to draw an absolute distinction between these strata and those who have 'succeeded' academically – being subject to similar forms of social, spatial and racial discrimination and disadvantages, there is a great deal of 'porosity' between categories.

It would not be excessive to claim that the high social and political voltage experienced in 2005 had prepared the terrain, in some senses, for what was to erupt the next year – namely the most spectacular and successful of all these recent struggles, the anti-CPE protest movement of February–April 2006. Indeed, the de Villepin government proposed its 'Loi pour l'égalité des chances', adopted on 31 March, which included an amendment creating a 'Contrat Première Embauche' (First Job Contract), as a supposed response to youth unemployment, and thus to the social conditions that had produced the riots the previous year. In fact, the CPE was simply an extension of the provisions of the Contrat Nouvelles Embauches (CNE), which had been passed fairly easily in 2005: the CNE allowed companies of fewer than twenty employees to sack an employee during the first two years of their contract without having to cite any grounds; with the CPE, this increased 'flexibility' of the labour market was to be extended to cover all under-twenty-six-year-olds, regardless of the size of the company. Following a neo-liberal syllogism, the government claimed that such a measure would 'reassure' employers about hiring, without fear of being 'locked in' to a particular employee, and that it would also bring business and the universities closer together – the latter being accused of producing 'unemployable' graduates and being too distant from economic realities. It is perhaps difficult to recall now, but, at the time, the US model of the 'flexible' labour market was being held up as an example to follow, especially in the field of youth unemployment. However, as David Howell from the New School of Social Research argues, the disparity between US and French rates is a statistical illusion:

> [A]ctual unemployment as a share of the total youth population is about the same in the two countries. Why? Mainly because American students often hold part-time jobs (and are thus counted as 'employed'), while French ones don't.
>
> [F]or male youth the unemployment-to-population rate is 8.3 percent in the United States and 8.6 percent in France . . . The unemployment-to-population rate for female youth is lower in both countries: 7.4 percent in France and 6.5 percent in the United States. So, using the proper yardstick, the ratio of unemployed youth to the youth population, the youth unemployment problem in France and the United States is almost indistinguishable.

What is true, however, is that French students, even prior to the CPE, were subjected to 'flexploitation' or *précarité*, with the result that the gap between the earnings of workers in the 51–60 range and those between 26 and 30 has increased from 15 per cent in 1977 to 40 per cent in 2005, and 57.1 per cent of fifteen- to twenty-nine-year-olds live with their parents. It is estimated that around 47 or 48 per cent of university students work alongside their studies, and, of course, many of these jobs are minimum-wage and highly insecure, and this is to say nothing of the veritable scam of 'internships'.

One of the first, most striking features of the anti-CPE movement – which spread more slowly, like an ink blot, than previous more explosive processes – was the mass pedagogical work carried out, which was very similar to the demystification of the European Constitutional Treaty by ATTAC and others, and which persuaded young people who, after years of 'normalization' of precarious employment originally saw the CPE measure quite favourably, that it should actually be opposed. Moreover, the campaigners were able to broaden out the question to envelop all sorts of transformations of the nature of work in ways that affected all *salariés*, younger or older, thus pulling the trade unions in behind them – indeed, in sharp contrast to the 'failed rendezvous' of May '68, in 2006 students went out in great numbers to workplaces, especially before the big demonstrations, in order to create links with the unions and involve workers. It should be added that Villepin's aggressive refusal to engage in any real negotiation also helped strengthen the case for all-out refusal by his opponents.

The movement – one the longest-lasting student movements in France – was characterized by several important features. Firstly, there was widespread adoption of the tactic of *blocages* – physical blockades with furniture and other objects, along with pickets and occupations – of the university premises. Second, despite internal tensions and friction, there was strong unity among the unions on the key demand of abrogation of the CPE, both at a student level (UNEF, FAGE, SUD-étudiant, Confédération étudiante and the anarchist CNT) and, crucially, with the workers' confederations, who supported the massive demonstrations and even called for strike action on 25 March and 4 April. Thirdly, the national *coordination*, comprising delegates – 144 delegations in all, elected by general assemblies open to all in each of the universities affected – played a very active role, with weekly meetings taking place, each time in a different city (Poitiers, Rennes, Aix, Lille, Dijon, Lyons – indeed, the 'provincial', extra-Parisian roots of the movement must also be underlined). The *coordination* was considerably more radical than the student unions, and included an important presence of radical leftist and 'autonomist' sensibilities; but it also maintained a high level of democracy, refusing to appoint spokespeople as interlocutors for the media. In the universities themselves, general assemblies – in some cases, assemblies of thousands of individuals (in Limoges, a rugby stadium was used and the meeting was covered by TV; in Rennes 2 and Poitiers, some five to six thousand students participated in the assemblies) – voted two or three times a week on the continuation of the strike and the blockades.

The tension was ratcheted up several notches on the night of 10 March, when CRS riot police expelled those occupying the Sorbonne. On 14 March, demonstrations assembled some 40,000 people; two days later, between 500,000 and 800,000 (447,500 according to police figures); on Saturday 18 March, between 530,000 and 1.5 million demonstrated across 160 towns; on the following Tuesday, a national strike was called, and between 1,055,000 and 3,000,000 turned out in the streets; on 31 March Chirac appeared on TV, but failed to calm the situation; indeed, on 4 April, large-scale strikes took place in public transport and the schools, and between one and three million demonstrators turned out. On 10 April, the government finally backed down – the law had been promulgated, but the president called for it not to be applied. This roll-call of monster marches should not lead us to neglect a whole series of direct-action measures, such as road, bridge, railway and motorway blockages, occupations of buildings of the ruling UMP party or of the employers' organization (MEDEF), and innumerable other 'spectacular' or ludic 'happenings' coordinated over the internet and by texting.

In many ways a textbook example of a radical, well-organized, democratic and, most of all, victorious struggle from below, the anti-CPE movement was by no means perfect – although a link was established with the working population, much less successful was the 'outreach' to the popular layers of the *banlieues*, and a certain number of incidents similar to those of the previous year tarnished some of the marches. Moreover, the activists paid a heavy price in terms of police repression – including more than 4,000 arrests and sixty-seven prison sentences. Yet these are but minor blemishes when put into a broader perspective.

The next expression of protest was seen in 2007, this time against the higher education reforms included in the 'Loi relatives aux libertés et responsabilités des universities' (LRU) of education minister Valérie Pécresse. In a context of increasing discontent in the universities and research institutes regarding absurd decrees on bibliometric quantitative evaluations, the growing 'precarisation' of staff and inadequate budgets, President Sarkozy's provocative and Philistine statements in relation to the teaching of 'useless' subjects and texts and his contemptuous reaction to the complaints of researchers helped spread a generalized sense of rebellion, leading to spectacular resignations, petitions and the foundation of the 'Sauvons la recherche' (SLR) network.

The Pécresse reforms, promulgated in August 2007, were seen as strengthening the power of university presidents against academic staff, as threatening the professional status of both teachers/researchers and administrative and technical staff, and as tending towards a 'twin-track' university system, between certain elite 'poles of excellence' and a mass of underfunded, substandard institutions with, on the horizon, the risk of increases in admission fees and an Americanization involving student loans, and so forth.

A first wave of protests was initiated in October, with, by 9 November, fifteen universities blockaded or closed by the administration and around forty on strike. After much frothing at the mouth by various authorities regarding the 'minoritarian' nature of these actions, Pécresse made some minor concessions and the movement died down by mid-December. In 2008 there was a small revival in this movement, linked to the announcement of the loss of 11,000 posts in the secondary school system.

However, it was in February 2009 that the protest really re-emerged, with a whole series of new criticisms and objections to the reforms raised all the way down the food chain, from renowned professors to graduate students, and the creation of a Coordination Nationale des Universités, which met eleven times between January and June 2009. On 5 February the first demonstration took place, assembling 50,000 (police figure: 36,000) across France; on 10 February, a march in Paris brought together 50,000 (17,000) alongside other *manifs* in other towns; on 15 February, a student *coordination* was created, and they came in to swell the ranks of the *enseignants-chercheurs*; on 19 February, another demonstration took place, with a short-lived occupation of the Sorbonne; on 5 March, despite the beginning of the academic holiday period, another demonstration attracted between 24,000 and 43,000 people; again, on 11 March, between 30,000 and 60,000 came together on the streets; on 24 March, between 5,000 and 15,000 demonstrated in Paris. Meanwhile, new occupations of the Sorbonne and CNRS took place; between 7,000 and 25,000 were back on the streets on 2 April. Between December 2008 to April 2009, seventy-five universities and thirty-three IUTs (technological institutes) were occupied.

As in 2010, with the protests against Sarkozy's pension reforms, the government in this event remained largely intransigent. In the latter case, there was no mass movement in the universities, although there was the beginning of a substantial school-student mobilization, which participated both in the marches and the various forms of road and transport blockades that were so important in paralyzing the country at various points during the conflict. The union confederations' choice of highly spaced out and ritualized 'days of action', however, allowed the government to sit out the protests until they dwindled.

Needless to say, the ambiguities of the Socialist Party on the question of the pension age did not aid the protestors. Nor is it an encouragement to dissenting movements that the candidate best placed for the party in 2012, Dominique Strauss-Kahn, is the very incarnation, as head of the IMF, of the neo-liberal consensus and austerity drives being forced down the throats of the Greeks, the Irish and now the British. When Nicolas Sarkozy underlines his support for and agreement with 'DSK', this is no mere feint.

Nonetheless, few of the participants in the enormous protests of autumn 2010 feel that they have suffered a definitive defeat, and more upsurges are most likely. In any case, what is undeniable is that student and youth movements in France have retained all their vitality and will remain a real force to reckon with for this administration and the next. Young people, including school students, have shown that they are capable and willing to defend even a pension system from which they may never benefit decades hence. A common anxiety for the future of French society has been bonded intergenerationally with a shared tradition of struggle 'tous ensemble'. This very experience of struggle has been successfully reproduced and transmitted from one cohort to the next, and this is undoubtedly strong grounds for hopeful expectations of further tumult ahead.

Flashback:

STRATEGY AND REVOLUTION IN FRANCE[1]

André Glucksmann

The May movement revealed the *nationwide crisis* tormenting France: not the revolution itself but the terrain which made it possible. 'Only when the "lower classes" do not want the old way and when the "upper classes" cannot carry on in the old way – only then can revolution triumph.'[2] While ten million strikers, the 'lower classes', launched a movement of a breadth unequalled in the history of the French workers' movement, the political crisis raged among the 'upper classes', the police brutality shocked average public opinion, and the first official statements, far from coping with the demands of the street, multiplied them. For three days (Tuesday 28 to Thursday 30 May), France no longer knew if it had a government, all the press examined alternative solutions, the parliamentary opposition declared its readiness to form a provisional government.

The physical inferiority of the forces of order was extreme, their morale low; the strike had only to hold, the demonstrations to continue and State power would have collapsed. De Gaulle's second speech (30 May) seemed to restore the situation, but in fact it revealed it: State power was not relying on its own too feeble strength, but on the weakness of the opposing camp. The 'left' proved its absence of will, and politics abhors a vacuum. On 13 May 1958, de Gaulle had conquered France in the name of order. Ten years later, the opposition could, but would not, repeat the operation to its own advantage; instead of an inverted 13 May we should have had a repeated 13 May. De Gaulle – Titan – found his feet once again on the ground that sustains his power: not the forces of order, but the fear of disorder; like a phoenix, the Gaullist régime was reborn immaculate, through the impotence of the parliamentary opposition.

---

1 From *New Left Review*, I/52 (1968), pp. 70–2.
2 V. I. Lenin, *Selected Works in Three Volumes* (Moscow, n.d.), vol. III, p. 430.

The workers and students had power in their hands, they found no organized force to which to entrust it. A nationwide crisis becomes a revolution, Lenin goes on, when the masses in movement can force their leaders to fight, leaders who *'are afraid of their own victory'*.[3] The May movement, despite the weakness of its opponent, was blocked in its rise to revolution; the parties and trade unions wanted none of it – lack of a revolutionary organization; the striking workers made no use of the power they held, and seeing the hesitations of their leaders some began to be afraid of victory, since they did not know what to do with it – lack of a revolutionary theory.

The field of battle, the nationwide crisis, was favourable, but the Communist Party only joined the battle to keep possession of its arms, not to open the road to socialism – it left the strikers in the lurch, sounding the retreat before the fight began. The two conditions for the transformation of a nationwide crisis into a revolution were lacking: no revolutionary organization, no general theory coordinated the struggle on a national scale.

At the beginning, the student movement, expanded to include the young workers, replaced the vanguard organization; its forms of extra-parliamentary action took the place of a strategy. The importance of the student 'detonator' seems miraculous to whoever cannot spot the tripwire that could unleash a chain reaction in French society as a whole. *It took the (empty) place* of revolutionary organization and theory; it played its part within the limits of its possibilities. The May movement suggests the perspectives of a revolutionary strategy for the second half of the twentieth century in the 'advanced' capitalist countries.

Spartacus began his epic with seventy slaves. They established themselves on the slopes of Vesuvius; at night the volcano's fire, in the day its smoke, proclaimed from afar the advent of an unprecedented revolt. Later, arriving within sight of Rome, Spartacus's army was immobilized: the world capital was almost defenceless, but the slaves did not dare take it, the collapse began.[4] The Sorbonne, occupied by revolutionary students, symbolizes Rome conquered from within: the intellectual citadel has opened, the ghetto of the workers' suburbs may begin to move, if the encounter takes place this place will be called revolution. An 'independent movement of the immense majority in the interests of the immense majority',[5] the May movement doubly awakened society: by violence and by speech.

---

3 Ibid., p. 431.
4 'The Soviets of Workers' and Soldiers' Deputies must seize power not for the purpose of building an ordinary bourgeois republic, nor for the purpose of immediate transition to socialism. This cannot be. What, then, is the purpose? The Soviets must seize power in order to take the first concrete steps towards this transition, steps that can and should be made. In this respect fear is the main enemy.' (Lenin, May 1917, *Selected Works*, vol. II, p. 106.)
5 Marx-Engels, *Selected Works*, vol. I, p. 44.

NEW CLASS STRUGGLES IN FRANCE[1]

Larry Portis

Flower power *dans la gueule*! – 'Flower power in your face!' This was my favorite slogan seen at the demonstration in Montpellier, France, on 16 October 2010. It emblazoned a cardboard sign and was carried by a young girl with curly hair and a headband. At the bottom of the sign was printed in very large capital letters: *Tous ensemble pour la Grève Generale* – 'All together for the General Strike.'

Curious, I asked the girl about the sign, and about the reverse side, on which was written, 'Never trust a hippy' (*Ne fais jamais confiance aux hippies*). 'Is this really a problem?' I asked, 'Are there still hippies around?' Respectful of my age, she hesitated to respond, before saying, 'Yes, there are. We are the hippies.' She is fifteen years old and, I found, as capable of discussing the issues of neo-liberal reform of public institutions in France as anybody. At least people like her understand what might be called simple common sense. Students at all levels and young workers know that requiring people to work longer, as the retirement reform proposed by the Sarkozy government calls for, will result in fewer jobs for the young.

This is an ineluctable deduction, but one avoided by almost all French politicians. Even the French Socialist Party, for example, also accepts that the retirement age must be raised, in accordance with the decisions of the sacrosanct European Union. Only the more radical organizations, such as the Communist Party, the Greens, the New Anti-Capitalist Party (the former Ligue Communiste Révolutionnaire) and, of course, revolutionary unions and political formations like the CNT (Confédération Nationale du Travail), Alternative Libertaire, Lutte

---

1   This text was first published in the print edition of *Counterpunch* ($40 a year to subscribe: PO Box 228, Petrolia, CT 95558).

Ouvrière, and the Fédération Anarchiste call for real progressive fiscal reform, the reduction of work time, and other radical structural changes.

We can analyze the facetious slogans as we wish, and there are thousands of them, conceived and formulated with humour and creativity. Whenever a movement in France lasts for more than a few weeks, there is an impressive explosion of imaginative sloganeering, the commandeering of popular songs provided with new and politically pointed lyrics (often far better than the originals), and street theatre of all types.

I've been to almost all the recent demonstrations in France, at least since 1986, when French students forced the government to withdraw a reform of entrance requirements to universities. What I have observed on these numerous opportunities to participate in mass mobilizations is what I learned during long-ago graduate studies focused on the history of France and its popular movements, and the ideas that accompany them or react to them: there is a revolutionary tradition in France.

And yet, paradoxically, I'm always surprised. For, in between the movements, I habitually lament the progressive loss of critical consciousness in France, the emergence of new, pernicious forms of media distraction (typically originated in the United States), the fact that there are more McDonald's restaurants per capita in France than elsewhere in the EU, the dumbing-down of education, and all the other symptoms of consensual one-dimensionalism.

But this is what a revolutionary tradition means. Regardless of adaptations to technological change, rebellious attitudes to authority persist. Popular uprisings in France are part of a heritage going back at least to the seventeenth century.

Resistance grows when a centralized state forces the populace steadily to relinquish more and more of its personal liberties and resources. In the present context, a good part of these liberties and resources are to be found in the fruit of former struggles. The eight-hour day and paid vacations were won through hard popular struggle in 1936. The resistance movements during the wartime occupation and then the Liberation in 1945 gave birth to the present system of social security, public health services, and retirement benefits. These institutional changes quickly came to be considered inalienable social rights.

The present government in France has pledged to overturn the situation. Already in 2007, President Nicolas Sarkozy had privately said he would be the French Margaret Thatcher. He would force through fundamental changes, reducing the power of the political Left and 'modernizing' France by dismantling state-financed social programmes. During his campaign, he declared, 'In this election, the question is to know whether the legacy of May '68 is to be perpetuated or if it must be liquidated once and for all.'

With his careful efforts to dissimulate his allegiance to powerful industrial and financial interests, Sarkozy impressed much of the electorate. He assured the young that he would provide jobs and increase purchasing power. He pledged to the elderly that he would crack down on crime and provide security for all. By recruiting members of the Socialist Party and carefully selected individuals from ethnic minorities to his new government, Sarkozy posed as a leader above political parties – neither Right nor Left. After several months in office, he divorced his wife and quickly married a former top model and pop-idol groupie turned singer (with the help of her family connections and fabulous inherited wealth). 'Super Sarko' was born.

It might have worked. But then, in 2008, a bit more than one year after his election, the crash of the New York Stock Exchange changed everything for Super Sarko. People in France, as elsewhere, began asking questions: Why are the banks and other financial institutions being given assistance, and not ordinary people? Why must the universities become unequal in status? Why are the numbers of schoolteachers being reduced when it is generally understood that more are needed? Why are post offices and railway lines being closed? Will programmed privatizations really result in better services?

At the same time, more and more became known about Sarkozy's connections to the industrial and financial elites. On the night of his election, he gave a party for them in one of the most expensive restaurants in Paris. Sarkozy is a funny little man with a large ego, and he tends to invite ridicule upon himself. Soon he became the butt of jokes, and the object of scurrilous speculations about his need to vaunt his virility and to demean his subordinates. Sarkozy came to be the most despised French president in recent history. Today his approval rating is in the vicinity of 26 per cent.

Far more important than Sarkozy's peccadilloes is what he represents socially. He is the point man for what the sociologists Michel Pinçon and Monique Pinçon-Charlot call the French oligarchy. In September 2010, these authors published *Le president des riches. Enquête sur l'oligarchie dans la France de Nicolas Sarkozy* ('The President of the Rich: Investigation of the Oligarchy in Nicolas Sarkozy's France'). The book establishes incontrovertibly that Sarkozy does the bidding of the powerful employers' association (MEDEF – Movement of French Enterprises) and the financial elites. His personal power base, in the exclusive western Paris suburb of Neuilly and the business centre of La Défense, is a centre of rampant political corruption and nepotism.

What distinguishes Sarkozy is his unadulterated contempt for people in general, and poor people in particular. It took French people (or, at least the 71 per cent of the French population supportive of the present mobilization in the streets) three years to become fed up with his attempts to gut social services in the country. The current protests focus on the regressive 'reform' of the state retirement programmes, but they go far beyond that. We learned just a few days ago, thanks to the online newspaper *Mediapart*, that a financial group was recently created to offer 'complementary retirement services' based on 'capitalization' to those who find the present (or reformed) system inadequate. A certain Guillaume Sarkozy, brother of the president, directs the group, and was a former number-two of the MEDEF employers' association.

Thanks to Nicolas Sarkozy, French people have learned much about the governance of their country. This is why they are now on the streets.

UPDATE

Richard Greeman

I ended my report last week (see below) with the hope that 'the French people, who are always full of surprises, will find some way out of this impasse in which their "representatives" – the union leaders and the official Left parties – are apparently their worst enemies'. A week later, the biggest 'surprise' is the entrance en masse of French youth, considered 'apolitical', into the arena of the social struggle. All over France, high schools are being blocked by their students, while the presence of beautiful young faces is overwhelming in the huge nationwide street demonstrations that keep intensifying. I'm not sure you're getting these exciting images on US and British TV, but you can view some at <www.libération.fr/societe/01012297576-les-jeunes-en-renfort>.

A poll in yesterday's Paris daily *Libération* indicated four out of five French people think the government should give in and negotiate, while 69 per cent support the demonstrators, who are demanding the withdrawal of the bill putting full retirement off to age sixty-seven. (Curiously, only 43 per cent actually favour outright withdrawal. I assume most of the others consider themselves 'realists' and hope for a favourable compromise with the inevitable, considering the move towards 'austerity' all across Europe).

Youth + labour = people power?

Actually, this massive mobilization of French youth should not come as a surprise. Last year there were weeks of strikes and protests among high school and university students against education cutbacks, and in November 2005 there was serious rioting among mostly French-Arab and French-African youth in the ghetto-like projects that surround Paris and other French cities (when Sarkozy, then minister of interior, made a name for himself by calling them *racaille* ['scum'] and threatening to scrub them with a high-pressure hose). In 2006 the French youth revolt became more political, when the right-wing government passed the CPE (First Job Contract) bill, a labour 'reform' (presumably aimed at encouraging the hiring of youth) which deprived workers under twenty-six of their legal rights as workers. All over France, students blockaded schools, went down into the streets, attempted to block trains, and eventually dragged the reluctant unions to support their demonstrations. In addition, the outpouring of us parents and grandparents in support of the kids was massive, and after six weeks of chaotic disruptions, the Villepin government was forced to throw in the towel and withdraw the bill.

A recurrence of 2006 is Sarkozy's worst nightmare, and he was recently quoted as saying in private: 'As long as the young people don't get involved, I can handle the movement against my pension reform.' The government's response to the youth involvement has been to try to drive a wedge between the generations by provoking violent incidents around the high schools and encouraging mysterious 'casseurs' to burn cars, presumably in the hope of alienating the adults with the spectre of 'violence'. At the same time, Sarkozy's spokesmen paternalistically maintain that teenagers shouldn't be meddling with an adult issue they don't understand, especially since the reform is actually designed to help young workers by lowering Social Security payments. On the Left, the head of the Force Ouvrière union, equally paternalistic, was quoted rejecting the help of the youth as 'the weapon of the weak' (presumably like 'women's tears')! On the other hand, generational solidarity is strong in France, as demonstrated by a handmade sign reading: '(Son, 26): Mom, what's work? (Mother, 57): You'll find out when you're 67!'

Elites versus masses

The massive entrance of the youth into the arena has changed the balance of forces in today's stand-off between an intransigent right-wing administration and most of the population. The second 'surprise' since last week has been the mobilization of the truckers (mostly independent) and the refinery workers, which has resulted in petrol shortages at service stations all over France and deliberate slowdowns ('snail actions') by trucks on the highways. This is all the more remarkable in that the French truckers, who can retire at fifty-five under a special dispensation, are striking purely out of solidarity. More and more, the movement is in the hands of local committees and worker assemblies, who vote to continue and expand the symbolic one-day strikes called by the cautious national union leaderships. In Marseille and elsewhere, there are ongoing tugs-of-war between demonstrators, who block refineries and oil depots, and the police, who disperse them only to find them back the next day.

The deepest fears of both the official Left (union leaders and Socialist politicians) and the Right are that the movement will 'get out of hand'. Editorialists wring their hands about a tragic descent into chaos. In place of the traditional struggle between Left and Right within the institutions, today's struggles are between the established elites and the rank-and-file – what in the US we prudishly call 'the working middle class'. The French, with typical Gallic irony, have adopted as their identity a government minister's contemptuous slur by calling themselves 'les Français d'en bas' ('the Frenchmen at the bottom of the heap').

Different interests, different tactics

As I see it, these struggles – between establishment leftist and rightist on the one hand, and on the other between elites and ranks – are being carried out in parallel, but they have different goals, and thus need different tactics. The goal of the strikers and the masses in the streets is clear. They want Sarkozy to withdraw the 'reforms'. Period. Their tactic is equally simple: all-out unlimited mass strikes until the government yields – as it did in 1995 (when the union-initiated movement against an earlier pension 'reform' got out of hand) and in 2006 (when the CPE went down in flames).

On the other hand, the goal of the official Left (Socialists, Communists and their affiliated unions) is to weaken Sarkozy, bring the government to the negotiating table, and re-legitimize themselves as a viable alternative to the Right with an eye on the 2012 presidential election. Their tactic: prolong the crisis by measured, periodic shows of force. Of course, this delaying tactic resulted in defeat for the workers in 2003, when the strikes predictably petered out during summer vacation and the government raised the minimum number of years you have to work to earn a pension from thirty-seven to forty-two (which particularly hurt women who have taken off years for childbearing). Nonetheless, after the success of yesterday's sixth successive national mobilization of up to 3.5 million in the streets, the union leaders are calling not one more but two more spaced, symbolic one-day national strikes: one in a week, and the other in two weeks!

Meanwhile, the whole country is going wild, and no one knows what will happen between now and two weeks from now. On the government side, Sarkozy, ever more intransigent, is pushing up the date of the final vote of his reform in the Senate, while among the youth and workers in transportation, petroleum, chemicals and other key industries the ongoing strikes and spontaneous, daily, local actions are intensifying all over France. One reformist union leader was quoted as saying: 'By marginalizing us, Sarkozy turned the power over to the streets.' So why did Sarkozy put his presidency on the line by uniting the fractious French unions against him, freezing them out of the action and refusing to negotiate?

My analysis
Short answer: 'France has the stupidest Right in the world', well represented by this little man with the big inferiority complex. (Demonstrators' slogan: 'Carla, we're like you: we both get fucked by the head of state.') Long answer: ever since 1995, when the Gaullists got back into power after Mitterrand's fourteen-year 'Plural Left' (Socialist–Communist) administration, the Right has been looking for a showdown with organized labour in an attempt to duplicate the neo-liberal triumphs of the 1980s when Thatcher, after stockpiling coal for years, crushed the miners' union in a prolonged strike, and Reagan fired all the air-traffic controllers. The Gaullists' first attempt at cutting benefits unilaterally under the Chirac administration was the ill-fated Juppé Plan of 1995, which provoked a runaway general strike and had to be rescinded. Villepin's 2006 attack on the labour rights of youth (CPE) had the same fate. In both cases, the premier took the rap and the president saved face. It took an egomaniac like President Sarkozy to take personal responsibility for the cuts, and thus paint himself into a corner.

Today's Right forgets that the official Left is their best ally. During the May–June 1968 general strike, the Communist Party and its affiliated CGT union leaders saved capitalist France by blocking the striking students from making contact with the striking workers, negotiating a modest wage-hike with the government on behalf of the strikers, officially 'ending' the strike despite a mass vote to continue it, and agreeing to channel the movement into parliamentary elections, which the Right won. Indeed, going further back in French labour history, in 1936 during the general strike and factory occupations, the CP-CGT leader Maurice Thorez famously declared: 'You have to know how to end a strike.' Ditto in 1944–45, at the time of the Liberation, when the workers were still armed and the French capitalists, having collaborated with the Nazi occupiers, should have been expropriated. The same Thorez joined de Gaulle's government and told French workers to 'roll up their sleeves' and rebuild the country under capitalism. Despite these betrayals and sell-outs, the French working class has not been seriously defeated by capitalism in the way that British and American labour have, and the French have learned the lessons that solidarity works, that resistance pays off, and that mass strikes are their strongest weapons.

There is no predicting what may happen as this conflict moves towards a showdown – desired both by Sarkozy and by the vast majority of the rank-and-file French, who in polls favour an unlimited general strike to bring the crisis to a head (even if half of them accept the necessity of pension cuts). So stay tuned for future developments.

Richard Greeman's first report on French strikes

People ask me what it is like living in France during these massive one-day strikes and popular mobilizations against the conservative Sarkozy government's pension 'reforms'. These cuts would push the minimum retirement age forward from sixty to sixty-two, and the minimum age for receiving full benefits from sixty-five to sixty-seven.

On the one hand, it is thrilling to see millions of citizens taking to the streets, as well as hundreds of thousands of workers striking in defence of their hard-won social rights, defying an increasingly reactionary government. Indeed, what is most heartening is that the 'troops' seem to be more radical than their official leaders, the union chiefs and Socialist Party politicians. Recent polls showed that the French public not only supports the one-day strikes (which make life hell for commuters and parents of schoolchildren); nearly half are in favour of an open-ended general strike to make the government yield – a strategy advocated by the far-Left parties like the NPA, as well as by militant rank-and-file workers and local unions who are champing at the bit.

Once again I am reminded of what I love about France: a still-living revolutionary tradition of popular mass mobilization and struggle that goes back to the sans-culottes of 1789, the revolutions of 1830, 1848, and 1871 (the Paris Commune), the sit-down strikes of 1936, and in my own lifetime, the nationwide student-worker uprising of May–June 1968 and the 1995 nationwide strike of public employees that went 'wildcat', paralyzed France for two months (during which Parisians cheerfully commuted by bike and event boat), and forced an earlier conservative government to withdraw its unpopular welfare 'reforms'. It's also a great pleasure to see a nasty right-wing SOB like Sarkozy humiliated by millions of angry, jeering citizens blocking the trains and taking over the streets.

On the other hand, I also have a disheartening feeling of *déjà vu*. Why? Because the unions used the same dilatory tactics of spaced one-day public sector work-stoppages in 2009, and the government simply bided its time until summer, when the French go on vacation, and rammed the cuts through parliament late one August night. And this wasn't the first time these tactics had failed.

Indeed, ever since the runaway general strike of 1995, every time the French have massively demonstrated and gone on national strikes in opposition to government attacks on their labour and welfare rights (as in 2009, 2008 and 2003), the official leaders of the unions have imposed the delaying tactic of spaced one-day national work-stoppages and demonstrations – marches and counter-marches designed quite precisely to 'demonstrate' to the government their ability to call out their troops (and thus presumably to rein them in). These demonstrations are great for letting off steam, but inevitably they run out of steam. Time is always on the side of the government and the capitalists in the class struggle. The masses' only strength is in their numbers and their resoluteness, and their most effective tactic, once they are mobilized, is to stay mobilized, spread the movement to all sectors of the economy, go for broke, and paralyze the country until the bosses give in – as they did in 1936, 1968 and 1995.

The apparent purpose of the leadership's military-style manoeuvres is to make a show of force and induce the government to invite the union leaders to a round table – thus recognizing their legitimacy as the official representatives of labour. This plays out in the media through competition over how many demonstrators went into the streets in each successive demonstration: social struggle reduced to sports statistics. The unions count 3.5 million people; the police count less than half. The union leaders go on TV and call it a success; the government says it is not impressed, and won't budge. Then the politicians get in on the act. With presidential elections looming and Sarkozy's popularity at an all-time low, the Socialists, who in power also imposed neo-liberal cuts, grandstand about their support for the movement. They, too, have an interest in prolonging the struggle against Sarkozy, as they hope to reap the results of his unpopularity at the polls. Former Socialist presidential candidate Segolène Royale encourages the youth, specifically high-school students, to join the demonstrations. The Right (which has been cutting back teachers like mad) cries 'scandal'. Another political horserace.

The goal of the mass movement is quite different. The strikers and demonstrators sincerely want to use their mass power to force the government to rescind the cuts, as the Chirac-Juppé government was forced to do in 1995 when rank-and-file assemblies ignored the unions' cautious tactics and took matters into their own hands. Those 1995 strikes got out of hand and continued for two weeks, until they achieved complete victory and the cuts were rescinded. Paradoxically, this victory was a stinging defeat not just for the government but also for the unions, who were de-legitimized as responsible 'social partners', and seen as unable to control their troops.

This is worrying for the leadership at the CGT, CDFT and other federations, since only about 23 per cent of French workers belong to unions, which are supported not by dues but by government allocations. Since 1995, the unions have tightened their control over the movement to prevent another wildcat breakaway. And you can't cynically turn mass enthusiasm and anger on and off like a tap without exhausting it, so such tactics inevitably spell defeat for working people, whose dream of retiring keeps receding into the future while they remain on the treadmill.

Similar mass struggles are happening all over Europe, where the same neo-liberal cutbacks are being imposed in the name of paying 'the debt' (created by bailing out the banks). Yet, here again, the Left politicians and union leaders, far from seeking strength through international solidarity, remain staunchly isolated within their national boundaries, despite the obvious fact that the European Union has created a common economic zone! But the unions and left parties depend for their 'franchise' on the national state, which subsidizes them directly.

One hopes the French people, who are always full of surprises, will find some way out of this impasse in which their 'representatives' – the union leaders and the official Left parties – are apparently their worst enemies.

Montpellier, France, 15 October 2010

Flashback:

1968

Angelo Quattrocchi

Barrages of black-clad *flics*. Leather and steel and plastic.
Forgotten nightmares. Masks of blindness. Lines of fear.
Sweet and sickening taste in the mouth. Dry palate. Bowels.
The first wave.
The black-clad army is now a wave of black-clad men, inflicting pain with white clubs. To be left alone is to be grabbed and clubbed; it is falling down and being kicked by many converging on the prey. A girl lies unconscious.
Grenades make bangs and blue clouds.
Cobblestones. Stones found near the trees.
Nauseating gases impregnate streets and lungs. Protection, regrouping, embryos of barricades, then – barricades.
Captured students are taken to Notre-Dame-des-Champs police station.
And then it starts to rain.
At eleven, the flics are masters.
The Sorbonne – ringed in black.

SPRINGTIME IN FRANCE

© Lea Guzzo

5

SIMMERING GREECE

THE FIRST BIG WAVE: 2006–07

Spyros Dritsas and Giorgos Kalampokas

At the beginning of the new millennium things seemed rather calm in Greek universities. The reforms in secondary education of 1997–98 had led to a more disciplined student generation entering universities, a generation much more accustomed to pressure, hard work and stress. Moreover, the change in the system of appointments of teachers in primary and secondary education, which added a new national exam and drastically undervalued university degrees, despite fierce opposition from teacher and student unions, meant that some of the strongholds of the student movement were recovering from defeat. The total number of students had grown rapidly, but many of them were in new departments without well-defined employment prospects and without collective traditions of struggle. The Greek university had changed much. In Greece and France the expression 'Universities at different speeds' (*Universités à plusieurs vitesses*) is used to describe the new hierarchies of universities and university departments according to the degree of adjustment to the imperatives of capital. In such a different social and political landscape, past victories of the student movement offered no guarantees that the new wave of restructuring could be resisted. The student mobilization during the summer of 2001, although successful in its demand for aspects of the Bologna Process to be abandoned, did not achieve a unity in struggle among all universities. Divisions remained, and there was a general feeling that the student movement could not offer a collective answer to the new situation.

But beneath the surface the tension was rising . . .
However, all these tendencies represented only one side of a complex situation. The capitalist strategy for the universities was facing a major contradiction because the majority of students, despite being influenced by aspects of the dominant ideology, were still expecting to achieve

decent employment through obtaining a university degree. This was the result of a broader capitalist strategy, exemplified in the Bologna Process, to widen access to higher education, and at the same time to make sure that higher qualifications are not translated into better working conditions or increased bargaining power. According to this strategy, educational mobility should not be translated into social mobility. This gap between collective aspirations and the harsh reality of deteriorating work prospects, along with the attempt to discipline students and the high cost of studies (of tutorial courses in order to enter universities, of living and transport, especially in provincial universities), further strengthened a widespread feeling of a sacrifice made in vain.

Consequently, the material tendencies that led to the student movements of the 1990s, in particular the deterioration of work prospects for degree-holders, were now more intense than ever. But although the situation seemed ripe for all these contradictions to be expressed, the student youth seemed passive, even consenting, as if the State had finally managed to win the wager of discipline and conformism in relation to the student youth.

The calm before the storm . . .

In 2005, few could have predicted or been optimistic about what was going to happen. The government passed a series of laws that had to do with the very essence of the capitalist restructuring of universities, such as the introduction of assessment and evaluation processes, despite strong student resistance in the past. The minister of education, Marietta Giannakou, seemed particularly strong, and in a position to survive the job she had been assigned unblemished, despite its traditional description as an 'electric chair' because of the high number of education ministers that had resigned in the past.

But in lecture halls all over the country the anger against the government was rising. The United Independent Left Movement (EAAK), the radical left group in student unions, was systematically trying to delegitimize government policies that politically and ideologically confronted the DAP – the student wing of the then ruling conservative New Democracy Party, which offered fervent ideological support to these policies. At the same time, all other student tendencies were taking anti-government positions. All these factors had been fuelling a sense of growing discontent that was searching for a way to be turned into active resistance and movement.

In this climate, the government announcement in early 2006 that it was going ahead with legalizing private universities, despite an explicit constitutional ban on private higher education, was raising tensions within the universities, with the sporadic occupations in March 2006 offering the first signs of what was to come. The spark that ignited the movement was created by the arrogance of the government and its assessment that the student movement was defeated, and by its consequent decision to choose an aggressive strategy for implementing an authoritarian neo-conservative reform. The new law that it proposed included provisions such as expelling students permanently if they did not manage to complete their courses two years after the minimum four, five or six years required for the completion of university, polytechnic and medical degrees respectively; abolishing the university sanctuary; running universities according to corporate management standards; and reducing funding. This was the tipping point . . . On the one hand, the attack was global, affecting all students – those in schools and departments with militant traditions and those without any history of struggle; the institutions of technical higher education, but also the provincial universities, in many of which there were no collective experiences of struggle. On the other hand, the authoritarian character of the attack, its openly neo-conservative 'law and order' rhetoric, the sense of a violent disciplinary endeavour, and the attack on public education and whatever gains the popular movements of the past had managed to obtain, made much more evident the image of a government trying to intimidate the students who were fighting for their dignity. The victory of the French movement against the CPE, in March 2006, was more than encouraging. The baton had been handed to the Greek student movement . . .

How it all started: 2006
The first protests began in March 2006, with the first assembly decisions for occupation taking place in schools with a long tradition of militancy: the schools of the National Technical University of Athens, the Medical School of the University of Athens, the polytechnic schools at the University of Patras and the University of Thrace. But soon the movement spread to big student unions that had not previously shown signs of mobilization. Mass assemblies, each with more than 1,500 students present, voted in favour of occupations at the Faculty of Letters of the University of Athens, the Economic University of Athens, and the University of Macedonia. The student wing of the ruling New Democracy Party started abandoning auditoriums and lecture halls, even in schools where its electoral presence was strong and it controlled the union. At the University of Macedonia, angry students surrounded its student union representatives demanding they co-sign the decision of the assembly in order for it to be put into effect, and then proceeded to a spontaneous march of 2,000 students through the centre of Salonica. By the end of May 2006 almost all Greek universities were occupied: 404 university departments . . .

Universities were becoming vibrant social spaces again. A new paradigm of collectivity and resistance was born. Schools were full of students. Struggle was combined with social and artistic creativity and with the search for radical political answers. May '68 seemed less distant and more familiar.

On 25 May 2006 the Coordination of Student Unions' Assemblies and Occupations was formed, to coordinate and organize the struggle. The decisions of the Coordination were then used as a starting point for student unions all over Greece, some of them without even the experience of an assembly until then. In the streets of Athens and other cities with university departments, mass student rallies were organized. The magnitude of the demonstrations was a surprise both to the government and ourselves. Having no political arguments to offer to the students, they resorted to the use of riot police. On 8 June 2006 a big demonstration of students, university professors and teachers, and other workers in solidarity, was violently attacked by the police. But police violence could not stop the movement. After every demonstration students were more confident that they could win the battle. Under pressure from the movement the government announced that it was postponing the introduction of the law to parliament. The Coordination declared that a first battle had been won.

It had been a battle not only against the government, but also against passivity and a defeatist mentality, against the attitude that we could do nothing; a battle against the movement's own 'bad self'. Now everybody knew what they could accomplish if they organized their struggle, built solidarity and collective identity, and articulated those demands that indeed expressed the needs of all involved. The government was aware of this, as were the students and the wider society.

Blocking the amendment of the Constitution

Encouraged by the struggle of the students, from the beginning of the next school year (2006–07) primary school teachers entered a prolonged struggle against austerity measures. The Congress of the Federation of Primary Education Teachers, which took place on June 2006, at the same time as the mass student rallies, made the historic decision to go on strike at the beginning of the school year. The assemblies at local teachers' unions voted in favour, and a two-month strike began. It was obvious that the government could not cope with the situation. The initial minor ruptures offered an outlet for feelings of discontent and anger, and led to prolonged struggles that the government could not easily manage; they were unable to rely on mainstream unions, since they, also, could not control the strike. Thus, the government chose the strategy of confrontation, refusing to negotiate with the striking teachers. However, the teachers' strike provided an example of collective struggle that was going to be instrumental in the development of the student movements.

As 2006 approached its end, there was optimism on the part of the students. The occupations of May–June 2006 and the teachers' strike offered the possibility of a broad front of struggle across education that might alter the balance of forces, and possibly lead to a wider popular movement against neo-liberal policies. The militant stance of the university teachers' association (POSDEP) during the movement of May–June 2006 was also a reason for optimism. Both the president of POSDEP, Lazaros Apekis, and its general secretary Yanis Maistros, were outspoken critics of neo-liberal reforms.

In such a conjuncture, the attempt to amend Article 16 of the Greek Constitution that explicitly bans any form of private higher education, as part of a greater process of constitutional amendment that was to be completed in early 2007, became a major political battle. Defence of the Article suppled an objective for a new wave of student mobilization, but also for a wider front of movements throughout the education system. Student unions began occupations right after the return from the Christmas holiday, despite the dominant rhetoric in the media that they were 'minorities', and that private universities were a necessary form of modernization – and despite the fact that both the ruling New Democracy Party and the PASOK, the socialist party in opposition, supported the amendment. Student assemblies were organized all over Greece, and for the second time in just a few months all Greek universities came under occupation by the students, with mass rallies in all cities, side by side with university professors, teachers and other workers. All over Greece, committees of struggle in defence of Article 16 were formed by teachers, professors, students and workers, organizing local debates and rallies and creating a large movement in support of public education. Faced with such a movement, the government resorted to police violence, and on 8 March 2007, at the peak of the movement, a huge national demonstration in Athens was violently attacked by riot police, with mass arrests. The government was obviously aiming at dispersing the demonstration and defeating the movement. However, under the pressure of the movement and in the face of growing discontent among large segments of the population, PASOK, using some minor procedural technicality as a pretext, announced that it was not going to take part in the process of constitutional amendment, thus depriving the government of the majority it needed. For the first time in recent history, a process of constitutional amendment – the highest parliamentary procedure – had been severely undermined and blocked though the intervention of a social movement. This completed an historic victory for students and for the movements in education in general. Although the government managed to pass a slightly amended version of the law it had proposed a year earlier (whose full implementation remains at stake even now), the fact that Article 16 remained in place meant that the movement was politically victorious.

The government had been defeated, the image of its ability to implement whatever policies it chose had been tarnished, and one of the biggest attacks on public education had been successfully answered. The political scene was becoming unstable, and young people were becoming the uncontrollable variable that made an easy return to normality rather difficult.

THE SECOND WAVE: 2010–11

Ilias Kefalas

This text is being written during the first days of 2011. Greece for the past ten months has been under the supervision of the EU–IMF–ECB troika. Wage cuts have been implemented in the public sector, and drastic changes in the system of collective bargaining have also led to wage cuts in the private sector. The official unemployment rate is over 13.5 per cent, and is expected to reach or even exceed 15 per cent in the months to come. A mass wave of layoffs is under way in many companies and factories. The government is attempting the complete dismantling of public universities. The Greek youth movement is fighting once again for a better future.

This is the situation in Greece, after the full eruption of the debt crisis and the beginning of the implementation of the measures included in the 'Rescue Programme' – in fact the ceding of control of the economy and of policy-making to the EU–IMF–ECB troika. For Greek society it is an historic watershed. In the conjuncture of the global capitalist crisis, 'actually existing' neo-liberalism is combined with an aggressive neo-conservatism, with the aim of reversing any social and political gains the struggle of the labour and student movements have accomplished in the last century.

After the attack on salaries and wages, the so-called 'socialist' government attempts to dismantle completely what is left of the welfare state. Public institutions are being closed, public utilities and companies are going to be privatized, and the public health and education systems are facing severe cuts, with the possibility of hospitals and schools closing. The subaltern classes are facing rising living costs due to increases in VAT.

Universities could not be left out of the scope of this attack. From 1991 onwards the Greek student movement had managed to stop or delay important aspects of the capitalist restructuring of education and especially of the 'Bologna Process' and the strategy for a 'European Higher

Education Area'. However, there has been constant pressure from the forces of capital for universities to produce a new type of university graduate: cheap, flexible and disciplined. In a conjuncture of crises this pressure has increased, leading not only to a new wave of university reforms but also to profound changes in the ways youth enters the labour market.

At the beginning of 2010, as part of the process of restructuring dictated by the EU and the IMF, the Greek government introduced a new legal framework for employees under twenty-five. According to this reform, which is in many ways reminiscent of the French CPE (First Job Contract), young workers would receive 70 to 80 per cent of the minimum wage. At the same time, unemployment among those between the ages of fifteen and twenty-four has reached 34.5 per cent, and Greek youth seem to be condemned to flexible and precarious employment and a constant inability to survive on their own, without support from their families.

On September 2010 the Greek government announced plans for new university reforms, calling for consultation with the academic community. The proposed reforms include changes that not only undervalue degrees and the employment prospects they offer, but also fundamentally alter the very essence of university education. Universities are to be run according to business standards and benchmarks, in full compliance with the imperatives of markets and employers. The introduction of the European Credit Transfer System (ECTS) will lead to individualized degrees and competition between graduates. Many departments are going to be closed or merged, thus severely shrinking higher education. Any form of democratic procedure within universities is going to be abandoned, since universities are going to be run by 'academic councils' comprising mainly non-elected 'experts' and 'representatives of the business community'. The system of entry to universities is going to change, with extra exams added at the end of the introductory university year.

Students have reacted to these proposals. The starting point was the big demonstrations on 17 November 2010, organized to commemorate the student and popular uprising of November 1973 against the dictatorship. More than 20,000 students took part in the demonstrations, expressing their will to fight not only against the proposed changes in higher education but also against the whole austerity package imposed by the government under EU–IMF–ECB supervision. On 25 November and 2 December there were new massive student demonstrations, and the Coordination of student unions called on students to struggle against the proposed reforms and austerity policies. The police deployed aggressive tactics, and there were clashes with riot police. A few days later, on 6 December, thousands of students took part in demonstrations organized to mark the two years that had passed since the December 2008 revolt. Across the country, tens of thousands of demonstrators marched, and again there were clashes with the police.

The highest point of the first round of confrontation was the 15 December general strike. Thousands of students took part in mass rallies along with labour unions all over Greece. Workers and students were united in the common struggle to get rid of the EU–IMF–ECB supervision and the austerity package. The 'socialist' government is finding it more and more difficult to implement its policies, and its parliamentary majority is shrinking. Since May, four PASOK MPs have broken ranks with their party to protest against the measures taken.

At the beginning of 2011 the Greek government is facing rising discontent and anger, and Greek society looks like a powder keg ready to explode. The Greek government is aware that the history of the student movement proves it can ignite a wave of social protest and contention that will be very difficult to control. That is why it is trying to adjust its tactics and the timing of the introduction of reforms.

At the time of writing, students are again preparing for a new round of general assemblies in order to discuss a new wave of occupations and mass protests. Greek youth are fighting for their survival and their dignity. Hope for tomorrow begins with struggle today.

THE DECEMBER EXPLOSION

Eirini Gaitanou

December wasn't an answer, it was a question

– a slogan on a wall in Athens

Welcome to the desert of the real

A bullet in the body of a fifteen-year-old boy on a Saturday night in Exarcheia (the area in the centre of Athens which is still a laboratory of radical political ideas and alternative social practices, and the meeting place of the radical youth) was enough to bring tens of thousands of people – youths, immigrants, precarious workers – onto the streets in protests that lasted over a month. This signalled the emergence of a new wave of resistance and contention in Greece, but also all over Europe. An era of insurrection began in response to an era of fear.

But was this bullet enough? In reality, the December insurrection was the answer of the youth to the oppressive regularity to which it had been condemned. It was also the first social explosion of the period of the economic crisis, and a reaction to a social disaster that everyone could sense was coming. The revolt grew out of an awareness that, for the first time, a generation was facing a future that was worse than that of previous generations. Mass unemployment, austerity, flexible work, rising inequality, retreat of the welfare state, fragmentation and individualization of social subjects – all these on the one hand meant an unbearable situation for the lower classes, and on the other hand intensified processes of social exclusion and marginalization and a constant denial of any prospect of upward social mobility. This social and political reality also induced a profound ideological crisis, leading the state to choose the road of repression against social movements. At the same time, the tear in the social fabric was deepening, while the state could no longer guarantee the minimum conditions of social reproduction. A crisis of legitimization of the political system was thus created, through the dominance of bipartisanship, the widespread disillusionment with political parties, and a growing feeling that state power was acting with indifference and authoritarian rigidity towards social demands and protests. This was accentuated by the intensification of repressive practices and a widespread perception that traditional channels of political communication and representation, such as political parties and trade unions, were no longer functioning as they had in the past.

The end of discipline – magic life

Just when everyday life seemed to be rather predictable, an 'accidental' event changed things violently. The media and the representatives of the political establishment tried at first to attribute the murder to a 'tragic misunderstanding'. The immediate answer of the demonstrators in posters that were circulated was: 'Everybody in the streets. Occupations, marches, clashes . . . No misunderstanding!' Athens was suddenly set ablaze for a whole month, an insurrectionary climate swept through the country; the smell of tear gas and violent clashes became part of ordinary life.

But December was more than that. At the same time, it was characterized by massive initiatives of self-organization, by innovation and experimentation regarding forms of struggle, by extensive collective reappropriation of public space, by the creativity and activism of a multitude of social subjects engaged in these initiatives and collective experiences.

December was a movement like no other. It was a mass movement without specific political demands or a political programme, apart from a demand for radical change based on the spontaneous action of the people involved, and on non-hierarchical forms of self-organization in the absence of a definite vanguard. The political organizations and collectivities of the Left and anarchist or autonomous groups were part of the movement (not all of them: the Communist Party was hostile), but did not act as its leadership. The demand of the student occupations in California – 'Occupy Everything, Demand Nothing' – could easily also express the spirit of the December revolt, describing a collective reappropriation of both politics and space, beyond the traditional norms of social movements with specific demands. However, it was an insurrection with great political depth, which, through its experimentation with new forms of struggle, tried to set new limits to our understanding of politics.

Money to the banks, bullets to youth: our time has come

The December insurrection was determined by the social forces involved in it. Young people played a leading role in the development of the movement. The student movement of 2006–07 against educational reforms facilitated the development of a collective culture of struggle among both students and other segments of Greek youth. Furthermore, the way youth was constituted as a social category both in apparatuses of social reproduction and in the productive process, the prospect of job insecurity for young employees, the violent reforms in the educational system as a part of a greater capitalist restructuring of the conditions of production and reproduction of labour power – all these contributed decisively to young people being at the forefront of protest. At the same time, the participation of immigrant youths in the movement was important, and the same goes for workers facing flexible and precarious employment. This insecurity, both for now and for the future, but also the inability of youths to express their rage within traditional forms of representation (given the non-existence of organized student unions in secondary education; the exclusion of immigrants from political representation; the bureaucratization of the trade union movement; the lack, in most cases, of union representation for precarious workers in most sectors), a sense of repression and at the same time of being increasingly marginalized – all of these unified a wide spectrum of social categories and strata under a common identity of being oppressed. The accumulated rage and dissatisfaction was ready to be expressed.

Welcome to December 2008, welcome back to your life

And this rage was indeed expressed. One hour after the murder of the fifteen-year-old Alexis Grigoropoulos by a police officer, thousands of people were flooding the centre of Athens. At the same time, protests and demonstrations were organized in many cities in Greece. In Athens violent clashes began almost an hour later. University buildings at the centre of Athens were occupied – although, particularly during the first night, almost everybody stayed in the streets, erecting barricades and reappropriating public space from the forces of order. During that night, but also for many of the days that followed, the street belonged to the insurgents. The next day a big rally was organized by political and social organizations, and the clashes continued, while the police tried unsuccessfully to quell the crowd. It was then that 'Down with the government of murderers' was first heard, and became a central element of the political discourse of the movement. Monday, 8 December was a milestone for the rebellion. On that morning, high-school students occupied their schools and organized spontaneous demonstrations targeting police stations all over the country (these local demonstrations would continue for many days), and the assemblies and occupations of the universities began. In the evening, during the big demonstration in Athens, the centre of the city turned into a real battlefield. Tens of thousands of protesters participated, prolonged attacks were made against government buildings, the government lost control of the city, and the police only managed to protect symbols of the political system (parliament, the Presidential Palace). Most banks were attacked, as were many stores (contrary to a widespread impression, most expensive stores were simply smashed up as symbols of wealth and consumerism; looting was not so widespread). The infamous Christmas tree at Constitution Square was set on fire, in one of the most emblematic images of the movement (for the next few weeks Athens had the privilege of possessing the world's only Christmas tree under constant police protection!). The government flirted with the idea of declaring a state of emergency, forbidding demonstrations, although the idea was finally abandoned. The insurrection was a fact.

'A spark in Athens, a fire in Paris, it's the coming insurrection'

First, the next day (the day of the funeral of Alexis, at which thousands of people gathered, and the police attacked them!), marches were organized on a daily basis, the police departments were besieged – but the movement also constantly invented new forms of action. When the GSEE (Trade Union Confederation) cancelled a mass rally on 10 December, the day of a scheduled general strike, 'in order not to make things worse', the grassroots unions and the student unions took the initiative, and a mass rally took place. The division between the union bureaucracy and workplace militancy was more than obvious. In the days that followed, many public buildings were occupied (town halls, prefectures), and opinion poll companies and radio and television stations were accused of disinformation. Particularly important was the occupation of the building of the GSEE, by the 'General Assembly of the Workers in Revolt'. Mass rallies and actions of solidarity with those arrested during the rebellion were also organized in many cities of Greece. Moreover, new forms and practices of ideological and cultural counter-hegemony were developed. The Athens Opera was occupied, and for some days it was used as a venue for discussions and performances. Theatrical shows, including a premier at the National Theatre, were interrupted; abandoned buildings were occupied and turned into cultural centres. The reappropriation of public space also took the form of occupying empty building plots and converting them into self-managed parks – some of them are still in use. Interventions were made even during New Year's Eve celebrations. Finally, marches and demonstrations were organized in more than sixteen cities abroad. At the same time, even foreign governments began to worry: Could the 'Greek virus' spread to their countries? The answer was given by the French president, Nicolas Sarkozy, who postponed the introduction of new educational reforms – in fear, as he stated, of a potential expansion of the Greek rebellion into France.

History, here we come

The magic of December lay exactly in its polymorphism, its creativity, and the mobilization of the masses – in step with the intensity of the violent forms of struggle against state mechanisms and the police, and the clearly anti-systemic character of the movement. 'All the flowers were left to flourish.' At the same time, the insurrection and its forms of struggle enjoyed broad legitimation within Greek society (even to the point of ordinary people throwing pots at the police and approving of attacks on the banks 'that took our houses'). Participation in demonstrations was impressive, despite the mobilization of the media to delegitimize the rebellion. December expressed the need for a return to politics, but not in the dominant or established forms of party politics or traditional political representation. It articulated the need for politics as self-organization and collective self-management. This was exactly the element that terrified the political scene. And if one aspect of the effort to delegitimize December was suppression, the other was the attempt to devalue it as an explosion without political demands – as a simple expression of violent anomie. However, the difference between an insurrection and a social movement organized around a specific demand is that the former can only be defeated if it does not take place! In this sense, December 2008 exemplified the rage that was growing within Greek society – a cry that 'things cannot go on as they used to!' Besides, as was often repeated at the time, the insurrection was not legal, or moral: it was only just!

YOUTH UNREST IN GREECE

Panagiotis Sotiris

From the 1973 anti-dictatorship occupation of the National Technical University of Athens to the 1979 wave of university occupations, and from the 1987 occupations to the high school and university movement of 1990–91, and subsequent waves of unrest in 1995, 1997–98 and 2001, Greek universities and high schools have never been very peaceful.

The current cycle of unrest began in 2006 with a wave of university occupations, demonstrations and clashes with the police that forced the Greek government to delay the passing of neo-liberal reforms. It continued in 2007 with the combination of student occupations and a university teachers' strike that overturned a process of Constitutional amendment that included lifting the ban on private universities. Then there was the mass revolt of Greek youth in December 2008.

Currently, following the economic crisis, the implementation of a draconian austerity package under the supervision of the EU, the IMF and the ECB, and proposals for a total overhaul of higher education that will include the elimination of any democratic process and the introduction of business management practices, there are clear signs of a new wave of protest.

Despite the persistence of student unrest in Greece, most mainstream theorists tend to explain youth unrest mainly as an expression of anomie and a lack of discipline (Kalyvas 2008). Contrary to this, we insist that the actions of youth movements in Greece have roots in the contradictions of Greek capitalism and in specific traditions of social and political militancy.

'Merry crisis and a happy new fear': economic crisis and youth unrest

The intensification of the economic crisis provides the material background for current youth unrest in Greece. The sequence that led to the austerity package enforced by the European

Union, the European Central Bank and the International Monetary Fund had begun earlier, when after the artificial euphoria created by the 2004 Olympics the contradictions of the Greek economy became more acute. In 2008 the Greek economy was already sliding into recession (Bank of Greece 2009), in sharp contrast to the high growth rates attested from the mid-1990s. Rising social inequality has become an integral aspect of the Greek social landscape (Kouvelakis 2008), along with insecurity for the future.

The crisis of the Greek economy is not a simple manifestation of the global capitalist crisis. It is a crisis of the 'developmental paradigm' of Greek capitalism that was based upon low labour costs, the exploitation of immigrant labour, the use of European funds, and increased household consumption fuelled by debt. These contradictions were overdetermined by the financial and monetary structure of the EU. The introduction of the euro and the provisions of the EU treaties meant a continuous loss of competitiveness, a constant pressure towards capitalist restructuring, deterioration of wages and labour relations, and a vicious circle of indebtedness.

Labour militancy in the public sector, student and youth movements, and increased legitimation of radical protest, show that the 'modernization' of Greek society is still an 'unfinished project'. Consequently, through the austerity package dictated by the EU, the ECB and the IMF, Greece is becoming a testing ground for the possibility of a 'shock therapy' of structural reforms in social formations with long traditions of struggle.

Students have taken part in the continuing wave of protests that began in spring of 2010, the result of a growing sense of a 'stolen future' or of a 'lost generation' exemplified by the rise of youth unemployment, insecurity and the inability of working families to meet the cost of studies. In statements from the student movement, the struggle against educational reform is presented as part of the broader struggle against the policies of the Greek government, the EU and the IMF.

'A lost generation': deterioration of work prospects for Greek youth

The unemployment rate among youth (those between fifteen and twenty-four) in Greece in 2008 stood at 22.1 per cent, with the EU-27 average standing at 15.4 per cent; by the end of 2009 it had reached 27.5 per cent, (with an EU-27 figure of 20.3 per cent), and in October 2010, 34.6 per cent. In 2008, six years after graduation, one out of three higher education graduates, two out of three secondary education graduates, and one out of three compulsory education graduates could not find any form of stable employment (Karamesini 2009, p. 21). The term '700 euro generation' has been widely used to describe the over-exploitation of young employees, many of them highly qualified. A survey of the employment prospects of Greek university graduates has shown that they face workplace flexibility and/or are obliged to accept positions that do not match their formal qualifications. The current austerity package allows paying young employees less than the minimum wage. Moreover, a picture emerges of a 'unity in difference' among Greek youth. Despite the differences in employment and social status between the segments of youth, they all face deteriorating employment prospects, leading to a rather unitary identity for youths in Greece, something especially obvious during the December revolt.

'They shall not pass': education as a terrain of struggle

Educational policy has been a contentious terrain in Greece. Historically, education has been a mechanism of upward social mobility, hence the reason for families' investing in their offspring gaining a university degree, hitherto associated with better employment prospects. However, from the 1990s increased access to higher education has not led to guaranteed employment. In the 2000s the combination of a highly competitive system of entry exams for higher education – requiring tremendous amounts of study and many extra hours of expensive tutorial courses – with the prospect of obtaining a university degree that will not lead to secure employment has produced a widespread feeling of insecurity. Attempts to bring higher education closer to business interests and to discipline the student movement have also fuelled unrest. The 2006–07 reforms included changes in the status of university degrees in line with the 'Bologna Process', which de-links degrees from professional qualifications, as well as harsher disciplinary measures, attempts to undermine the university sanctuary (the ban on police forces entering university campuses and buildings), intensified study schedules, and an attempt to legalize private higher education in Greece, through the amendment of Article 16 of the Greek Constitution.

Current proposals by the Ministry of Education, introduced in autumn 2010, represent the most aggressive attempt at university reform for many decades – a complete undermining of the public character of higher education. In line with similar developments all over Europe, the government is planning to introduce capitalist-style academic management in place of democratic process, by taking decision-making authority from senates and departmental assemblies to 'academic councils' that might include representatives of the business world and a non-elected rector-manager. Consequently, universities will lose any academic autonomy. Processes of assessment and evaluation will determine university funding, with humanities and social sciences facing major cuts. Universities will be forced to consider introducing tuition fees, leading to greater commodification of higher education, along with a race towards direct funding or 'sponsorship' from private corporations. Many departments and schools will be forced to merge, or even close, sharply reducing overall access to higher education. New flexible study programmes at school level will mean further fragmentation and devaluation of degrees. Working conditions will deteriorate, with tenure eliminated for assistant professors, while lecturers will lose any possibility of reaching professorship.

University reform is an aspect of a broader process of capitalist restructuring. Commodification and entrepreneurialization of higher education are important aspects of it, but equally important are changes in the role of education in social reproduction. Educational reforms tend to 'internalize' the changes in the labour market and the capitalist labour process within the educational apparatus, especially the need for a labour force more skilled but with fewer rights, more productive but also more insecure, overqualified but underpaid. This pre-inscription of the realities of capitalist production, this subsumption to the imperatives of capitalist accumulation, is not limited to changes in university funding. It takes the form of changes not only in the relative value of university degrees, but in the very notion of the degree, leading to new fragmentations, educational hierarchies, processes of individualization that respond to the new realities of the workplace. It can account for the emphasis on training instead of education, for the changes in curricula, for the current entrepreneurial culture in higher education, for the emphasis on the individualistic 'investment' in one's qualifications. It can explain why youths in higher education have a stronger perception than before of the realities of the workplace. As also observed during the French student movement against the CPE (First Job Contract), students tend more easily to associate with the labour movement and think in terms of common demands and solidarity. Although disputes about professional qualifications associated with degrees have been crucial in the development of student movements against the Bologna Process, student movements are not just a reaction to the devaluation of degrees, but, as Stathis Kouvelakis has suggested, part of a greater social mobilization against the neo-liberal 'restructuring of the totality of capital–labour relations' (Kouvélakis 2007, p. 279).

'Money to the banks – bullets to youth': police violence and youth unrest

Police violence was also a contributing factor to youth unrest, especially in December 2008. However, a focus on the inability of the police to deal with youth protest or on rituals of collective youth delinquency misses the point. Moreover, it is not enough to link hostility towards the police to the historic association of the police in Greece with state authoritarianism and the persecution of left-wing militants. Police violence mainly acts as a metonym for the systemic social violence of capitalist restructuring and neo-liberalism. The murder, in cold blood, of fifteen-year-old Alexis Grigoropoulos was perceived as the 'tip of the iceberg' of all forms of social inequality, insecurity and oppression, exemplifying all forms of everyday aggression and discrimination, and the treatment of young people as the new 'dangerous classes'.

Legitimation crisis!

Youth unrest in Greece has been fuelled by a wider sense of a crisis of legitimacy of the dominant policies, because of the economic crisis and the apprehension of widespread political corruption and direct links between business and the political system in recent decades. A few months after the December revolt, a special Eurobarometer survey captured aspects of this social climate of dissatisfaction with the current situation and negative expectations for the future. The alienation of large segments of the population from traditional party politics led to high rates of abstention and null or blank votes in the 2010 local elections.

'You cannot put revolt into a museum': a tradition of militancy and struggle

Apart from social and political grievances, the persistence of youth unrest in Greece also has to do with particular traditions of collective struggle. Greek universities have had a strong tradition of left-wing and anarchist militancy, with roots in the student struggles of the 1960s and 1970s. At the same time, at secondary schools the tradition of using occupations as a means of protest is still strong. The organization of university student unions is rather unitary. There is strong participation in elections for student unions, which take place each year on the same day for all universities, and most political parties have a student branch. There is a strong electoral presence of the Left, especially of the Communist Party Youth. Particularly important is the presence of the United Independent Left Movement (EAAK), representing radical Left groups in almost all universities, and which has been a major force behind most student movements since the 1990s. Despite the tendency of the mainstream parties' student representatives to depoliticize and bureaucratize the student movement, a strong democratic culture persists. Mass student assemblies are the main decision-making bodies, especially since their decisions cannot be overturned by union steering committees. The predominance of the assembly as a forum for discussion, of democratic decision-making and self-organization has helped prolong student struggles and radical forms of protest such as occupations, disruptions of university senates and departmental assemblies, and the halting of academic and research activities.

The ability to overturn laws and create obstacles to aggressive capitalist restructuring has inspired confidence in collective resistance. Student movements can account for the repeal of a law in 1979, forcing a minister to resign and to withdraw proposals for privatization in 1991, reversing plans to make students pay for textbooks in 1995, delaying the passing of a law in the spirit of the Bologna Process in 2006–07, and stopping a Constitutional amendment process in 2007.

Currently there are also signs of political and ideological radicalization. In the 1990s collective resistance coincided with a general disillusionment with left-wing politics. The 2000s saw a youth and student radicalism more massive and more political in its expressions – in some ways comparable to the radicalism of the post-dictatorship period. The fact that this generation is being treated as 'lost' can only fuel this radicalism.

Conclusion
Student unrest in Greece has deep roots, and a long and continuing tradition of struggle. The conjuncture of the economic crisis, rising unemployment and job insecurity, and the continuous attempt to implement reforms in line with a more general trend towards entrepreneurialization, commodification and flexibilization of education, can only fuel discontent and unrest. Unrestrained by union bureaucracy, and in most cases independent of political manipulation, movements of Greek youth can always retain a capacity to surprise. One hopes . . .

THE MOVEMENT SPEAKS

From the 2006–07 student movement

Coordination of Student Unions' General Assemblies and Occupations, 25 May 2006
Through the proposed reforms the Ministry of Education and the government aim at:

- *Creating a new type of worker, flexible and cheap and at the same time productive and disciplined*, according to employers' demands and priorities, a worker that will not cost much, will not struggle for better conditions of employment and life, will be fully adjusted to the imperatives of the market and business competitiveness. This will be accomplished through the devaluation of degrees and the fragmentation of qualifications and employment prospects, but also through the intensification of study programmes and the attempt to discipline the student movement and to prevent it from resisting the restructuring of education.
- *Operating public universities within private economic norms and undermining the public and free-of-charge character of education, raising new class barriers.*

The introduction of an assessment and accreditation mechanism and the emphasis on life-long learning only help the above aims.

Coordination of Student Unions' General Assemblies and Occupations, 28 June 2006
Our movement has proved wrong all those who insisted our struggles were 'premature' and impossible to win. On the contrary, it has been proved again that uncompromising mass struggles can be victorious. We also proved that it was wrong to depict our generation as being

apolitical and adjusted to dominant policies. Contrary to regarding politics as having to do with experts and being far removed from collective practices, a new conception of politics emerged in the movement based upon a culture of collectivism, direct democracy and solidarity. The student movement was born out of general assemblies, coordinating committees and non-hierarchical cooperation. It is a movement of the students themselves in a struggle that is independent and guided only by their needs and the needs of society.

Coordination of Student Unions' General Assemblies and Occupations, 17 January 2007
We choose the road of struggle alongside other movements in education and the labour movement. Today, we can coordinate our struggle with high-school students, with teachers, both in primary education (local unions and the Federation of Primary Education Teachers) and in secondary education (local unions and the Federation of Secondary Education Teachers), who have shown their militancy and their willingness to participate in the mobilization against the amendment of Article 16 of the Constitution, and with the Federation of University Professors that opposes private universities. We can form a militant, radical and victorious front across all sectors of education that will take the responsibility for the battle against the amendment of Article 16. We can unite the dynamics of the student movement with the labour movement, creating a united front against the policies of the government. We appeal to each union and federation to support our struggle and to participate in it in an uprising of the whole people.

Communiqué of the Coordination of Student Unions' General Assemblies and Occupations Concerning the demonstration of 8 March 2007[1]
For the past twelve months the student movement has been giving lessons in collective struggle. After forcing the government to cancel the passage of new legislation last summer and blocking the reactionary amendment of Article 16 of the Constitution, it is now facing the challenge of fighting against the new legislative framework for higher education. The government is using brutal repression, its last resort, since it cannot gain consensus for its policies regarding both education and labour. In the 9 March demonstration, repression took a much more violent form. Police forces attacked students with extreme brutality, made widespread use of tear gas and arrested over sixty

---

1   The national educational demonstration of 8 March 2007 was violently attacked by special police forces, with tens of students wounded and many arrests.

protesters. This escalation of repression is reminiscent of the most savage moments in recent history. The attempt to terrorize the student movement makes evident the intent of the government and its allies to attack any form of resistance against their reactionary policies.

From the December 2008 explosion
Letter from Alexis's friends to the media
We want a better world. Help us.

We are not terrorists, 'people with masks', the 'known-unknown'.

WE ARE YOUR CHILDREN. These known-unknown . . . We have dreams – don't kill our dreams. We have impetus – don't stop our impetus.

REMEMBER. One day you were also young. Now, you chase money, you care only for the 'cover', you got fat, you got bald, YOU FORGOT.

We were waiting for your support. We were waiting for you to care, to make us, for once, proud. IN VAIN.

You live fake lives, you have bowed your heads and you are waiting for the day you will die. You don't imagine, you don't fall in love, you don't create. You only sell and buy.

Where are the parents? Where are the artists? Why don't they step outside?

HELP US

THE CHILDREN

P.S.: Don't we use more tear gas, WE cry by ourselves.

First Communiqué of the Athens Law School Occupation[2]
The same government that implements politics of austerity for workers and at the same time offers 28 billion euros as bail-out for the banks, the same government that uses police as an answer to the social inequality that it is creating, is the same government that, following the policies of the PASOK governments, is drafting within the European Union framework anti-terrorist legislation against movements and militants, that murders and kidnaps immigrants in police stations, that arrests protesters, that represses and penalizes workers' struggles. It uses the judicial system to issue decisions that make strikes illegal, that put militants behind bars, and that justify police violence and brutality. It is investing in fear and is

---

2 During the first night of demonstrations in December, radical Left and autonomist groups, along with students and workers, occupied the Law School of the University of Athens.

intensifying the attack on all fronts (privatizations, pension reform, education, health, social rights). These are the policies that armed the hands of policemen and murdered a fifteen-year-old student.

Communiqué from the Athens Coordination of Student Unions' General Assemblies and Occupations, 12 December 2008
The revolt of the youth is an expression of social anger against the politics that murder life, education and work, against the government that attacks the youth and at the same time is handing 28 billion euros to the banks. It is a political answer to state murder and repression, and is linked with the more general struggle of the movements against anti-labour policies. Our movement is organized on the basis of general assemblies, occupations and strikes, and we will win! All over Greece, from Thessaloniki to Crete, there are huge demonstrations of a youth that is resisting, fighting, demanding and struggling against dominant policies.
[. . .]
The government, in its attempt to suppress the youth revolt, is trying to turn segments of society and workers against the revolt. They are trying to suppress the growing radicalization of the youth (who are blocking police stations, occupying schools, universities and public buildings) by publicizing scattered cases of looting and using lies to discredit the movement and attack its increasing strength and the radicalization of its political appeal. Workers, the majority of the society that is under attack by anti-labour laws, are the natural allies of our movement that is expressing the anger of high-school students, university students, precarious young workers of the '700 euros generation', the unemployed, and immigrants.

From the Occupation of the Headquarters of the Trade Union Confederation (GSEE)

We will either determine our history ourselves or let it be determined without us.

We – manual workers, employees, the jobless, temporary workers, locals or immigrants – are not passive TV-viewers. Since the murder of Alexandros Grigoropoulos on Saturday night, we have participated in the demonstrations, the clashes with the police, the occupations in the city centre or in the neighbourhoods. Time and again we had to leave work, and our daily obligations, in order to take the streets with the students, the university students and the other proletarians in struggle.

WE DECIDED TO OCCUPY THE BUILDING OF GSEE

• To turn it into a space of free expression and a meeting point of workers.

• To disperse the media-touted myth that the workers were and are absent from the clashes, and that the rage of these days was an affair of some 500 'mask-bearers', 'hooligans' or some other fairy tale, while on the TV-screens the workers were presented as victims of the clash, while the capitalist crisis in Greece and worldwide leads to countless layoffs that the media and their managers treat as a 'natural phenomenon'.

• To flay and uncover the role of the trade union bureaucracy in the undermining of the insurrection – and not only there. GSEE and the entire trade union mechanism that supports it for decades and decades, undermine the struggles, bargains away our labour power for crumbs, perpetuates the system of exploitation and wage slavery. The stance of GSEE last Wednesday is quite telling: GSEE cancelled the programmed strikers' demonstration, stopping short at the organization of a brief gathering in Syntagma Square, simultaneously ensuring that the people will be dispersed in a hurry from the Square, fearing that they might get infected by the virus of insurrection.

• To open up this space for the first time – as a continuation of the social opening created by the insurrection itself – a space that has been built by our contributions, a space from which we were excluded. For all these years we entrusted our fate to saviours of every kind, and we end up losing our dignity. As workers we have to start assuming our responsibilities, and to stop assigning our hopes to wise leaders or 'able' representatives. We have to acquire a voice of our own, to meet up, to talk, to decide, and to act. Against the generalized attack, we endure. The creation of collective 'grassroots' resistances is the only way.

• To propagate the idea of self-organization and solidarity in working places, struggle committees and collective grassroots procedures, abolishing the bureaucratic trade unionists.

General Assembly of Insurgent Workers

From the Occupation of the Town Hall in Agios Dimitrios[3]
There has been a lot of talk about violence. For the people in authority and the media violence is only what destroys order.

---

3   A municipality in the greater Athens area. The Town Hall was occupied by a popular assembly throughout the December revolt.

But, for us:

- Violence is to work for forty years for extremely low wages and to wonder whether you will ever be able to retire.
- Violence is the bank bonds, the robbery of pension funds, the stock exchange fraud.
- Violence is to be forced to take a housing loan that you are going to have to repay with massive interest.
- Violence is the right of the employer to sack you whenever he pleases.
- Violence is to be unemployed, precarious, to be paid 700 euros per month, sometimes without insurance.
- Violence is workplace 'accidents', because the bosses are reducing costs to the detriment of workplace safety.

[. . .]

- Violence is to be an immigrant woman, to live in constant fear of being thrown out of the country, and to have a permanent feeling of insecurity.

From the 2010–11 Student Movement

Statement of the Coordination of Student Unions' General Assemblies and Occupations, December 2010
We are facing a new law that wants universities to function according to private and entrepreneurial standards, that is dismantling degrees and collective professional qualifications and workers' rights, and that wants to put research under the command of capital. It is a law that wants fewer and fewer people to reach higher education, that makes cuts to funding for student accommodation, and that is attempting to introduce tuition fees. It is trying to deprive student unions of any means of struggle; it is creating an authoritarian framework and is increasing the study workload [. . .] It is also aiming at disciplining youth and abolishing the university sanctuary.
[. . .]
Youth is facing a return to the Middle Ages in relation to workers' rights. The new legislation for reduced wages for young people and the attempt to undermine the system of collective bargaining and agreements means we are facing the prospect of being the '592 euros generation', having to cope with mass layoffs and a return of child labour. Flexible labour relations, job insecurity, unemployment, and working off the books is the bleak future they are offering us. [. . .] We are talking about a youth that sees its future 'mortgaged' because of the accumulated debt that we have paid again and again.

[. . .]

In this conjuncture we are fighting the battle of our generation. We must make our own history. The only way is to continue with the demonstrations and occupations, and to broaden the front both geographically and socially. [. . .] We will not allow the government, the EU, the IMF to wreck out present and our future. We, through prolonged struggle alongside high school students, workers and the youth, will reverse the policies of the Memorandum. [. . .] With occupations, demonstrations, and the coordination of general assemblies, alongside the workers' struggle, we will fight to the end! To victory!

A CITY BURNING IS A FLOWER BLOOMING

6

TUNISIA: THE TOPPLING OF A DESPOT

'HE WHO CULTIVATES THORNS WILL REAP WOUNDS'

Leila Basmoudi

Dictators rarely relinquish power of their own accord. They either die or have to be pushed out by force. Just before this stage is reached, when they're about to be ejected by a mass movement, they try everything possible to stay in power. They torture. They kill. It was when we lost our fear of death and when the funeral processions of our dead comrades were being saluted on the streets by uniformed soldiers, that the end was nigh for President Zine Ben Ali, a useful Washington ally in the 'war against terror'. His security thugs, composed of criminals, misfits and clansmen, were seen attacking men and women. An old historian reflected: 'It's like Scipio's armies in Carthage over two thousand years ago. They looted, killed and raped our women. But they were Romans seeking revenge. Ben Ali and his gangsters are Tunisian mercenaries. They do the dirty work for Washington and Paris . . .' A staunch ally of Washington, recipient of Saudi largesse, admired as a model by the president of the IMF and visiting Western journalists (most recently, the easily flattered Christopher Hitchens in *Vanity Fair*) and politicians, supported to the end by the French president, Nicolas Sarkozy – but to no avail. Ben Ali had failed. His unsentimental friends in the West hurriedly organized his exile and then washed their hands. Ben Ali was given asylum in Saudi Arabia, a good home for tyrants: they can easily access their foreign bank accounts. Will they freeze them and seize them and return the money to our country and its people? Only if hell freezes. This was one of their guys. He did their bidding, and in return they let him amass a fortune. We want our money back, and we want this criminal tried for his crimes – not at The Hague but in the court of our people. Our poet of the last century Abu al-Kasem El-Chebbi, wrote that 'he who cultivates thorns will reap wounds'.

We have not yet won the war. The structures of the dictatorship are still in force. Three hundred people died to get rid of the tyrant, mainly young men shot in the head and dumped in the streets. While their menfolk watched at gunpoint, Ben Ali's militia thugs raped the women. That's why we will carry on the struggle for a new democratic constitution that will get rid of the filth that is elite corruption and give us the right to work and provide a better future for all our citizens. We have won the first battle, and Ben Ali's sponsors in Washington and Paris told him it was time to leave. Things had to change so they could remain the same, they thought. And that gives us heart to carry on. Other Western-backed dictators – the decaying Bouteflika in Algiers, and Hosni Mubarak in Cairo – will be soiling their trousers in fear. So will Muammar Gaddafi, who took power in 1969 and has still not managed to educate his people. He may be eccentric. He may be mentally unbalanced. But those who depend on him keep him in power, a laughing stock of the Arab world. He's upset at what happened here, and with good reason. He might die in office, but what we have achieved will make life difficult for the sons of Mubarak and Gaddafi and Ali Saleh (Yemen's dictator since 1978), being groomed for power by Western intelligence agencies, just as here. And what of the King of Morocco, whose dungeons echo with the screams of Saharan prisoners? How long will he last? Listen to the bells of Tunis, you corrupt, monstrous, moth-eaten dictators. They're ringing for you. Listen to the bells in Tunis, Presidents Obama and Sarkozy. They're ringing for the torturers that you sustain. Citizens are burning themselves in Algiers and in Cairo, hoping to trigger a revolution. It will come.

THE UPRISING OF TUNISIA'S YOUNG PEOPLE IS A REAL POLITICAL REBELLION

Taoufik Ben Brik[1]

At least fifty dead. People burning themselves to death every day. Whole cities rising up all over the country. The army entering the fray. Greater Tunis under curfew. What can put out the fires of rebellion?

When blood was spilled in Kasserine and Tala in the winter of 2011, the protests became more radical and we saw the beginnings of a rebellion for which there was no precedent in a Tunisia that had been caged up for so long. A rebellion that makes no social demands. A rebellion that does not give a damn about bread or jobs. This is a political rebellion, a complete rebellion. It is not a rebellion on the part of a few handfuls of individuals. Towns, villages and whole housing estates are in rebellion. This is a radical political rebellion. A rebellion whose positions are non-negotiable. A rebellion that opposes individualism in the name of the collective, the rule of might in the name of the law, privileges in the name of equality, and clients in the name of citizens. A rebellion that hunts down the lukewarm, the spineless, the waverers and the parvenus. A Tunisia that believes – still – in revolution and not involution. And that is telling Ben Ali to clear off: 'Twenty-three years is enough!'

The government's reaction, naturally enough, was to increase the repression. The process was inexorable: it became a massacre.

No one wanted things to turn out this way. The tiny opposition did not want this; it is falling apart and has little enthusiasm for confrontation. Nor did the protector-powers who worry about the good-natured image of this little country in the Maghreb.

---

1   This article first appeared in *Le Monde* on 14 January 2011.

Quick! Save Ben Ali before his regime collapses in an orgy of bloody violence! As MEP Hélène Flautre put it: 'If the Tunisian government drifted in that direction, it would damage the reputation of the country's Western protectors, and public opinion at home would ask them to justify their actions.'

Throw him a lifeline? The West obviously wanted to encourage the man in Carthage to opt for change in continuity, and to convince public opinion that a change that meant no change had some credibility. It could be done either by Ben Ali's supporters or a loyal and conciliatory opposition.

For that to happen, there obviously had to be no more talk of what really had to change: the pauperization, the confiscation of public money, the mafia's hold over the government, the blatant corruption, the reliance on the police, the widespread use of torture, the rigged trials, the *omerta*, the dependency of all institutions . . .

The topics, the tone and the arguments that were put forward all had to assert and promote the certainty that Tunisia is, above all, an ordinary, banal country. So relations between the government and society are in crisis? 'What government doesn't have to deal with that crisis?' asks the well-known publicist Borhène Bessaies. Young people are disillusioned? 'It's the same all over the world', protests newly appointed minister for communications Samit Laâbdi. Frustrated intellectual activists are showing signs of rebellion? Béchir Tekkari, minister for higher education and another apologist for Ben Ali, again attempts to play down the threat: 'That's what people in the media are supposed to do: denounce the government and appeal to universal values.' They forget that it is too late for procrastination. Ben Ali had met his match: the street has decided to have its say.

And the most revolting forms of persecution are said to be 'isolated incidents': the attempted murders, the manhunts, the beatings, the theft and looting of property, the passports seized, the phone lines cut . . . And then they say with a straight face that they agree that these abuses of power are counterproductive. Any attempt to challenge the legitimacy of those who hold power in Tunis is 'counterproductive'. Which is one way of validating the ends by questioning only the way the means are abused. Basically, people have to be convinced that the shackles are stupid rather than wicked, and that those who can't avoid being shackled or who can't get used to it are wicked and not intelligent. And to complete Ben Ali's rehabilitation they dwell at length on the slight improvement he has promised: he intends to release the demonstrators, has promised to create 300,000 jobs, and wants to set up a commission of enquiry to look into corruption and abuses of power. And Prime Minister Mohamed Ghannouchi is trying to speed things up.

The subtext is actually quite witty: the killings, we are assured, don't affect many people (a handful of thugs wearing hoodies, as Ben Ali once put it). So they are clumsy, rather than typical of the regime. They call for tactical adjustments and need to be managed more flexibly, but not really challenged. Especially as the real demonstrators are worried about bread and other day-to-day issues. They couldn't care less about the political ambitions of the ten or twelve stars created by the foreign media. So these are not the death throes of the repressive police regime they have been criticizing. So this is not really the beginning of a revolution. A palace revolution will do. Michèle Alliot-Marie, Frédéric Mitterrand or Bruno Lemaire will argue that: 'To say that Tunisia is an out-an-out dictatorship . . . seems to me to be a gross exaggeration. People often get the wrong idea about Ben Ali.'

Defining common ground where different visions can compete

Ben Ali is supposedly unable to choose between the various clans that are arguing about what policy should be adopted. He has yet to come to a decision. So he is a thoughtful man who knows what is at stake and who has inner resources he can draw upon. A call to action is cleverly passed off as a semblance of change: a minister for communications leaves, a new minister of the interior arrives, and the regional governors play musical chairs. Dictators may not enjoy this game, but they play it often enough. And this so-called handover of power may open up a gap. And Ben Ali himself does not know where that might lead.

The one thing certain is that the rebels, who are the real protagonists in the current cataclysm, will be excluded from the process so long as external pressures are strong enough to guarantee the continued existence of a government that is in hock to the interests of free trade and that is willing to play the part of docile partner that Tunisia has been cast to play in international geopolitics.

And yet today's young rebels have, potentially, more room for manoeuvre. Can they occupy that space? If they rest their case on basic rights, both individual and collective, on building a living democracy, shared values and laws that apply to all, they can put down roots in both the population and the political landscape. It is not a matter of hoping that your own horse wins. It is a matter of defining in democratic terms the common ground on which different ways of seeing things can compete. A call for the establishment of a decentralized, pluralist and non-sectarian national convention would obviously be welcome. But who is in a position to guarantee that it will be recognized, that it will be pluralistic in political terms, that there will be a range of different actors, and that it will have its roots in the people?

THE TUNISIAN REVOLUTION: A SOURCE OF INSPIRATION TO OUR *QUARTIERS*

Parti des Indigènes de la République

The Arab people of Tunisia have driven out their tyrant. This is a huge victory for all Arab people and, more broadly, all the people of the world. The fantastic uprising of the Tunisians – huge, determined, spontaneous and uncontrolled – proves once more that nothing can stop the strength of the popular will once it has resolved to cast off its chains.

This victory is part of the revival of anti-colonial struggles all over the world. It will help to shift the regional and international balance of power in favour of oppressed peoples. The Tunisian people have given a good slap to a French government that supported Ben Ali to the last and, in the person of Michèle Alliot-Marie, went so far as to offer its technical assistance in repressing popular demonstrations. The despot has gone. That was the goal of the revolution, and it has been achieved. A lot remains to be done before the Tunisian political system can be profoundly changed, and before the Tunisian people can be freed from those who exploit and oppress it, but the barriers are beginning to break down. The mobilization in Tunisia will continue, will liquidate the dictatorship's institutions and will strengthen the anti-colonial dynamic.

We – immigrants and heirs to colonial immigrations – give and will continue to give our support to the ongoing Tunisian revolution in our working-class *quartiers* and wherever we are. Its victory is our victory.

We demand, among other things, that the French authorities refrain from interfering in any way in the internal affairs of the Tunisian people, and that they solemnly apologize not only for colonization but also for the unfailing support they gave to Ben Ali's dictatorship. We demand the immediate resignation of the minister for foreign affairs, whose recent statements are the embodiment of France's imperialist politics. We demand that all property in France belonging to Ben Ali's family and to all agents of the Ben Ali regime be confiscated and restored to the Tunisian people. We demand that legal proceedings be taken against all those members of Ben Ali's family and all agents of the regime who are resident in France.

People of the working-class *quartiers*, and heirs to colonial immigration, the Tunisian people have shown us the road to our liberation.

SOLIDARITY

A MAFIA-LIKE DICTATORSHIP[2]

Moncez Marzouki

A wind of political and social rebellions has been blowing across Tunisia for the last three weeks. The violence of the repression, which has resulted in twenty-three deaths, demonstrates that the Ben Ali regime feels for the first time that it is under threat. But the power and persistence of the mobilization of the Tunisian people give European public opinion and European political representatives an opportunity to open their eyes to what Tunisia really is. For over twenty years, their perception has been distorted by the received ideas put about by the government and many of its French sympathizers.

1. 'The Tunisian regime is certainly not a democracy, but it is not a dictatorship. At most, it is an authoritarian regime.' No, recent events prove to those who did not or would not see it: the Tunisian regime is the worst kind of police and mafia dictatorship. Having Ben Ali in Carthage is like having Al Capone in the White House.

2. 'The country owes its economic miracle to Ben Ali.' The Tunisia of the 1990s in fact owed its relative prosperity to the three decades of the Bourguiba presidency, which were characterized by huge investment in education, in family planning and the establishment of a healthy market economy capable of generating an annual growth rate of 7 per cent. That was the situation Ben Ali inherited. Over a period of twenty years, he transformed Tunisia into a corrupt economy whose mafia-like tendencies are there for all to see.

---

2 This article first appeared in *Le Monde* on 12 January 2011.

3. 'Ben Ali eradicated the Islamist threat.' If we do not support him, there is a great danger that we will see the establishment of a Taliban regime on the southern shores of the Mediterranean, Nicolas Sarkozy argued in 2008. Ben Ali in fact destroyed Ennadha, a conservative, bourgeois Islamist party, violating human rights on a huge scale in the process. Ennahda had nothing to do with Jihadi violence. And as for the political troubles, the 'beards' are nowhere to be seen: witness the secular slogans chanted by the demonstrators.

4. 'There is no credible opposition. The Tunisian opposition is weak, divided and powerless.' Those who live or have lived under a dictatorship know that it is only in a democracy that there can be an opposition, and that under a dictatorship there can only be resistance – either armed or unarmed. When he was elected and re-elected three times with more than 90 per cent of all votes cast, Ben Ali organized his own 'opposition' in order to allay suspicion – muzzling, jailing and torturing the hundreds of brave and honest men and women who fought one of the most repressive and perverse machines that has ever existed.

5. The fifth cliché takes the form of a faux-naif question. 'What alternative is there to Ben Ali?' If a Tunisian asked a French citizen the same question –'What is the alternative to Sarkozy?' – the answer would seem both natural and obvious: 'Whoever the French choose in the next presidential election.' A Tunisian should be able to give his or her French friend the same answer: Ben Ali's successor will be whoever the Tunisian people elect in free and transparent elections. Who says that we are sentenced to life under a dictatorship?

Ben Ali has long been described as the man who could guarantee Tunisia's stability. Now that a rebellion has broken out in the country, he is the main destabilizing factor; his departure is the only thing that can restore calm. French public opinion and politicians must open their eyes and see what the Tunisian government really is. If they do not, there is a real danger that France will lose the sympathy it enjoys in Tunisia. France would no longer be able to play a role in the peaceful transition towards the rule of law, or help to create a stable and prosperous Euro-Mediterranean space that shares the same democratic values.

THE REVOLUTION OF DIGNITY

Sadri Khiari

People have been asking me the same question ever since Zine Ben Ali fled the country. Why has there been such a great upheaval in Tunisia, which was famous for its 'stability'? How could a man who ruled with a fist of iron fall from power so suddenly?

There are all sorts of possible explanations. I will give only what seems to me to be the most important. The mafia-like clique that surrounded the deposed president had no structural basis in any consensus or consent. It had, in other words, no moral authority over the population. Now, no political system can survive when it has absolutely no moral authority. Ben Ali, his wife and their family were the object of complete contempt as well as fear, even for the privileged strata of the population, even for those who profited from the regime.

When he came to power in November 1987, Ben Ali immediately began to construct a gigantic machine to repress the population, to keep it under control and surveillance and to turn it into a clientele. From time to time, the French press reported the arrest of political activists or union officials, the torture of opposition members and the brutal intimidation of human rights activists, but the actions of the police were directed mainly against the population at large. The police pressure was constant. It came from the Ministry of the Interior, but also from the many unofficial militias, including those working for the Rassemblement Constitutionnel Démocratique. The RCD is no ordinary political party. It is an extension of the state, and its role is to keep the population under control and surveillance, and to punish, buy off, corrupt, and extort money from everyone in every sphere of society. In addition to these institutions, there are the structures of the administration, which are deployed not, as one might have thought, to serve citizens but to use all their power to hand down directives from the highest levels of the state. They act, in other words, as agencies for repression, control, surveillance and clientelization. The workings of the Ministry of Justice are a perfect example.

I am not suggesting that all civil servants are to blame. Most of them are decent citizens who are badly paid, who work in atrocious conditions, and who are themselves at the mercy of their all-powerful superiors. I am simply saying that the police system was responsible for making everyone an agent who colluded with and supported the government.

Make no mistake about it: the police and bureaucratic mechanisms established by Ben Ali were not just designed to inspire fear and obedience. They were designed to kill the human element in all of us – and that is both more pernicious and more effective than fear itself. Ben Ali built a huge machine to destroy the dignity of Tunisians, a terrible technology of indignity. The compromises, or even the collusion, the corruption and all the shameful wheeling and dealing that went into surviving or simply finding some peace, were just some of the mechanisms that were used systematically to take away our dignity. The whole of society had to know that the government held the people in complete contempt. The whole of society was taught to despise itself, and everyone was made to despise him- or herself and everyone else.

I will say it again: repression and fear would never have been enough to protect a government that had absolutely no moral authority. Given that they had no moral legitimacy, Ben Ali and his gang of hooligans had no choice but to destroy morality, break solidarities, abolish respect, spread contempt, and constantly humiliate everyone. 'You are nothing and you will never be anything.' 'You are sub-human.' That was the social and moral message of the Ben Ali regime. Bourguiba, who was certainly an elitist, regarded Tunisians as nothing more than a swarm of individuals; turning them into a nation was his responsibility. Ben Ali did just the opposite, and turned a nation into a swarm of individuals. He lost his bet, as the nation refused to become a swarm. The mud from the palace in Carthage never succeeded in burying the whole of Tunisia. In my view, talk of poverty, of social difficulties, of the abstract need for democratic freedoms, or even of the way repression creates fear and submission, explains only one minor aspect of what has been happening in Tunisia over the last month. Mohamed Bouazizi did not kill himself in such a terrible way simply because he had no job and because a police officer prevented him from making a few coppers by selling his vegetables. He set fire to himself because, when that police officer spat in his face, he told him what the Ben Ali regime told us every day: 'You are just dog shit. I can do what I like with you!' Bouazizi had certainly had enough of being poor, very poor. He could no accept the fact that he was no longer a human being. May his soul be at peace. We are all thinking of him. We all identified with him, even though some of us have jobs and live comfortable lives. The Tunisian revolution has driven out the tyrant: the driving force behind it was the desire to restore the dignity that Bouazizi had been denied. Were Tunisians demanding wage increases? Were they demanding the freedom of the press? Were they demanding some right or other? No. they were expressing their dignity, and saying that their dignity meant that Ben Ali had to go. And they made him go. Even if he had understood that, he would not have wasted his time making what only he would have seen as concessions: price cuts, free access to the internet, elections, and a promise to resign within three years. That would have been Ubuesque. His life was at stake, and he knew it.

Is it at all over? Not by any means. The revolutionary effervescence has not died down. Dignity is still fighting indignity all over the country. The Tunisian people is no longer a collection of individuals who survive as best they can and try to preserve their human qualities. It is a collective body that loathes the idea that the men of the Ben Ali regime, and a few politicians who are eager to share the cake of victory, might dispossess it of its own victory. The Tunisian people trusts only itself, and it is right. The second act of the revolution will focus on the destruction of the institutions created by the former president – starting with the RCD – and the democratic election of a Constituent Assembly that will restore to the people the political sovereignty that was taken away from it decades ago. And then, we shall see.

SOCIAL REVOLTS IN ALGERIA AND TUNISIA

Yassin Temlali

Today's social revolts in Tunisia and Algeria were triggered by the same socio-economic discontent, which mainly affects young people who are poorly integrated into the economic system.

They take the same form in both countries: violent clashes with the security forces and attacks on symbols of the state. There are, however, differences, and it is worth looking at them. The youth revolt in Algeria began in Oran and Algiers, and then spread to the east and the west, the mountainous regions and the Hauts-Plateaux. The countryside, which has been in turmoil for many years if the frequency of social protests since the 'black spring' of April 2001 is anything to go by, has passed on the torch to the traditionally rebellious neighbourhoods of Algeria's two biggest towns, and especially to those of the capital, where the intifada of October 1988 began over twenty-two years ago.

Although the protests in Tunis are widespread in geographical terms, they still centre on the disinherited regions of the centre (Sidi Bouzid) and the west (Kasrine, Gafsa, and so on), where Zine Ben Ali's regime is seen as a coastal-based clique that favours the capital and the Sahel at the expense of the interior. There have been no real 'riots' in the four governorates of Greater Tunis (Tunis, Menouba, Ariana, Ben Arous) or in the tourist area of Cap-Bon (Nabeul, and so on), and there has been less social agitation in the Sahel governorates (Sousse, Sfax, and so on). In all these regions, the protests have tended to take the form of demonstrations on the part of school students, or action in support of the insurgent youth on the part of political and union activists in Sidi Bouzid and Gafsa. The social protests in the countryside, which has (with the notable exception of a town such as Gafsa) been less involved than Tunis in democratic struggles, are a reminder of the serious regional imbalance between the two Tunisias. Tunis monopolizes investments and job opportunities, whereas the rural areas, which are primarily agrarian, have been relatively unaffected by the benefits of the 'Tunisian miracle'.

In Algeria, the contrasts between the development of the towns and the countryside, or between north and south, are not negligible, but they appear to have been eclipsed in people's minds by the even more shocking contrasts between the wealth of the state and the stagnating incomes of wage-earners, between the enormous need for jobs and the squandering of public funds by corrupt officials, or on big projects that have been given to foreign companies for electoral reasons. This growing awareness of growing inequalities was heightened by the boasting of Ahmed Ouyahia's ministers, who never missed an opportunity to come out with astounding statistics about foreign-exchange reserves, income from hydrocarbon exports and receipts from the 'Fonds de régulation', which have for the last tens years been used as a 'secret fund' that is beyond any parliamentary scrutiny. This explains both the violent resentment of the authorities (expressed, for example, in attacks on public administrations) and the national character of the uprising.

Algeria: a counter-example for some, a model for others
The intifada in Sidi Bouzid was not a bolt from the blue. It was preceded, in January 2008, by the long (five-months) intifada in the Gafsa mining basin and, in August 2010, by violent demonstrations in Ben Guerdane (near the Libyan border) against government measures aimed at restricting cross-border trade. But until January 2008, the Ben Ali regime succeeded in reducing these social protests to their trade-union dimension. Together with the good reports it got from the IMF and the EU – so repetitive that they became boring – this relative civil peace convinced the regime that its 'development model' had the support on the whole population, and that Tunisians were mainly concerned about the last of their rights, or what Jacques Chirac, speaking in Tunis in December 2003, called 'the right to eat'. The Tunisian government spent this long period of relative social peace (1987–2008) dismantling Islamist organizations (in the 1990s) and struggling against the democratic movement (in the 2000s), which has grown all the stronger now that the El Nahda party appears to have been greatly weakened by unusually savage repression.

The official and semi-official press was quite happy to invoke the spectre of the security threat to justify the clampdown. As the Islamist rebellion in Tunisia's eastern neighbour lost its intensity, Ben Ali lost his edifying status as a 'counter-example'. The popular uprisings that Algeria experienced from 2001 onwards demonstrated that, if the 'imperatives of the war on terror' could no longer smother the social front in that turbulent country, the same might be true in a 'stable' country like Tunisia. The democratic battles fought in Tunisia from 2001 onwards (the actions in support of the journalist Taoufik Ben Brik) kept political mobilization at a surprisingly high level, given the harshly repressive climate. They brought hundreds of activists together in a broad front against the 'police dictatorship' that was able to welcome new actors such as bloggers opposed to censorship, artists, and so on. There is no such front in Algeria, where the 'democrats' are profoundly divided by their old differences as to how to deal with armed Islamism and with a regime that fought Islamism in the name of 'safeguarding the Republic'. The steadfastness of the Ligue tunisienne des droits de l'homme (LTDH) and of the 'prisoner of conscience' committees has kept alive international interest in civil liberties in Tunisia. Publicized by satellite TV and the internet, the struggles of these collectives have acted as an antidote to the fatalism that the authorities are trying to encourage. It is political, union and third-sector militants who are now organizing actions in solidarity with the people of Sidi Bouzid, Gafsa and Kasserine. They are also ensuring that their voices are heard in the international media.

Tunisian unions: an effective support

While the Ben Ali regime has eliminated important actors who might have been able to mediate between it and the population (credible parties, voluntary associations), it has not succeeded in turning Habib Bourguiba's long-cherished dream of turning the Union générale tunisienne du travail (UGTT) into a tame union. A counter-balance to the power of the government ever since independence, and a space in which the radical left could speak out, the UGTT did more than support the young people of *la profonde Tunisie* with sit-ins (including two outside its headquarters on 25 December 2010 and 7 January 2011). It also supported it by giving it a voice in the world press, which continues to gather news from 'union sources'. The UGTT did support Ben Ali's presidential candidacy in 2004 and 2009 (at the cost of an internal crisis), and most of the members grouped around Secretary-General Abdesselam Jerad are far from independent. But the organization does have middle-ranking leaders (in the civil service union, health and education) who are sufficiently radical to have hailed the Sidi Bouzid intifada in much more open terms than the executive bureau. And it is well known that tens of trade unionists have become involved in democratic struggles in recent years.

Their radicalism explains why the central leadership has not completely given in to the pressures brought to bear by the authorities, why it is supporting popular revolts, and why it is even calling for greater freedoms (in a statement of 4 January 2011). The same cannot be said of the

Union générale des travailleurs algériens (UGTA), which has become subservient to the regime since Bouteflika took power in 1999. Most of its national secretaries are members of the two 'official parties' (the FLN and the RND). This subservience to the government has led to the departure of many members, who have left to join more militant unions. This explains why the UGTA takes almost no notice of the protests that are going on in the country. They have been mentioned in only one statement (made public on 7 January 2011), in which the UGTA defended the government's view that blames 'speculators' for the present crisis.

A NEW ERA, OR MORE OF THE SAME?

Yassin Temlali

Is the democratic transition to be conducted after all by the official party, the RCD (Rassemblement Constitutionnel Democratique), following a light facelift and the sacrifice of a few disgraced figures as a sop to popular vengefulness? As euphoria gives way to mounting anxiety, signs of radical political change are far from evident. The new-look RCD could profit from dissensions in the opposition to cling to power. A brief survey follows of the forces in play and analysis of their positions in a turbulent Tunisia.

There are few signs of the radical political change that would make the fall of Zine Ben Ali the start of a new epoch and not just another 'Era of change'. The country is being governed by an old warhorse of the official party, Fouad Mbazaa, who only recently, in November 2010, was urging the former president to stand in the 2014 election. The image of his prime minister, Mohamed Ghannouchi, whose government repressed the street demonstrations of recent weeks, may be that of a simple 'technocrat', but cannot be separated from that of the RCD state. The presidential elections scheduled to be held in two months' time will be organized by these two men, burdened by their association with a regime rejected overwhelmingly during a month of upheavals. The demonstrators arrested since 18 December 2010 have been released, but some political militants remain behind bars. They include Ammar Amroussia, a leader of the PCOT (Parti Communiste des Ouvriers Tunisiens), the journalist Fahem Boukeddous, and Hassan Ben Abdallah, leader of the popular dissent in the Gafsa mining basin between January and June 2008. The army, projected as 'neutral', appears determined to ensure continuity of the existing system in a rearranged form. It may have arrested some former interior ministers, but is protecting other former officials equally implicated in the police excesses of the past twenty-three years. The 'Tunisian model' extolled by the IMF and World Bank, whose failure has been demonstrated in magisterial fashion, is not being reconsidered: already it is almost forgotten that the flame of revolt that led to the fall of one of the oldest despotisms in the region was first ignited in the deprived back-country, marginalized by an economic system heavily dependent on the European economy. Only corruption is being denounced, and only Ben Ali and his family are earmarked for popular vindictiveness, as if the pillaging of Tunisian resources were the unassisted accomplishment of a handful of men and women; as if no one in the state party had benefited from their largesse or given them its protection.

The new context finds the opposition split into two camps. One consists of supporters of a soft transition leading to a coalition government. These include Mohamed Nedjib Chebbi's PDP (Parti Democratique Progressiste), Mustapha Ben Djaaffer's FDTL (Forum Démocratique pour le Travail et les libertés) and El Tajdid (the former Communist Party) chaired by Ahmed Brahim. The first two personalities were both prevented from standing in the presidential election by a law requiring their candidature to be supported in advance by dozens of elected representatives. Ahmed Brahim did stand against Ben Ali in the 2009 election, but predictably obtained a fairly miserable 1.57 per cent of the votes cast. The three men have widely differing backgrounds, however. Mohamed Nedjib Chebbi comes from the radical left, more specifically a Maoist-leaning organization called El Amel El Tounsi ('The Tunisian Worker'), from which the PCOT also originates. Mustapha Ben Djaafer is a former militant of Habib Bourguiba's Socialist Destour Party, forerunner and ancestor of the RCD, but left before founding, with other dissidents, the MDS (Mouvement des Democrates Socialistes) in 1978, and the FDTL in 1994.

The other camp considers that a proper transition would require 'the Ben Ali system to be dismantled', followed by the election of a constituent assembly which would write a new Constitution. It includes the PCOT and the Islamist movement El Nahda, which does not reject the option of a government of unity (Habib El Louz, *Al-Jazeera*, 16 January 2011) provided that it is not led by one of the symbols of the RCD in the image of the present prime minister (Rached Ghanouchi, *Al-Jazeera*, 15 January 2011). This attitude is shared by some democratic militants – for example Sihem Ben Sedrine of the National Council for Freedoms (CNLT). The Congress for the Republic (CPR), led by the former chairman of the Tunisian Human Rights League, Moncef Merzouki, seems to share, more or less, the radical attitudes of his former partners in the '18 October Democratic Front'. Like the leadership of El Nahda, he accepts the idea of a unitary government, but not in the framework of the RCD system (*El Watan*, 15 January 2011).

It is not without significance that the first group comprises officially recognized parties (the PDP since 1988, the FDTL since 2002 and El Tajdid since 1981, under its old name of Tunisian Communist Party) which hope to go down in history as the artisans of the transition while having a go at managing public affairs. These parties do not regard the current constitutional framework as totally inadequate for starting a democratizing mutation, and see the present prime minister, Mohamed Ghannouchi, as a 'non-corrupt individual' (Attia Athmouni of the PDP political bureau, quoted in *Le Journal du Dimanche*, 16 January 2011). They set no conditions on participation in a government of unity other than the proclamation of a general amnesty and recognition of movements which 'have already applied for [official] approval without ever getting it' (a formulation that could exclude El Nahda). They propose, of course, recasting the juridical arsenal inherited from the Ben Ali era (electoral law, and so on), but do not envisage doing this in a context of entirely new institutions. As for the second group, it consists of parties that have been subjected not only to major restrictions on their activities (PDP, El Tajdid), but to outright denial of their right to exist, and suspect that this unjust situation may persist. The PCOT and El Nahda point out that the Tunisian Constitution was made to measure for the two presidents who have governed the country since its independence, and that there have been fifty-five years of it. They recall that, on 7 November 1987, Ben Ali made promises of greater openness to the opposition, which he then subjected to harsh repression.

Divergent views could soon lead to another split in the opposition between supporters and opponents of legalizing the Islamist movement. A priori, the PDP, the PCOT and the CPR (the last two themselves illegal) will not mind El Nahda being recognized; but this is not necessarily the case with other forces – El Tajdid, for example – resistant to the idea of giving political legitimacy to religious bodies. The former Communist Party's views on this matter are supported by other (unrecognized) groups like the Parti Socialiste de Gauche (a splinter of the PCOT), which were its allies in the Democratic Initiative (during the 2009 presidential elections). They may also find support from associations which fear that legalizing El Nahda may presage the end of Tunisia's specific brand of secularism and threaten women's rights. On the other side, Fouad Mbazaa's face-lifted regime could parade the scarecrow of a seizure of power by the Islamists, hoping to persuade the big powers to endorse the supervized change it has started to put in place and divide the opposition, just as Ben Ali successfully did after the coup d'état of 7 November 1987.

RADICALIZATION OF THE YOUTH MOVEMENT IN ALGERIA

Omar Kitani

For the first time, every wilaya, region and town has risen up at the same time and put forward the same 'demands'

The riots started in the last week of 2010, when there were strong protest movements in the working-class neighbourhoods of Algiers. The inhabitants of some neighbourhoods took to the streets to protest at the way some housing had been allocated, and raised the issue of the housing crisis. The same neighbourhoods, which are known as 'slum areas', had already made political news for months in 2009. After a bitter struggle, the Algerian government retreated in the face of the people's determination and decided to rehouse them in newly built estates.

On Tuesday 4 January, riots broke out in several places to the west of Algiers. This time, the demonstrators were protesting about the general rise in the price of basic foodstuffs that had been introduced two days earlier. The next day, it was the turn of Bab El-Oued, a neighbourhood in central Algiers famed for being the stronghold of the revolt of October 1988. Within two days, the whole of Algeria was ablaze. There had never before been a popular uprising like this: for the first time, every *wilaya*, region and town in Algeria had risen at the same time and was putting forward the same demands.

The main actors are young people aged between fifteen and thirty, and they have won the sympathy of almost the whole population

This is only to be expected, given that the youth unemployment rate is over 25 per cent and that this age group accounts for over 65 per cent of the population (government propaganda gives the much lower figure of 10 per cent). An educational system that had become a laboratory for testing various neo-liberal theories of education – in an attempt to find the best way of inserting young people into the labour market – has had the perverse effect of 'training' millions of unemployed young people with no social prospects. It has been a conspicuous failure: one study shows that one pupil in four gets into the sixth form. The thousands of young people who leave school earlier do not have the right to any training. Even cultural associations have been banned in recent years, and restrictions on the right to organize and the right of association have come to a head.

The rise in the price of basic foodstuffs: the straw that broke the camel's back

The food crisis that is now affecting Algeria is an extension of the food crisis that hit several countries in the South in 2007: Egypt, Tunisia, Morocco, Mexico, Haiti, Pakistan, Mozambique, Bangladesh, Bolivia, Niger . . . Millions of people took to the streets to express their anger and hunger. This is a structural crisis within the world capitalist mode of production, and it has been triggered because the big food-processing companies have a stranglehold on every stage in the food-production process (production, processing, distribution). As a result, these international companies can determine the state of the world market by controlling the price of food.

Algeria was not spared the protest movements of 2007, even though the state subsidized the price of some basic foodstuffs. The movement did not, however, take the form of 'bread riots', as it did in other countries. Algeria saw an upsurge in working-class and union struggles that raised the question of wages and purchasing power. Indefinite and rolling strikes were called in all sectors to pursue demands for wage increases. This outbreak of working-class struggles was the direct result of the increased price of foodstuffs on the world and national markets. As usual, the government's only answer was repression: several union activists were arrested or sacked, but the government then backed down in the face of the workers' determination. The workers did win some insignificant pay rises, but they were soon wiped out by more price increases.

In 2010, the authorities recorded over 11,500 riots

Riots are commonplace in Algeria: they are the only form of expression available to young people in a country where the neo-liberals in power have blocked all channels of communication and expression. From 2000 onwards, popular protests and strikes became much more frequent. Some think that the explanation for this lies in a return to 'calm' after ten years of Islamist terrorism. This simplistic explanation is often put forward by the ruling classes in a bid to conceal the real reasons for the movements that characterize the Algerian political landscape.

The austerity policies forced upon the country by the IMF and the neo-liberal policies adopted by the state in the 1990s began to 'bear fruit' at the beginning of the twenty-first century: millions of unemployed men and women, hundreds of thousands of young people in a 'free' job market that could not absorb them, the dismantling or destruction of public services, the pauperization of whole sectors of society . . . These are the real cause of the increase in social struggles over the last ten years. In 2001, the movement in Kabylia signalled the beginning of a new cycle of popular protests, and it is not over by any means: the anti-people policies and economic choices that sparked it are still in operation.

The extent and radicalism of the movement have caught the government off-balance

On the first day of rioting, the government and the neo-liberal parties had nothing to say about what was going on. On the second day, only the parties of the left had anything to say, and they supported the young people. On the third day, the movement took on a national dimension, and the government and the right broke their silence. They all had their own explanations to offer for the insurrection, but none of them admitted that the crisis was the result of the neo-liberal policies they themselves had recommended and supported. Far from apologizing, the state blamed shopkeepers and wholesalers. In their view, it was speculation that has caused the price rises. Other neo-liberal parties – those not in the government – used the mainstream press to attack the policy of 'economic patriotism' adopted by the government in late 2009. This 'economic patriotism' was just for show, as no real measures have been introduced since then. Even though the right initially 'supported' the young rioters, with some attempting to surf the wave of protest (calling for legislative elections in 2012) and others trying to rush through neo-liberal reforms, they quickly realized that they were playing with fire.

The insurgents' targets reveal the class nature of the revolt

Even though the young people are not organized and are not putting forward clearly formulated political demands, their targets reveal the class nature of their revolt. Their first targets were police stations, but they then attacked the international companies that have moved into Algeria: Renault, Peugeot, Dacia, Volkswagen, Toyota and Suzuki concessionaries, multinational mobile phone companies like Djezzy, Nedjma and Samsung, and international banks like PNB Paribas and Société Générale were all targeted and looted by the insurgents.

The multinationals reacted by using their media influence to try to extinguish and discredit a revolt that was beginning to threaten their interests in Algeria. The mainstream Algerian press, which the multinationals use as a crutch, seemed to change its tune. One of the main French-language papers, which ran the headline 'Something is Rotten', devoted one quarter of a page to an advertisement for Dacia cars, indicating the power of foreign capital in Algeria – as did all the other papers that rely for their survival on paid advertising from similar companies.

European governments were also ordered to come to Algeria's rescue by the holders of international capital. France even offered to send police reinforcements to help the Algerian and Tunisian police, who had been swamped by the scale of the revolt, to secure the premises and property of these firms. Michèle Alliot-Marie categorically stated that their lordships must not be exposed to the rage of the rebels in Tunisia and Algeria. The government, for its part, decided to respond with repression: 1,500 young people were arrested, hundreds were wounded, and five were shot dead. The government built thirty-five prisons in 2010 alone. An extraordinary inter-ministerial commission then took economic measures favouring the importers of the raw materials used to produce foodstuffs. In practice, this meant the removal of and exemption from 41 per cent of import duties payable on such products until 31 August 2011. The same firms were also exempted from VAT (at 17 per cent) and from tax on their profits.

These hasty economic measures were another gift to the bosses of the big private companies

The government's measures met the demands put forward by the employers and the food-packaging industry at a press conference organized by the CEO and owner of the Cevital group on the third day of the rebellion. They were very satisfied with what they described as 'salutary', 'helpful', 'forward-looking' and 'important' measures. They had good reason to be satisfied: they were being given 300 million euros on a silver plate. We have to state the obvious: the role of the bourgeois state is to serve the social class that controls it.

These economic measures are not a solution to the crisis, which is not restricted to foodstuffs (sugar, oil), whatever the government may say. It is a structural and multi-dimensional crisis brought about by twenty years of neo-liberalism. The neo-liberals have destroyed both public economic establishments and agriculture, and therefore Algeria's only chance of reacting to the world food crisis. Both domestic and foreign trade have been handed over to private monopolies. These measures are another step in the direction of a new crisis that will be worse than those already undermining Algerian capitalism.

Algeria and Tunisia: one fight!

If we ignore the details, there are more similarities than differences between the popular uprisings in Algeria and Tunisia. Both were triggered by a socio-economic crisis affecting the most disadvantaged social classes. The reaction has been almost the same: a social explosion taking the form of riots, mostly involving unemployed youths. The demands are the same: jobs, housing, freedom – and the departure of Ben Ali, in the case of the Tunisians. The reasons for the crisis are also the same: the neo-liberalism and austerity policies prescribed by international financial institutions (the IMF and the WTO).

The Algerian and Tunisian governments are both very good at implementing these policies. If the IMF awarded Nobel Prizes to presidents who applied their austerity policies literally, it would find it difficult to choose between Bouteflika and Ben Ali, but the latter would probably carry off the prize, given that he has been in the pay of the IMF for the last twenty-five years. His dictatorial management of Tunis should also please the architects of neo-liberalism, who are constantly encouraging the presidents of other countries in the South to follow his example, just as they encouraged the bloody Augusto Pinochet in the Chile of the 1970s. Having murdered fifty Tunisian citizens who were simply demanding the right to life, he has now moved to the much higher stage of using the army to crush the youth revolt. The people of Algeria and Tunisia will not know any prosperity until they get rid of these acolytes of the IMF.

Freeing the young people who have been arrested

A number of union, political and student organizations, human rights leagues, and left intellectuals have been brave enough to appeal for solidarity with the young insurgents, including our party (the PST), and the Comité pour la solidarité avec les luttes populaires. They have called upon workers and young people to block these neo-liberal attacks on the people by organizing solidarity meetings in the universities, like those organized by the Nedjma student association at Béjaia University, and the student march held at the University of Algiers. Bridges are being built between the neighbourhood struggles and the worker–student struggles. But the movement's battle-cry must be for the liberation of the young people who are in prison, given that the revolt ended on the sixth day. They have twice been the victims of repression, and we must mobilize to have them released.

The movement must also give thought as to how to break with neo-liberal policies: they have revealed their limitations and their inability to satisfy the people's most basic needs. A different social and economic system is required to satisfy the aspirations and day-to-day needs of workers, women, young people, and all the other underprivileged strata. That is the only solution to the crisis.

AN OPEN LETTER

Amin Allal

Dear All,

A few words about the situation in Tunis before and after Ben Ali's flight . . . 'in real time', as the journalists say.

Thursday, 13 January

As you leave the capital's airport, you can see where the army has been deployed along the main roads since yesterday. There is an anxious calm in Tunis and its suburbs. The schools have been closed since the day before yesterday, and few people have gone to work. People are in a hurry to get home as the curfew comes into force at 8 p.m. Everyone is waiting to hear the president speak. The speech has been announced many times, and has now been put back to 8 p.m.

The ten or so friends and family members around me roar with (nervous) laughter as he finishes his last sentence. Unusually, he is speaking in dialect, sounds unsure of himself and nervous, and tries to make strange jokes. The man in Carthage gives the impression that he is begging to be allowed to finish his mandate, which lasts until 2014. He is trying to sound like Bourguiba, and sometimes like a clumsy version of De Gaulle. 'I understand you.' 'No more censorship.' 'No more bullets.' 'I have been received.' The dictator seems cornered, frightened.

Once the speech is over, a few activists from the government party organize and orchestrate their joy at 'the changes announced by the president' with a chorus of car horns. They can defy the curfew, but the police tell us to go home. Thousands of bloggers and tweeters immediately react on the web, and work through the night to make sure that we are not robbed of our victory.

Friday, 14 January

About three thousand 'politicized' people gather in the place Mohamed Ali in front of the headquarters of the Centrale Syndicale, whose leaders have been swept aside by opposition unionists and federations. We set off at 9.30 and are joined by more and more people – a lot of young people. The demonstrators: over 100,000 outside the Ministry of the Interior spend three hours chanting 'Ben Ali out!' 'Give us bread and water!' 'Ben Ali, No!' Things never get out of control. Groups from the ruling party make a few attempts to counter-attack and break up the demonstration, but they get nowhere.

The police had completely dispersed, but they are back and firing gas grenades into the crowd.

As we go home, we learn that the government has been dissolved. The army is on the streets, but is powerless to do anything. The police are firing live rounds, and the number of dead is rising.

5 p.m.

Rumours that the president is trying to flee.

8 p.m.

The prime minister, flanked by the presidents of both houses, officially announces that the president really is no longer in power. The prime minister will take over for the moment.

Saturday, 15 January

The dictator has gone, but the atmosphere is ugly today. The army is everywhere at once, and nowhere to be found. Gangs from the party mafia are supervising the looting.

I had to take refuge at a friend's because there's been more gunfire in Bad Jazira. Helicopters keep flying over Tunis. The TV says that everything is back to normal, that the airport is reopening. It doesn't feel like it here. People are organizing themselves into neighbourhood 'safety committees'.

Afternoon

Driving through a new neighbourhood in the capital and the inner suburbs, it's obvious that the looting people are talking about has been very targeted. Most of the targets are supermarkets belonging to rich families and families related to the president. A few police posts are on fire, but most of the fires are in premises belonging to cells of the ruling party. Ultimately, there has been very little infrastructural damage, and no one has been lynched.

The army is in control of the main roads, and is stopping thieves and stolen cars. Soldiers are controlling the traffic, and have arrested RCD activists and some bent cops. The danger that activists from the ruling party will use 'security' as an excuse to blackmail them seems to be receding.

The people are in control of their own streets, and the RCDists are keeping their heads down. The state of emergency is still in force.

Today's joke-slogan is: 'The people demand a TEFLON presidential chair to make sure that the next president does not stick to it.'

Evening
We control the street in Bab Jdid.

'Citizens' groups', consisting mainly of young men from the neighbourhood (no RCD, or at least not here) are posted at the corner of every street, armed with sticks to 'secure' the street, with white flags to prove who they are to the army helicopters that are constantly overhead.

For these men, it's like a learning process. They are learning to take on new responsibilities. And, though it might not seem like it, the women are not far away. They are in control of the streets too. People are quietly talking about politics. 'Never again. We won't be fooled again.' 'We've driven him out. He's run away, but we'll bring him to justice.'

There is some excitement when a car goes past, or when emissaries talk about where the gunfire is coming from. An incredible scene: a passing police car is stopped, and the plainclothes officers are asked to produce their identity papers. They do so.

Gunfire in the distance, and sometimes close at hand.

Negotiations with the legal opposition parties in Carthage lead to the formation of a Government of National Unity. It will organize presidential elections within sixty days, as the Constitution requires.

The main thing is that a peaceful citizens' movement has defeated the authoritarian regime.

Sunday, 16 January
Still some gunfire, but 'back to normal' is the slogan, and it is beginning to happen. The cafés are opening one by one in central Tunis.

People are full of hope. There are no more taboos, and people are talking themselves hoarse.

During the mobilizations, there was little indication that political conditions would allow the Islamists, who have been repressed for so long, to express themselves politically. There was not much sign of them. How to pass judgement on the old regime's wrongdoings? What role for the younger generation, who supplied most of the foot soldiers? An end to the state of emergency – pull out the troops – elections now. A lot of basic questions are already on the agenda

Best wishes,

Amin Allal

TUNIS, JANUARY 2011

© Nasser Nouri

Postscript:

EGYPT AWAKENS – 'MUBARAK, YOUR PLANE IS WAITING'[1]

Adam Shatz

Mahmoud, my driver in Cairo when I reported from Egypt last year, didn't talk much about politics, and – an understandable precaution – kept his views to himself unless he was asked a direct question. But when he dropped me off at the airport, he launched into a sharp attack on the Mubarak regime. 'The Egyptians are a very patient people by nature, but their patience is running out', he said. 'They could explode.' (Once his calm returned, he begged me not to mention his name, which isn't in fact Mahmoud.)

I thought Mahmoud's warning was the sort of crystal-ball punditry you hear from taxi drivers throughout the developing world, where life continues to grind on as usual even though autocratic governance, corruption and poverty give people every reason to revolt. Leftist militants, reformist politicians, Muslim Brothers and human rights activists had been telling me for the previous two weeks that, for the moment, the regime had been reasonably successful in neutralizing dissent, that Egyptians were too caught up in everyday worries to mobilize politically, and that the hopes raised by the Kifaya protests of 2005 had collapsed.

But that was before the murder of Khaled Said, a twenty-eight-year-old Alexandrian beaten to death last June by plainclothes officers for asking whether they had a warrant when they searched him. That was before the flagrant rigging of the parliamentary elections in December, which left the Muslim Brotherhood – the country's largest opposition movement – without a single seat. That was before the New Year's Day bombing of a Coptic church in Alexandria, in which twenty-three died, followed by the usual official claims that there are

1   From 'Mubarak's Last Breath', *London Review of Books*, Vol. 32, No. 10, pp. 6–10.

no sectarian tensions in Egypt. And that was before the popular uprising against the regime of Zine Ben Ali in Tunisia.

Yesterday, tens of thousands of demonstrators – men and women, young and old, working- and middle-class, religious and secular – took to the streets in a 'Day of Rage' protest against Mubarak, who has ruled the country since 1981. The protests weren't restricted to Cairo: there were demonstrations in Alexandria, Suez and the Nile Delta village of Mahalla, a centre of labour insurgency in recent years. Inspired by the Tunisian uprising, the protesters showed extraordinary defiance and courage, going so far as to tear up a poster of Mubarak in Tahrir Square in central Cairo: something unimaginable until yesterday. Outside the offices of the ruling National Democratic Party, a crowd of a thousand chanted: 'Mubarak, your plane is waiting for you' (Zine Ben Ali fled by plane from Tunis to Saudi Arabia). Protests in Egypt usually involve a few hundred (or a few dozen) people, vastly outnumbered by police; this time, the relation of forces was reversed.

Caught off guard, the police responded with tear gas, water cannon, rubber bullets and live ammunition; three protesters in Suez were killed, more than 800 have been arrested, and the regime has moved to ban demonstrations in the capital. Predictably, Mubarak's spokesmen in government and the press have blamed the protests on the Muslim Brotherhood, but no one takes these claims seriously: the Brothers did not even participate officially. The chief organizers were internet activists involved in the campaign to remember Khaled Said. He has become Egypt's Mohamed Bouazizi, though it wasn't until Bouazzi's self-immolation – and the Tunisian revolution – that Egyptians mobilized en masse in Said's name. (The Egyptian government is now blocking Facebook, where a page called 'We Are All Khaled Said' has been used to organize the protests.)

Despite the Mubarak regime's efforts to invoke the spectre of the Muslim Brotherhood, Egyptians aren't demonstrating for an Islamic government any more than the Tunisians were; they're demonstrating for an honest government – one that will improve education and infrastructure, reduce poverty and inflation, end the Emergency Law, stop torturing people in police stations, stop doing the bidding of the US and Israel in Palestine, stop rigging elections, and, above all, stop lying to them. And whatever their differences, they are united in the conviction that neither Mubarak nor his son Gamal, who is being groomed to succeed him, is capable of meeting these demands. As one young activist said to me last year, 'We need a radical shake-up. We have a saying in Egypt that you can't make a sweet drink out of a rotten fish.'

Is this the explosion Mahmoud was talking about? That remains to be seen: a day of rage does not make a revolution. But it's the most dramatic expression of popular anger since the 1977

Bread Riots, which were crushed by force at the cost of 800 lives, and it could be a rehearsal for what's to come. Revolution in Egypt would have enormous consequences for the region, as the US – Mubarak's indispensable source of protection – well knows. Egypt is America's closest Arab ally, a key partner in the 'peace process' and in the policing of the Gaza Strip: it is as central as Tunisia is peripheral. And so, as police were dispersing protesters in Tahrir Square, Hillary Clinton did her best to scatter seasoning on the rotten fish: 'The Egyptian government is stable and is looking for ways to respond to the legitimate needs and interests of the Egyptian people.' Later that day, in his State of the Union address, Barack Obama hailed the people of Tunisia, but said nothing about the Egyptians who hoped to repeat their example, and in whose capital city he had delivered a grand speech full of promises yet to be fulfilled.

NOTES ON CONTRIBUTORS

UK: DECEMBER DAYS

Elly Badcock is SOAS Union Secretary and part of NUS Women's Committee.

Jo Casserly is a student and activist member of the University College London Union.

Noel Douglas is an artist and designer who works across a range of media. He exhibits internationally and his work has featured in *Art Monthly*, *Dazed and Confused*, *The Economist*, the *Guardian*, *Mute*, *NME* and *Time Out*. His website is www.noeldouglas.net.

Amy Gilligan is a research student at the University of Cambridge and member of the Cambridge Defend Education Campaign.

Joe Harvey, **Kaity Squires**, **Stuart O'Reilly** and **Adam Toulmin** are students in further education.

Peter Hallward is Professor of Modern European Philosophy at Kingston University. He is the author of several books including *Absolutely Postcolonial* and *Damming the Flood*.

James Haywood is Campaigns Officer at Goldsmiths Students Union.

Jody McIntyre is a British activist and freelance journalist.

Ashok Kumar is Education Officer at LSE Students Union.

Susan Matthews is a Senior Lecturer in English Literature at Roehampton University.

James Meadway is a PhD student in the Economics Department at the School of Oriental and African Studies. He is a member of the editorial board of *Counterfire* and a senior economist at the New Economics Foundation.

Nina Power is a Senior Lecturer in Philosophy at Roehampton University. She is the author of *One-Dimensional Woman*.

John Rees is a British political activist, broadcaster and writer.

Kanja Sessay is NUS Black Students Officer.

Clare Solomon is President of the University of London Union.

Hesham Yafai is a student at King's College London.

ITALY

Elisa Albanesi is a student at La Sapienza University in Rome.

Marco Bascetta writes for *il manifesto* and is editor-in-chief of Manifesto Libri.

Giulio Calella is cofounder of the radical publisher Edizioni Alegre and coauthor of *Studiare con Lentezza* and *L'onda Anomala*.

Martina Cirese is a photographer and student at La Sapienza University in Rome.

Giacomo Russo Spena writes for *Micromega, il manifesto* and *Il Riformista*.

Uniriot is the network of rebel universities across Italy. See www.uniriot.org.

Benedetto Vecchi is a journalist and editor of *il manifesto*.

OCCUPIED CALIFORNIA

José Laguarta is a member of the Puerto Rican Association of University Professors (APPU).

Evan Calder Williams is a writer, theorist and doctoral candidate in literature in Santa Cruz University, California. He is the author of *Combined and Uneven Apocalypse* and writes the blog *Socialism and/or barbarism*.

FRANCE

Sebastian Budgen is a Verso editor and a member of the editorial board of *Historical Materialism*.

Richard Greeman is a veteran activist, writer and eminent scholar on the works of Victor Serge.

Lea Guzzo is a PhD student in Arts Management at Birkbeck College, University of London.

Larry Portis is the author of books on France, including *Georges Sorel* and *French Frenzies: A Social History of French Popular Music*.

SIMMERING GREECE

Spyros Dritsas is a Resident Physician in Surgery. He was a member and spokesperson of the Coordination of Student Unions' General Assemblies and Occupations in 2006–07.

Eirini Gaitanou is an electrical engineer, currently studying for an MRes in Political Science at the Ecole des Hautes Etudes en Sciences Sociales (EHESS) in Paris.

Giorgos Kalampokas is a chemical engineer and a student in Political Philosophy and Social Theory. He was a member of the Coordination of Student Unions' General Assemblies and Occupations in 2006–07.

Ilias Kefalas is a student at the School of Mechanical Engineering of the National Technical University and a militant activist in the United Independent Left Movement (EAAK).

Panagiotis Sotiris teaches Social and Political Philosophy at the Department of Sociology at the University of the Aegean in Mytilene, Lesvos. He has published widely on Marxist philosophy, social theory and educational policy.

TUNISIA: THE TOPPLING OF A DESPOT

Amin Allal is a PhD student in Political Sciences at the Institut de Sciences Politiques in Aix-en-Provence, France and has conducted fieldwork in Morocco and Tunisia.

Leila Basmoudi is a painter who lives just outside Tunis. She describes herself as a 'Carthaginian dissident'.

Taoufik Ben Brik is a Tunisian journalist and writer.

Sadri Khiari is a Tunisian activist exiled in France since early 2003. One of the founding members of the Party of the Indigenous of the Republic, he has published, among other titles, *Pour une politique de la racaille* and *La contre-révolution coloniale en France de de Gaulle à Sarkozy*.

Omar Kitani is active in the Parti socialisiste des travailleurs d'Algérie and a supporter of the Committee for the Abolition of the Third World Debt.

Moncez Marzouki is a Tunisian opposition leader and coauthor, with Vincent Geisser, of *Dictateurs en sursis*.

Nasser Nouri is an Egyptian photographer.

Parti des Indigènes de le République [*Party of the Indigenous of the Republic*] was born out of the homonymous movement founded in France in 2005. It 'constitutes a space of autonomous organization for all those who want to fight against racial inequalities'.

Yassin Temlali is an Algerian writer and researcher.

POSTSCRIPT

Adam Shatz is a Senior Editor at the *London Review of Books* and a former literary editor at *The Nation*. He has reported from Lebanon and Algeria for the *New York Review of Books* and has contributed numerous articles on politics, music and culture to *The Nation, The New York Review of Books*, the *Village Voice, American Prospect* and the *New York Times*.